W9-BZA-315

# THINK
# ORANGE

# THINK ORANGE

Reggie Joiner's ideas in *Think Orange* will empower and motivate Christian leaders around the world to rethink how the church and families can and should function together.
—**Craig Groeschel,** pastor of LifeChurch.tv and author of *It: How Churches and Leaders Can Get It and Keep It*

As one of the founders of North Point Community Church and a proven innovator in family ministry, Reggie Joiner is in a terrific position to offer insight into how the church can align its strategy with families for the benefit of preschoolers, children, and teenagers.
—**Dr. John C. Maxwell,** best-selling author of *The 21 Irrefutable Laws of Leadership*

For those of us who are passionate about the potential of the church and the importance of the family, this book offers a critical and refreshing perspective. That is a rare combination. Reggie helps us consider how the integration of these two organisms can be leveraged in powerful ways to reach the next generation.
—**Nancy Ortberg,** author of *Unleashing the Power of Rubber Bands: Lessons in Non-Linear Leadership*

If there is an institution that can bring American families back together, it's the church. The infrastructure is there, the heart and the will. What we need, then, is a plan. If churches and families practiced the ideas in this book, our entire culture could be regenerated.
—**Donald Miller,** author of *Blue Like Jazz* and *To Own a Dragon*

This is a must-read for every church leader wrestling with the number of students walking away from their faith at age eighteen. It's time to close the back door! Reggie's fresh and unique approach is just what we all need to strategically partner with parents.
—**Sue Miller,** former director of Promiseland at Willow Creek Community Church

Reading this book is like having coffee with Reggie. It's warm, friendly, thought-provoking, and fun! You won't want to miss this conversation!
—**Christine Yount Jones,** executive editor of *Children's Ministry Magazine*

# THINK ORANGE

IMAGINE THE IMPACT WHEN
CHURCH AND FAMILY COLLIDE ...

REGGIE JOINER

David C Cook®
*transforming lives together*

THINK ORANGE
Published by David C. Cook
4050 Lee Vance View
Colorado Springs, CO 80918 U.S.A.

David C. Cook Distribution Canada
55 Woodslee Avenue, Paris, Ontario, Canada N3L 3E5

David C. Cook U.K., Kingsway Communications
Eastbourne, East Sussex BN23 6NT, England

David C. Cook and the graphic circle C logo
are registered trademarks of Cook Communications Ministries.

All rights reserved. Except for brief excerpts for review purposes,
no part of this book may be reproduced or used in any form
without written permission from the publisher.

The Web site addresses recommended throughout this book are offered as a resource to you. These Web sites are not intended in any way to be or imply an endorsement on the part of David C. Cook, nor do we vouch for their content.

All Scripture quotations, unless otherwise noted, are taken from the *Holy Bible, New International Version®. NIV®*. Copyright © 1973, 1978, 1984 by International Bible Society. Used by permission of Zondervan. All rights reserved. Scripture quotations marked MSG are taken from *THE MESSAGE*. Copyright © by Eugene H. Peterson 1993, 1994, 1995, 1996, 2000, 2001, 2002. Used by permission of NavPress Publishing Group. Italics in Scripture are added by the author for emphasis.

LCCN 2009924463
ISBN 978-1-4347-6483-6

© 2009 Reggie Joiner
Published in association with the literary agency of
D. C. Jacobson & Associates LLC, an author management company
www.dcjacobson.com

The David C. Cook Team: Don Pape, Thomas Womack, Amy Kiechlin, and Jaci Schneider
The reThink Editing Team: Sarah Anderson, Kristen Ivy, Mike Jeffries, Cara Martens,
Beth Nelson, Greg Payne, Karen Wilson
Design: FiveStone, Jared Erickson and Ryan Boon

Printed in the United States of America
First Edition 2009

1 2 3 4 5 6 7 8 9 10

031609

# DEDICATION

This book is *mostly* dedicated to
My wife, Debbie
*The only one in my family, or on the planet,*
*who has chosen to live with me the rest of my life.*


But it is also dedicated to
My children: Reggie Paul, Hannah, Sarah, and Rebekah
*They have all worked hard and patiently to raise a father.*

My parents, Rufus and Dee
*They have believed in God and me for as long as I can remember.*

My brother, Jimmy
*He still believes in God, even though I have been in ministry most of his life.*

My mother-in-law, Betty Dean
*She raised my wife to love God and her family.*

# ACKNOWLEDGMENTS

Thanks to those on the reThink staff
who are advocates of these principles every day.

Thanks to those on the Family Ministry staff
of North Point Community Church
who lived these principles for over a decade.

Thanks to Orange leaders everywhere
who champion this cause by investing in the lives of kids, teenagers, and families every
week on the front lines of ministry.

A special thanks to
Joel Manby and the reThink Board of Directors
*for believing in this vision.*

David C. Cook
*for believing in this book.*

Don Jacobson
*for making me believe this book should be written.*

Lanny Donoho
*for believing in this enough to stand by me, literally, for more than a decade.*

Karen Odom, Colette Taylor, Betsy Wright, Greg Payne, and Sue Miller
*for years of telling me I should write this book.*

The reThink design team,
Ryan Boon, Jared Erickson, and Jason Locy, and the FiveStone team,
*for making this book more fun to read.*

The reThink editing team,
Beth Nelson, Mike Jeffries, Kristen Ivy, Cara Martens, Sarah Anderson,
Greg Payne, and Karen Wilson,
*for wrestling with the words and concepts in this book*
*(and for all the times they stayed awake with me).*

# CONTENTS

# FOREWORD

When we started North Point Community Church in 1995, many of our staff and core volunteer leaders were parents with young children. The idea of partnering with the family seemed natural. We were church leaders and we were parents. In a way, what we were attempting to build was for our own families and the futures of our own kids. Reggie Joiner took on the responsibility of creating those environments for families.

When I was asked to write this, I thought of the ways we still benefit from his time at North Point as our director of family ministry. Elementary-age kids insist their parents get them to church on Sunday mornings because they don't want to miss their small groups. Hundreds of high school students serve in ministry areas on Sunday mornings and then drive back to church on Sunday afternoons for their own worship, teaching, and small-group time. Reggie's fingerprints are all over these environments.

Reggie believed from the beginning that we needed to come alongside parents in their efforts to grow their children spiritually. He knew the environments we established for kids were crucial, but that our influence was limited. We only have about forty hours a year with their kids. At the same time, he knew that parents' influence was also limited and that other adult voices were needed in the lives of their kids.

For ten years at North Point and now through the reThink Group, Reggie continues to change the way thousands of church leaders interface with families. Through his newest contribution, *Think Orange*, you have the opportunity to "pick his brain." In the pages that follow, he shares everything he's learned about how to do church, how to do family, and, most importantly, how to do them together.

In *Think Orange*, Reggie argues convincingly that developing a strategy to maximize the influence of both the church and parents is not only effective, but also scriptural. As you work your way through this book, pay attention to what Moses said to parents and leaders at a turning point in Hebrew culture. Imagine

Nehemiah touring the broken walls of Jerusalem as he developed a systematic plan to rebuild a nation's faith. These narratives, along with others scattered throughout the book, make it clear that God not only calls us as leaders to grow our people spiritually, but He also calls us to lead strategically.

*Think Orange* is not just another model or formula. It's a paradigm shift. It is a brand-new approach to capturing the hearts and imaginations of this generation's parents and kids. And from fourteen years of experience, I know it can make a huge difference in the dynamic of any local church. So find a comfortable place to read and a couple of fresh highlighters, and prepare to learn!

*Andy Stanley*

# Part One
## Two Influences

Two combined influences make a greater impact than just two influences.

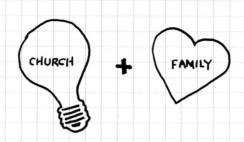

## ORANGE

2 COMBINED
INFLUENCES
MAKE A GREATER
# IMPACT
THAN JUST 2
INFLUENCES

# PLEASE READ THIS FIRST

It's okay to disagree with me.

I even disagree with myself quite often. I hear myself say something and think, "I'm not sure that's right … I'll have to come back to that later and examine it more closely." I'm not making excuses, just suggesting that a certain process energizes my creativity and thinking. I have been tentative about writing this book because I am sure I will pick it up as soon as it is released and disagree with parts of it. But that's okay. If I am personally a work in progress, then my personal work is progressing. How many people in their forties agree with what they said in their twenties? I am not trying to write something down that can never be challenged or that stands the long test of time. I am not trying to be Moses, Paul, or even one of the minor prophets. This is not intended to be infallible and inerrant. I just hope to continue a conversation that I believe is worth a thoughtful dialogue. Let me tell you what this book is *not*:

- the answer
- always right
- theologically profound
- deep
- the final thoughts on any issue

If some guy holds this book up and suggests that it is the solution for the complexity of issues facing this generation, *please hit him with it.*

At times it may seem
oversimplified,
overstated,
shallow,
idealistic,
sarcastic.

(By the way, if you struggle with sarcasm or have a difficult time telling when someone is sincere, this may be a frustrating experience for you.)

Also it's important to note that any inconsistencies or irreverence you may perceive in reading this book do not represent the publisher's thoughts or, in some cases, even my own.

This book is simply the attempt of a pastor/dad to explain why it is important for churches and families to work together to impact kids.

Smarter leaders than me have spent their lifetimes speaking to issues related to the church and family. They are all my heroes, and this list is not necessarily in any order:

Andy Stanley
Billy Graham
Mother Teresa
Bill Hybels
James Dobson
Sue Miller
George Barna
John Trent
Gary Smalley
Barbara Bush
Bill Bright
Martin Luther King Jr.
Howard Hendricks
Jeff Foxworthy
Bill Cosby

A host of people helping in this cause are younger than I am, but I chose to include only those who are older than me because it makes me feel better.

I started working as a full-time student pastor when I was nineteen. I don't think I would have hired me, but some compassionate leaders believed in my potential. Later, I was one of the founding staff members at North Point Community Church, where I served as the executive director of Family Ministries for over a decade. A few years ago, I started an amazing adventure with a nonprofit ministry I founded called the reThink Group. It is a team of innovative writers, thinkers, planners, creators, and doers who are devoted to influencing those who influence the next generation.

I am extremely grateful for their investment in this project. The mission this book describes is why we do what we do. Every day I am thankful that I have been a part of incredible ministries and learned from amazing leaders. I will often use the word *we* in this book when speaking from the author's perspective. When I do, I am usually referring to those who work with me on the reThink team, along with a handful of other key Orange thinkers who serve on our board or informal advisory teams. They have all challenged me to love the church and to fight for the family.

*Think Orange* is our effort to get a lot of smart leaders to start thinking about some of the same things.

If you're a sports enthusiast, you may have to get over the color implications as they relate to your favorite team. The color orange may represent something you loyally support or maybe even adamantly oppose. Try to remember this is much bigger than football or basketball or hockey. Okay, maybe not. But it is very, very different.

If you just don't think you look good in orange, that's also okay. The right shade of orange can go with blue, brown, black, green … you don't have to cover yourself in orange to make an orange statement. But then again, if you feel really passionate about it, why not?

What if every time you saw the color orange you thought about the changes that need to happen to reach the next generation?

What if the blending of red and yellow always reminds you of the importance of partnering with each other and especially with the *family*?

What if whenever you came across something orange you thought about *leaders* who are investing their lives to influence kids and teenagers?

We picked a color because it seemed like a great way to remember the cause. And we picked orange.

We believe in churches. Or at least in the churches who believe Jesus is who He said He was and that what the Bible says is true is true. Multiple expressions of the church are important in communicating God's story to a diverse culture.

Some leaders suggest that institutional churches can never be relational,
that traditional churches can never be relevant,
that megachurches can never be intimate,
that attractional churches are not missional,
that missional churches don't draw people,
that emergent churches never teach anything substantial,
that seeker churches don't have depth, and
that organic churches don't have any direction.

We love to neatly package another leader's style of church into a box and label it irregular or defective. We accuse the church we abandoned and defend the version we have customized.

No one is more opinionated about church models than I am. Throughout my life, I have realized God is doing something in a lot of different styles of church. We need to be careful about demonizing those who don't practice church the way we do, and learn from every version of church whose mission is to lead people into a better and more authentic relationship with Jesus Christ. God is a lot bigger than our definitions or labels, and I am sure He is not worried about how your church compares to the one down the road.

I believe some important things unite most of us—things like Jesus, our mission, and the value of the church and the family. I hope whatever version of church you are leading (or for those of you who are organic, whatever nonversion of church you are not leading), that you are willing to *rethink* how your church partners with and influences families.

If you are institutional, it can create more stability.
If you are attractional, it could make you more relevant.
If you are emergent, it will create a meaningful dialogue.
If you are missional, it helps build a bridge to community.
If you are traditional, it can reclaim your heritage.
If you are nondenominational, it will give you the flexibility to adapt.

Okay, I'm kind of kidding. But one effect crosses all these expressions: Partnering with the family may give you greater influence in the spiritual direction of the next generation.

You don't have to agree with everything that I say.
But could you agree with me on the following observations?

*There are two powerful influences on the planet—
the church and the home.*

*They both exist because God initiated them.*

*They both exist because God desires to use them
to demonstrate His plan of redemption and restoration.*

*If they work together they can potentially
make a greater impact than if they work alone.*

*They need each other.*

*Too much is at stake for either one to fail.*

*Their primary task is to build God's kingdom
in the hearts of men and women, sons and daughters.*

If you at least agree with these thoughts, I hope you're ready to start a conversation with some of us who think Orange.

You can draw your own conclusions and make your own applications, as long as in the end, you are fighting for the destiny of every generation … because you believe in the potential of the church and the family working together.

Throughout the book, we've placed a few resources to guide you in thinking Orange:

Slices are a collection of key terms and tools that facilitate the Orange principles. We've arranged them on individual pages you can cut out, frame, and place in your offices or ministry environments to help yourself and your team remember to think Orange.

Podcasts can be downloaded from OrangeLeaders.com. These audio lessons elaborate on Orange principles, terms, and topics.

*See*
*Concentrate 6.1*

Concentrates are case-studies, best practices, personal applications, and practical illustrations. You'll see references to them in the margins as you read, and you'll find the complete text of the Concentrates in the back of the book.

# 1

## ORANGE-OLOGY

I've never really liked orange. Until recently, I avoided wearing orange or painting anything orange. Maybe it was a subconscious aversion to the baby aspirin I took as a kid, or the fact that orange clothes make my skin look pale, or the rowdy nature of Florida Gator fans. I just know I have always had a personal resistance to that particular color.

That's why it's hard for me to believe I am actually writing a book called *Think Orange.* The truth is, after extensive Internet searching and countless images, I am developing a favorable opinion about orange. You might even say I am becoming an orange fanatic.

### What's so intriguing about the color orange?

Orange sends a variety of interesting messages. It symbolizes health—orange foods like tangerines, sweet potatoes, and carrots suggest a proper diet packed with beta-carotene or vitamin C. Orange stands out among the family of colors as distinct and bold. Those who work in safety or emergency professions choose it for its visibility. Advertising agencies use it to make a brash statement. Interior decorators strategically place it in a room to add flare or draw attention to an area. Organizations choose it to attract awareness for critical issues; dozens of causes from hunger to leukemia are represented by the color orange. A host of schools raise orange banners and wear orange jerseys to celebrate team spirit.

I could even be convinced that it's one of God's favorite colors—He stuck it right there between red and yellow as the second color in the rainbow. He decorates entire forests with shades of orange every autumn. It shows up in sunrises at the start of the day, sunsets at the end of the day, and in the glow of the moon at the right time of night.

So maybe you can see why I'm gaining a new respect for orange.

Even with all these reasons to love orange, we have discovered new cause to highlight this often-overlooked hue. It's why this book is called *Think Orange.* Orange is a secondary color, created when you combine two primary colors—red and yellow. I'm sure you remember finger painting in preschool. A magical moment probably occurred when you learned that mixing two colors produced something new and distinct. It was exciting to see how two pigments could merge to create something even more powerful.

Orange is what red and yellow can do when they combine efforts. If you paint only with red, you will get what only red can do. If you paint only with yellow, you will get what only yellow can do. But when you paint with red and yellow, you'll get new possibilities, fresh solutions, vibrant outcomes.

Are you beginning to see the potential? It's the advantage of using two colors to create a third option. When you think Orange, you see how two combined influences make a greater impact than just two influences.

Clearly, this isn't a new concept. Positive change and innovation have often resulted from the merging of two independent entities to accomplish a greater effect.

In New Mexico's Children, Youth and Families Department, Ellie Ortiz and Diane Granito have dedicated their lives to finding homes for older children and sibling groups. Ortiz suggested that the right photos of the children could give potential homes a look into the personalities and spirits of each child. Until that time, the photos that accompanied the children's files resembled mug shots, with plain backgrounds and unkempt subjects who rarely smiled. Recognizing an opportunity, they began to approach world-famous photographers and art galleries with requests to photograph the children in a more cheerful style.

In 2001 the first Heart Gallery opened, featuring photographs and information about various children available for adoption. Over a thousand people attended, and inquiries about children more than doubled. Since then, national coverage has abounded. From *Parade* magazine to ABC's *World News Tonight* and from NPR's *All Things Considered* to numerous articles in local newspapers, Ortiz and Granito's efforts have resulted in the formation of more than sixty new Heart Galleries all across the country. In city after city, the best

WHEN YOU THINK ORANGE, YOU SEE HOW TWO COMBINED INFLUENCES MAKE A GREATER IMPACT THAN JUST TWO INFLUENCES.

photographers in the business—some of whom typically require thousands of dollars for a portrait—have volunteered to take free pictures of kids who need homes. It's hard to imagine that a child's life could change because of the impact of one photograph, but these galleries are proving that it's true.

Heart Galleries are a perfect example of thinking Orange. Adoption agencies everywhere are discovering that combining their passion with the resources of art galleries gives kids a better chance. When two entities leverage their talents and influence, together they can do remarkable things.

When we open our eyes, we see examples of thinking Orange everywhere. When Harvard University leveraged its influence with the power of television, the mix of entertainment and education gave us *Sesame Street.* When a young father decided to combine the concept of family time with the amusement park industry, the world was introduced to the phenomenon of Disney.

Combining red and yellow always creates an Orange effect, and thinking Orange challenges the norm and has the potential to introduce something revolutionary.

## So what exactly is this book about?

In principle, this book is about two entities partnering to make a greater impact or to create a better solution. In practice, it explores the possibilities of what can happen if the church and the home combine efforts for the sake of impacting the next generation. For us, the church can be represented with yellow (chapter 2, "Bright Lights") and families with red (chapter 3, "Warm Hearts").

The premise of this book is simple: As long as churches do only what churches are doing, they will get only the results they are presently getting. And as long as families do only what families are doing, they will produce only the outcomes they are presently producing. To experience a different outcome, we have to embrace a different strategy. So if you are reading this book and you are genuinely satisfied with the results you see from kids growing up in our churches and homes, you should stop now. This book just isn't for you.

But if you have a heightened sense of concern about what appears to be a growing spiritual and moral dilemma in the next generation, I hope you will consider each page carefully. Thinking orange can be risky—reading this could stir you to initiate the kinds of changes that seem radical and incite controversy.

Many of us believe that both the church and the family are at a crossroads. It seems we have arrived at a potentially defining moment in society in which the church is losing its influence and the home is losing its heart. Some say it's time to give up on the church, or at least abandon the idea that the church in the form of an organized institution can have any lasting effect on the next generation. Others seem to suggest it's time to give up on the home. It's only logical to assume that since the family unit is continuing to disintegrate and parents are failing in their responsibilities, it's time to replace the home with a more effective model. Some churches are embracing the idea that the church needs to become a substitute for the family, while others are endorsing a movement that encourages the home to become a substitute for the church.

As a result, church and home represent a polarization of ideas instead of a convergence. Those who love yellow are determined to create brighter shades of yellow, while those who believe in red are determined to make richer, deeper versions of red.

But what if the solution for the next generation is neither yellow nor red? What if the answer is both, blended in a new and radical way? What if the church and the home combined their efforts and began to work off the same page for the sake of the children? We propose that the answer is Orange, seeing the potentially revolutionary effect that a true merger between the church and the home could have on the lives of children.

The critical question is *who* is going to initiate the strategy to get churches and families to think Orange? For the Orange effect to become a reality in the next generation, a new breed of leadership must emerge. We need leaders who will recast themselves, becoming catalysts to change the way the church and the home partner. Church leaders are the most logical people to champion this cause, as most churches have the platform and the network needed to rally the home and the church and to synchronize their efforts. But the church has not experienced leveraging its influence to truly engage the family. Too many churches are so accustomed to painting in yellow that they have difficulty thinking in terms of

**WORKING ON THE SAME THING AT THE SAME TIME IS NOT AS EFFECTIVE AS WORKING ON THE SAME THING AT THE SAME TIME WITH THE SAME STRATEGY.**

Orange. Rather than synchronize their efforts, they attempt to convince parents to start painting in yellow.

What's really at stake when the church and the family don't think Orange, when they are not advancing the same strategy? There are a number of adverse consequences to isolated red and yellow thinking:

- The church forfeits its potential to have greater influence on kids' and students' lives.
- Churches miss critical opportunities to meet the needs of unchurched parents in their communities.
- Communities continue to perceive the church as institutional, insulated, and irrelevant.
- The church is characterized by superficial relationships.
- Productions or programs are positioned as the answer.
- Parents and leaders fail to teach the same truths in a synchronized effort.
- Parents avoid or abdicate to the church the responsibility to be spiritual leaders.

I am not suggesting that the church and the home merely need to work concurrently and effectively in order to accomplish more. In many cases, the church and the home are each trying to do the best job they can for their children. Churches are full of programs that inspire families, and countless families participate regularly in their local churches. Both groups are simultaneously hard at work to build faith in children, but the problem is that they are not working in sync. Working on the same thing at the same time is not as effective as working on the same thing at the same time *with the same strategy.* When you creatively synchronize the two environments, you get more than just red or yellow—you get Orange.

Orange Babies is a group that has dedicated itself to protecting the future of children in an unusual way. Originating in Holland, the group's members are committed to rescuing children in Africa from falling victim to AIDS. A dose of the drug nevirapine during the last month of pregnancy can help prevent an HIV-positive pregnant mother from transferring the disease to her child. Here's the amazing thing: One pill gives the unborn child a 50 percent chance of being born without the deadly virus. The cost of the pill is a whopping six dollars. So Orange Babies has developed a simple plan to fight AIDS: Give the pills to as many mothers as possible so as many kids as possible can have a better chance to live.

Imagine you are a doctor who holds in his hands a drug that would stack the odds in a child's favor. Would you use it? Absolutely! Likewise, we as leaders are called to save lives and to give every kid the best chance possible. Although parents don't have a pill they can give their kids to help them have a better chance spiritually and morally, you can implement a strategy that will improve their odds.

Will you consider it?

It may mean that you have to abandon your existing methods.

It may require you to redesign your present programming.

It may radically change everything you do if you become convinced that partnering with parents could give kids a better chance.

# 2

---

## BRIGHT LIGHTS

As a college sophomore, I studied English literature under a professor who was overtly agnostic and anti-Christian. I had encountered individuals before who rejected Christianity or who didn't like church, but never had my foundational beliefs been confronted in such an antagonistic way. He frequently railed about the atrocities committed by the church, recounting the indecent acts of those who led the Crusades and poking holes in the inconsistent tactics of fundamentalists. He seemed to include all Christians in the same category, painting them as the most ignorant, narrow-minded, and prejudiced people in the world. Sometimes other students would gang up on the Christians and start adding their own reasons why the church was irrelevant and dangerous to society.

One day the conversation became particularly intense, and the handful of Christians in the room grew quiet. One of the more vocal students blurted out, "Everybody would be a lot better off if we just got rid of all the churches!" As the entire class erupted with applause, our professor interrupted with a statement that shocked everyone.

"That would be a tragedy," he said. "If we got rid of the churches, it would be like turning the lights off in our society. We need churches like we need our consciences."

It has always been intriguing to me that someone who was so skeptical about the church still believed and understood its mission. Even he knew that the church exists to illuminate.

We could attribute a number of different qualities to the church.
Before we start thinking Orange, it is important to understand the distinct and essential task the church has been designed to do. There are as many views of the church's role as there are theologians and experts and even churchgoers. But I'd like to suggest that there seems to be one primary function of the church in society—the one thing every church seems to have in common regardless of size,

denomination, theological slant, or location. *As one of the two primary entities that God has positioned to have influence in the world, the church is uniquely and strategically placed on this planet to display God's glory to the world.* The role of the church is simply to turn on a light.

If you search long enough you can find a host of smart leaders who have put their personal spin on why the church exists. I have read a lot of contradicting opinions on how to do church, or what the church should look like, and I think they probably agree on this issue more than they would like to admit. If you lose all the analysis and reduce some of the wordiness, most people agree on why the church exists. See if you can find that common thread in some of the following perspectives about the church.

> The Church exists for nothing else but to draw men into Christ, to make them little Christs. If they are not doing that, all the cathedrals, clergy, missions, sermons, even the Bible itself, are simply a waste of time. God became Man for no other purpose.
> —C. S. Lewis[1]

> The church is the single, multiethnic family promised by the creator God to Abraham. It was brought into being through Israel's Messiah, Jesus; it was called to bring the transformative news of God's rescuing justice to the whole creation.
> —N. T. Wright[2]

> The main reason [I make my son go to church] is that I want to give him what I found in the world, which is to say a path and a little light to see by. Most of the people I know who have what I want—which is to say, purpose, heart, balance, gratitude, joy—are people with a deep sense of spirituality.... They follow a brighter light than the glimmer of their own candle; they are part of something beautiful.
> —Anne Lamott[3]

> The church is missionary by nature because God through the Spirit calls, creates, and commissions the church to communicate to the world that the redemptive reign of God has broken into human history.
> —Craig Van Gelder[4]

Regardless of which leader you like best, they all make a similar point: The church exists to show the world who Jesus is. Certainly, the church universal may be a little more complicated, and there's a lot more to the church than just one simple definition, but I'm personally encouraged that Christians have come so close to agreeing on something.

The last book of the Bible takes this concept a step further and gives us a powerful metaphor for the church's purpose: the lampstand in the tabernacle. When John writes in the opening chapter of Revelation that Jesus compares the church to a lampstand, we are given a strong reminder of the church's responsibility.[5]

Anyone reading these words in the early church would have immediately understood the image of the lampstand. In Exodus, it was one of the few pieces of furniture that God commanded to be put in the tabernacle. God gave specific instructions on how the lampstand was to be built, the kind of oil it should burn, where it was to be placed, and what it existed to illuminate. The Exodus passages are rich with descriptions about the lampstand and can give any church insight into its purpose. For example, except for God's presence in the inner sanctum of the tabernacle, the lampstand provided the only source of light within the tabernacle walls. It is also interesting that one of the priests' primary jobs was to make sure that the light of the lampstand never burned out.

### The lampstand was located in a strategic place.

One of the most intriguing details about the lampstand was where it was placed—next to the table that held the "shewbread," the loaves known as the "bread of presence." The lampstand was positioned strategically to do one thing: cast its light on the table and on the bread that represented God's provision and presence. For generations, the lampstand of the tabernacle stood to highlight the object that best represented God's goodness and provision, the same object that Jesus would one day use to symbolize His own body.

The church exists to shine a light into the darkness, a light that highlights God's goodness and reveals God's Son, in order that the world can understand and know Him. We could dig deeper into the symbolism, but really, that explanation alone gives me enough to think about for a lifetime.

I recently reread John's challenge to the seven churches, or the seven lampstands, in Revelation. Everything seemed to make more sense to me in the light of the lampstand's purpose in the tabernacle. Every warning, admonition, and instruction seemed to indicate that God was concerned about the church losing its influence and impact. Everything about these churches—their teaching, their practices, and their work—was challenged for one reason: They were losing their effectiveness as God's light to their communities.

It is important to note that the lampstand in the tabernacle did not cast a broad light, illuminating everything in the tabernacle; the focus of its beam was specifically on the bread of presence. Likewise, the church is not called to illuminate everything—its light should be concentrated on showing others who God is.

For church leaders, the application is not complicated. Our jobs are clear: We have to keep the wicks trimmed, the light burning, and the lampstand in its proper place. If the light begins to dim, we must immediately move into action. God's intention is for the church to be placed strategically in culture in order to show Himself to the world. Anytime the church becomes ineffective in its role to illuminate Christ, it must rekindle and reinvent itself around its core purpose.

The church's potential to influence is directly related to how it is positioned and what it illuminates.

Has it ever occurred to you that maybe the reason some churches have more influence than others is that they are more intentional about putting Jesus in the spotlight? Maybe some churches have lost influence with their communities because they no longer focus on what attracts the hearts of people.

Jesus said, "I, when I am lifted up from the earth, will draw all men to myself,"[6] knowing that the nature of a forgiving Christ on the cross would compel people to follow Him. As long as the church remains an effective platform for God's light to reveal to the world the sacrifice Jesus made, the church will be naturally irresistible. Light is inherently inviting—just think of a porch light left on late into the night. Light communicates comfort, warmth, and healing. It gives direction and hope so we can see better and understand more fully. Most people I meet are looking for light. The problem is that the emphasis of too many

THE CHURCH IS NOT CALLED TO ILLUMINATE EVERYTHING—ITS LIGHT SHOULD BE CONCENTRATED ON SHOWING OTHERS WHO GOD IS.

PERHAPS THE REASON
THE CHURCH HAS AN
IMAGE PROBLEM IS
BECAUSE THE CHURCH
HAS AN IDENTITY
PROBLEM.

churches has gradually shifted and changed. The farther the lampstand moves away from its designated spot, the less inviting its light becomes to those who are looking.

The reason they are not looking to the church is that we are not doing a very good job of displaying God's light. We have an image problem with this generation, and as a result people are walking away from us and from God. Perhaps the reason the church has an *image* problem is because the church has an *identity* problem. We have forgotten who we are and what we are supposed to be showing the world, and it's time to reinvent ourselves around our one primary function—illumination. In the minds of millions of unchurched people, the greatest thing we can do to *rebrand* the image of church is to *restore* it to its original purpose. If we want the church to have influence in our communities, we must become a bright yellow light—a golden lampstand.

The church has a tendency to drift from what it was originally designed to do. The church was intended to focus its light on just one thing—Christ. However, when we continually move the light, using it for personal agendas and political ambition, even those outside our churches can recognize our misuse of the lampstand.

Have you ever noticed our tendency to use the lampstand to highlight unrelated issues and to leverage it for our own purposes? Instead of using it to do the one thing God intended it to do, we let its light drift toward things other than Jesus. As church leaders, it is easy to get sidetracked and to take the lampstand with us, forgetting that our job is to make sure the lampstand concentrates its well-tended light on one thing only.

*We tend to drift when the lampstand is used to fight personal battles.* We all have personal agendas that, at times, we've tried to advance using the lampstand. As leaders, we must be careful how we use the light. We need to guard against the tendency to carry around the lampstand and use it to interrogate somebody or something we don't like. We must reject the temptation to use the light to justify our opinions or win debates.

When I served as the Family Ministry Director at North Point Community Church, it was not unusual for community leaders or well-meaning Christians to ask us where we stood on a variety of issues. They were unintentionally asking us to move our lampstand a few inches in another direction. They would ask what our church's stance was on some issue—usually one of those issues that became known to our staff as the 4-H Club: Hollywood, Homosexuality, Halloween, or Harry Potter. It was tempting to respond, but then we would remind ourselves, "Don't do it! Don't move the lampstand!"

I recall a number of times during my life as a leader in the church in which I would look around after becoming distracted by irrelevant issues and realize we had drifted. Why is the lampstand over there? What are we doing fighting with these people? Why am I so anxious about things that really don't worry God? I have a hard time imagining Him getting worked up about too many of those things. I sincerely doubt that God is in heaven saying frantically, "Oh no! J. K. Rowling is writing another one of those books!" or "Calling all angels: Disney is going to let those people into their park. I need you to rally some Christians to boycott." No, I can imagine God pointing at the lampstand and saying to us, "Who moved the lampstand? What are you doing? Why are you focused on that other stuff? Bring it back over here where it belongs. Show them who I AM."

As a Christian, you certainly have a right to an opinion, and you ought to have convictions. But as far as the church is concerned, *please* don't move the lampstand away from its rightful position. Don't use the church's valuable resources to wage a battle that God is just not fighting. Instead of fighting Harry Potter, maybe we should be spending our energies helping kids become intrigued with the mystery of a God who made the universe. Maybe we should turn the spotlight on the supernatural powers of a God who can do absolutely anything. If we put the lampstand where it is supposed to be, we can capture the imaginations of our children in a way where they will never lose the wonder of their Creator.

Just remember that when the lampstand is moved, our influence is weakened. When the lampstand is moved, we marginalize the light and make it harder for people to see what God is really like.

WHEN THE LAMPSTAND IS MOVED, WE MARGINALIZE THE LIGHT AND MAKE IT HARDER FOR PEOPLE TO SEE WHAT GOD IS REALLY LIKE.

*We tend to drift when the lampstand is used to make political statements.* I know faith and politics can combine to become an explosive issue, so I just want to make it public that I love America.

Even so, I am not sure where we get the idea that if we as the church can somehow control the political system, we can create a more Christian nation. I have lived through Republican and Democratic presidents in my life, and I don't remember any president who has not claimed the Christian faith. Even so, at no point were we a more spiritual nation because of those presidents. The idea that we can somehow change the world through a political system seems a little off to me. Christians should absolutely be involved in politics, but churches should not be campaign headquarters. We are crossing a line when we position the lampstand to highlight a political candidate or platform—keep the lampstand shining on its rightful focus.

The political issue isn't new to the twenty-first-century church. The disciples got sidetracked even in the Gospels. They were hoping Jesus would overthrow the Roman government system that had oppressed the Hebrew people. I suspect they were ready to pull out their "Jesus for Caesar" signs. In response, Jesus made a powerful statement about what He came to do and what He didn't come to do. He didn't come to set up an earthly kingdom; rather, He came to set up a kingdom in the hearts of men.[7]

It's frightening that we sometimes move the lampstand to promote a political party or candidate and leave the King of Kings in the shadows. We are called to put our *God* on center stage so the entire nation—and every nation—can get a glimpse of His true character. The work of the church is more important than the work of nations, because the church transcends government. So why are we minimizing and marginalizing the primary work of God's people? It's time for some of us to move the lampstand back into its proper place and be strategic about shining a light on Jesus, the God of all nations.

*We tend to drift when the lampstand is used to make our church look better.* Sometimes we act like the lampstand exists only to illuminate itself, having forgotten that the lampstand didn't exist in the tabernacle just so the priest could see it.

It's as if we pick it up and walk around saying,
"Look at my lampstand."
"My lampstand is bigger than your lampstand."
"My lampstand is better than your lampstand."
"My lampstand is holier than your lampstand."

We begin believing our mission is to get people to buy into our version of church. We start dogfights with others about minor doctrinal issues and styles of ministry. Some people claim that only their model of church is approved by God. We quote Scripture to defend our positions publicly, and anyone who doesn't agree is labeled. It seems important to blog about it so that people outside the church can watch the fight. Yet most of the issues being debated are the ones we will probably never get clarity on until we get to heaven.

The church is too institutional;
it should be more organic.

The church is too attractional;
it should be more missional.

The church is too traditional;
it should be more relevant.

The church is too inward;
it should be more emergent.

Everybody has a strong opinion, and leaders love to test-drive the newest model of the church, but we must fight the tendency to shine so much light on ourselves that we forget where the light is supposed to be.

It's not that you shouldn't be excited about your local church; you should be. I'm also not suggesting you shouldn't work to improve the church; that needs to happen. But there is a difference. Love your church, but don't deify your church. Love your pastors (they are probably wonderful), but don't deify them or their roles. Our churches must not exist to shine spotlights on themselves—only on the Son of God.

We need to be intentional about keeping the lampstand in its place.
As church leaders, we need to be courageous enough to stand up and ask, "Who moved the lampstand?" What God says to the churches in the book of Revelation seems very direct: "Repent and do the things you did at first. *If you do not repent, I will come to you and remove your lampstand from its place.*"[8] God warns the churches that they have the potential to drift away from their original purpose.

**OUR MISSION IS NOT TO PRESERVE THE LOCAL CHURCH AS IT PRESENTLY EXISTS IN ITS VARIOUS FORMS OR MODELS; OUR MISSION IS TO *BE* THE CHURCH.**

In this instance, John was speaking to a church that worked hard and believed what was true. The critical issue was not the people's effort or theology; the problem was that they had "forsaken [their] first love."[9] Something had distracted that church's focus from the one thing that was primary: a love relationship with Christ.

This passage suggests that it really doesn't matter what a church is right about if it is wrong about its relationship with God. *God is more interested in the heart of a church than He is with its size or intellect.* He is less impressed by our ability to debate church structure or theology than He is with our willingness to touch those living around us. We are called to love Him and to demonstrate His love to the world around us.

According to the text, God says, "I will come to you and remove your lampstand." I can't say I know exactly what God means by that; I assume it isn't good. It doesn't look like He loses much sleep over the death of a church; in some cases, He may even breathe a sigh of relief. This verse suggests it is possible that He is actively involved in reducing the number of churches that exist.

Consider this possibility: Your programs are not sacred. Your church is not sacred. What is sacred is the *mission* of the church. You are called to shine a light and demonstrate God's love and grace to those who need it. Our mission is not to preserve the local church as it presently exists in its various forms or models; our mission is to *be* the church.

Regardless of how you view the church, it is a critical part of God's divine strategy to demonstrate His redemptive story to the world. The really good news is that we are the church—you and I together *are* the church. It's amazing when you think about it. If people looking in from the outside really knew your story or my story, they'd probably question how we got this role. And if you knew me the way I know me, or if I knew you the way you know you, I suspect we would disqualify each other. Even so, God has chosen us in spite of our messiness or maybe even because of it. All along He has planned this thing called the church so we could send a collective message to a generation that needs to know Him. Life is messy, but even with all our faults and failures you and I are still given a chance to demonstrate the message of His love. We are in this together only because God put us together to show how much He cares for our broken world.

Somehow God is going to use you and me collectively to be the church. That's His plan, and only God could have thought of it.

Are you making it harder or easier for people to see?
It doesn't matter how you define your church—emergent or traditional, mega or mini, a Starbucks or a living room—our mission is the same. Historically, the church has had a tendency to get stuck on a few issues, and these issues have made it harder for other people to know God. When we are not carefully strategic, we tend to create barriers for the very ones we are trying to reach.

A few years ago I was at North Point having an in-depth discussion with Andy Stanley about this issue. We were planning a conference for church leaders and started discussing the reasons churches get sidetracked. He referred to Acts 15 as an example that this is not a new problem. Paul and Barnabas were being the lampstand by taking the gospel to the Gentile world, and thousands were becoming Christians. You would think that the church, established for this exact purpose, would be celebrating the mission efforts of the disciples, yet they faced a dilemma that resulted in an emergency meeting of church leaders.

It seems that this issue needed the attention of all prominent leaders in the young church, so Paul and Barnabas left the mission field to return to Jerusalem to address the issue. If you have ever been to a church business meeting, you can probably imagine the scene—members of the church up in arms about something crucial to the mission, like the number of hymns sung, the color of the new carpet, or whether to use the NIV or King James Bible. The wilder the topic, the bigger the crowd, and the topic facing the church in this instance was one of the wildest—circumcision.

Some prestigious religious leaders had voiced concern that the newly converted Gentiles weren't being circumcised, and they thought it was wrong to allow new believers into the faith without undergoing this important ritual. Don't tell me God doesn't have a sense of humor to include this in Scripture. Acts 15:7 says there was "much discussion." I can imagine. I'm sure Peter was frustrated, because whoever was taking minutes actually recorded him responding to the legalistic Christians by saying, "Why do you try to test God by putting on the necks of the disciples a yoke that neither we nor our fathers have been able to bear?"[10] My translation: "Come on guys, how many of *us* ever really liked the idea of circumcision?"

ONE HUNDRED YEARS FROM NOW THE ONLY THING THAT WILL MATTER IS SOMEONE'S RELATIONSHIP WITH GOD.

Can you imagine Paul and Barnabas listening to all this? They've been out on the front lines witnessing the most incredible revival in history and have stopped everything to enter into this debate. Paul might have jumped in at some point and said, "Okay, let me get this straight. You want us to go back to all the cities where people have become Christians and say, 'How's your faith going? Great. Oh yeah … um, there's just one thing we forgot to tell you …'"

Thankfully, there are a couple of moments in which smart leaders take a stand on what really matters. Peter says, God "made no distinction between us and them, for he purified their hearts by faith…. We believe it is through the grace of our Lord Jesus that we are saved, just as they are."[11] Finally, James drives home the right answer in one sentence. I wish every leader in every church would write this one down and post it where it can be seen every day: *"It is my judgment … that we should not make it difficult for the Gentiles who are turning to God."*[12]

There's a lot at stake.
It's easy to laugh and feel superior when we read about the New Testament heroes spending time debating *that,* of all things. Unfortunately, there are too many examples of churches today that essentially insist on forms of circumcision. They make lists of requirements and draw religious lines in the sand that make it difficult for people to turn to God. In doing so, they alienate a large part of the population, and they complicate the simplicity of God's message. We need leaders who are willing to stand up like James and say, "We should not make it difficult." We need priests who are determined to keep the lampstand where it belongs. Even if we come from different denominations and views of what we think church should look like, we should all agree about this statement: *One hundred years from now the only thing that will matter is someone's relationship with God.*

Experts around the country are trying to track the number of college-aged students who grew up in church, yet are walking away from their faith after they graduate from high school. The estimate is between *70 and 80 percent.*[13] That's staggering. These are not kids who have grown up in agnostic homes; these are kids who have grown up in our churches, but they're walking away, having decided Christianity and the church is not for them after all.

A man recently came up to me with concerns about the older generation as well. He shared that his mainstream denomination has found that the average age of their members is now over sixty. If these trends continue, within the next ten years half of that denomination will literally die off.

The bottom line is that the church is losing its influence with two entire generations. This is a pivotal time in history when the church needs to refocus its mission.

A number of things happen when the lampstand is in the right place doing what it is designed to do.

First, there are *spiritual implications*. If we want the next generation to really see God, then what we do with the lampstand is critical. It is important for leaders to recognize what is at stake if our children and teenagers walk away from our churches without a concept of God that captures their imaginations. We need to show them the wonder, mystery, and power of a God who is too big for them to define, yet who has proven through time and space that He loves them intimately. When the lampstand is properly illuminating God, He is in the spotlight and His character shines. When there is no light for the next generation to see God, they will be disillusioned with a flawed church and underwhelmed by shallow faith. It is just one of the reasons an entire generation is searching for something bigger than what they have perceived the church has to offer.

Second, there are *personal implications*. When we do our job of displaying the character and grace of God to this generation, it affects how people see themselves. There has been a lot of rhetoric in Christendom about how we need to instill a biblical worldview into the hearts and minds of the next generation. God intended for the lampstand to shine a light on Himself. When you see God for who *He* is, you can trust what He says about who *you* are. You can also trust what He says about everything else in the world. Trust is the link to the heart of the next generation. If children and teenagers grow up with a close-up view of God, they will know how much He loves them personally. His love for them has the potential to make a lasting impact on how they love and trust Him. The best way to help the next generation in their struggle for identity and significance is to give them a firsthand glimpse of their Creator.

WHEN YOU SEE GOD FOR WHO HE IS, YOU CAN TRUST WHAT HE SAYS ABOUT WHO YOU ARE.

When the church is doing what it was designed to do, there are, finally, *social implications*. When we see God and ourselves in the light of His sacrifice for us, we will never look at others the same way. The priest was reminded of God's goodness because of the light in the tabernacle. The lampstand cast a light on the table that held shewbread—bread that foreshadowed the day that the Bread of Life, Jesus Himself, would be broken for you and me. The implication is powerful: The same Jesus who gave Himself for humanity lives in those who call themselves the church. If He sacrificed Himself for others and He lives in us, there is a compelling force moving us to give ourselves to one another. If we hope to mobilize the next generation to be the church, then as leaders we need to be the church. When the lampstand shines the way God intended, the next generation will understand its mission more clearly.

# 3

## WARM HEARTS

I remember watching a documentary several years ago called *The Richest Kids in the World.* My second-grade son became animated when the reporter described a lavish birthday party hosted by an affluent sheikh for his young son. The sheikh had flown his entire family to London for a special celebration where they were privately entertained by the cast of *Teenage Mutant Ninja Turtles.* The price tag of the party was over one million dollars.

I thought about those reports of the extravagant lifestyles of billionaires' children, and I played a mental game imagining what I would do with that much money. A jolt of reality brought me back to my world, and the thought occurred to me that I would never be able to give my children that kind of wealth. I'm ashamed to admit that for a few moments I actually felt a degree of resentment, becoming envious of those parents who were able to provide more than I could. Then I had an epiphany. I didn't exactly hear a voice from heaven, but I had a distinct impression that brought some clarity and focus, at least temporarily, to my frustration. *Most parents can't give their children a lavish inheritance, but every parent will leave a personal legacy.*

With the excess that surrounds most Americans, a lot of families get sidetracked from what really matters. We become so preoccupied with giving kids an inheritance that we forget the significance of leaving a legacy. Sometimes I just have to be reminded that what I give *to* my children or what I do *for* my children is not as important as what I leave *in* them. Isn't it interesting how "stuff" can distract us from what is really valuable and how quickly we can get confused about what it means to be rich?

Parents don't really believe the goal is to make their kids happy, do they? There are moments when I will buy anything, do anything, and go anywhere if it will just make my kids *happy*. I pretend that, as a parent, I know better than my kids what will please them.

Even though most parents genuinely believe their jobs aren't to make their children happy, they often get worn down and give in. If you're a parent, you don't like it when your kids are in a bad mood. Things are just easier when everybody is happy. You are happy when they are happy, so you'll watch a blue dog on television, eat McNuggets, buy pet turtles, listen to the Wiggles, and mortgage your house if their happiness is at stake. You don't want them to be spoiled; you just want them to be happy.

An entire marketing industry is built around the idea that parents want their kids to be happy. The advertisers know that we will sign them up for anything and everything to make sure they are socially adept, experientially rich, and academically well rounded. We will recruit coaches, tutors, instructors, and mentors to make sure they can dance better, sing clearer, jump farther, throw faster, hit harder, and test higher than other kids.

But at some point parents cross a line. It's hard to tell where the line is because it's not always obvious in the moment, but I do know I have crossed it before. In my pursuit of what I thought would make my kids happy, I threatened what makes them come alive.

Sometimes it is easier to look backward and see the mistakes in retrospect than it is to notice them in real time. I can search through the memories of our family archives and pinpoint moments where it happened, when things got out of control and competing values and good intentions somehow crowded out what was really important. Families run the risk of becoming relationally poor in their pursuit of becoming experientially rich. In the desperate attempt to do what is best for their kids, parents trade what is essential. In many ways, families become like the church that moves the lampstand away from its original position, letting their hearts drift. Too many parents wake up one day and realize they have economized on the very relationships they vowed would always be a priority.

**WHAT I GIVE TO MY CHILDREN OR WHAT I DO FOR MY CHILDREN IS NOT AS IMPORTANT AS WHAT I LEAVE IN THEM.**

I have read hundreds of books, attended dozens of conferences, and had thousands of hours of conversations with parents smarter than I am, yet I am still amazed at how quickly I can lose perspective. I recently sat down to summarize for myself what I want to remember, just so I could stay focused. I'm not suggesting this is a comprehensive list; it is just my list:

- What matters more than anything is that my kids have an authentic relationship with God.
- All my children need to know I will never stop pursuing them or fighting for a right relationship with them.
- My personal relationship with God and with my wife affects them more than I realize.
- Just *being* together can never substitute for *interacting* together in a healthy way.
- A mother and father are not the only adult influences my children need.

After I wrote these phrases and reread them, I realized a common thread ties them together: They are connected by the value of relationships. These are matters of the heart. At this time in my life, all four of my children are moving through their college years and into adulthood. As I review the past and look forward to what's ahead, these statements seem to transcend every season of our experience together. I wish I had written them down twenty years ago and thought about them more frequently.

Parents have a role that is as critical as the church's role when it comes to influencing the next generation. We have assigned the color yellow to the church because of its call to illuminate, and we have attached the color red to the family because its role is to love and demonstrate God's character through an unconditional relationship.

There's something that bothers me. A lot of Christian parenting books I have read start with the premise that there is an ideal mom or dad. These superparents conduct morning devotions, pray together every night, play contemporary Christian music, put framed verses on their walls, stay neatly within their biblical roles as husband and wife, vote conservatively, and attend church every week, where they give 10 percent of their income.

**The problem is, I don't find a lot of good parenting examples in the Bible.**
I am not dismissing "religious" parents. I am sure the Pharisees would have made great revolutionary parents and could have been extremely focused on their families. I've searched for them, but I just can't find any paragons of parenting

in Scripture. The Bible certainly lends advice about parenting, and there are a number of universal principles we should apply as parents, but you would have a hard time convincing me that David, Noah, or Eli was an exceptional parent.

Don't even try to point at the Proverbs 31 mom. What was her name? Oh yeah, she didn't have one. You say, "What about Joseph and Mary? They raised Jesus and He turned out okay." That is true, but He had a divine advantage because of His *real* father. Adam and Eve might have been good examples had they not single-handedly caused the downfall of the human race and subsequently raised one son who killed the other.

My point is this: Parenting is hard. Families are messy. There are no clear biblical examples. Anyone who claims they have discovered the secret to effective parenting is probably covering up something, just had a baby, or recently graduated from Bible college with a degree in youth ministry.

### There is a degree of dysfunction in every family.
Mine is no exception. When my dad was fifteen, he ran away from home and joined the Air Force to get away from his manipulative stepmom. My mother's father and mother struggled with alcoholism and both committed suicide one year apart during her elementary years. Neither of my parents had the advantage of reading James Dobson or Gary Smalley books. They never attended a FamilyLife seminar. They simply got married (without any premarital counseling), had kids, and plowed their way through being family. The only thing that kept them going was their faith in God and their love for my brother and me. As a result, their values of faith and family were effectively passed on to me.

Unfortunately, they passed along a few other things too. Traits like control issues, stubbornness, moodiness, insecurities, tendencies to manipulate, and a few others. Why? Because they were bad parents? No, they are human parents. Human parents tend to have human issues. Human parents struggle with the humanness their own human parents passed down to them.

It all started with the first mom and dad. Talk about a dysfunctional family. Adam was quick to blame Eve for causing him to fall into sin, and Eve passed the buck directly to the serpent. Then one of their sons killed the other one, and it all went downhill from there:

Noah had a drinking problem.
Abraham offered his wife to another man.
Rebekah schemed with her son to deceive her husband, Isaac.
Jacob's sons sold their brother into slavery.
David had an affair, and his son started a rebellion.
Eli lost total control of how his boys acted in church.

In comparison to the parents described in the Bible, mine were incredible. Has it ever occurred to you that maybe God filled the pages of Scripture with bad parenting examples to encourage us? I know God desires for me to be a responsible parent, but my humanness sometimes gets in the way. When I read the variety of Christian books about parenting, they often make me feel overwhelmed and guilty. If I consider my own inherent faults and personality quirks, I am not sure I have it in me to be an A-plus parent. When I read the Bible, though, I am actually encouraged, and I am definitely aware that God has a way of doing something incredible in spite of my faults.

This motivates me: My parents were exponentially better at parenting than their parents.
They were much stronger parents than they could or should have been, especially considering how they were parented. They somehow managed to go against the odds, learn from their parents' mistakes, and raise the standard for my brother and me. In making a few pivotal decisions, they broke free of some of the patterns they had inherited.

Whenever I think about how far they actually came as parents, it gives me hope. It makes me optimistic that I can continue to raise the bar. It suggests to me that my son and daughters have the potential to be even better parents than I have been. I embrace the possibility that our legacy as a family can continue to strengthen as the next generation surpasses the previous one in becoming effective husbands and wives, mothers and fathers. I have hope because I watched my parents reinvent themselves. Maybe I'm naive, but I choose to believe that most parents desire to be better parents, and even minor improvements can result in a significant change in the direction of a family. When you factor in the promise of God's grace and a degree of His divine intervention, anything is possible.

If you're a church leader, you have the potential to give every parent hope. You may be in a better position to influence families than many parenting experts. Assuming that you believe in the importance of family, you have a decision to make about your approach to parents:

- You can decide that most parents will probably never change.
- You can challenge parents to an idealistic and unattainable standard.
- You can choose to believe that most parents, regardless of their baggage, have the desire and capacity to improve.

Whether or not you consciously embrace one of those decisions as a leader, your style of ministry and programming reflects one of those three assumptions. *Your perception of parents' potential to change can drive how you respond to them.* Some leaders have subconsciously given up on the family and, as a result, unknowingly communicate a lack of belief in parents' potential to change. Other leaders create an idea of family that is so unrealistic the average parent doesn't even try to attain it. Most parents need leaders with a strong sense of belief in their potential, leaders who are willing to become actively involved in helping them understand God's plan for their family.

### Examine the role of the family.
What would happen if parents began to see the family in the same way believers should view the church, as a human part of God's design to demonstrate who He is to the world? Don't miss the significance of that vantage point. Our humanness does not prevent God from using us; it is our humanness that actually becomes the platform from which He demonstrates His power, goodness, and love to His people. It is an amazing thought when you realize that both the church and the home are comprised of broken, imperfect people through whom God has chosen to tell His story.

What if it's not God's plan for parents or leaders to restore the church and the home to a sublime, utopian state? What if, instead, it's God's plan to do an amazing work within the church and the home in order to put His grace on display? Imagine the Supreme Creator visibly and actively involved in both entities—healing, loving, restoring, and re-creating a broken people in order to demonstrate His glory and plan of redemption. If this is true, then

BOTH THE CHURCH AND THE HOME ARE COMPRISED OF BROKEN, IMPERFECT PEOPLE THROUGH WHOM GOD HAS CHOSEN TO TELL HIS STORY.

every parent and leader should work to combine the influences of church and home with a very strategic mindset.

I am going to suggest something now that I hope you will never forget.

If you're a church leader, your purpose is not to equip parents to have exceptional parenting skills. If you set unrealistic expectations, you may create an atmosphere in which parents become discouraged and children get disillusioned. Christian authors are notorious for giving families lists of things they should do. Parents start working the lists, and in their quest to get it right, they usually wind up feeling defeated. If we are not careful in our zeal to partner with the family, we may actually create an unhealthy culture that paralyzes parents and sidetracks our ministries. It is critical to guard our mindsets and stay focused on the primary role of the family.

Unreasonable standards or ideals that are too lofty may be the reason that moms and dads who attend church get discouraged and give up, families going through divorce or crisis are tempted to drop out, unchurched families are skeptical about engaging in the Christian community, leaders become frustrated trying to motivate parents and opt to bypass the family.

It is important to help parents understand that their role is not to impress their children or anyone else with their ability to parent. Their role is to impress on their children the love and character of God. Does that mean you don't challenge parents to sharpen and improve their parenting skills? No, it just means you help them parent from the perspective of a bigger story, one that allows room for our missteps but still encourages us to participate.

I want to establish a simple perspective that drives our staff at the reThink Group as we work with church leaders and parents. I hope it will encourage you in your context.

*God is at work telling a story of restoration and redemption through your family. Never buy into the myth that you need to become the "right" kind of parent before God can use you in your children's lives. Instead, learn to cooperate with whatever God desires to do in your heart today so your children will have a front- row seat to the grace and goodness of God.*

The first priority of the family should be to establish a quality of relationship with each other that is a reflection of an authentic relationship with God. That may have been what Paul was aiming at when he wrote to the church in Ephesians 5 and 6 about the family.

Ephesians 6:1
*Children, obey your parents in the Lord, for this is right.*
A child's response to a parent should reflect the child's attitude about God.

Ephesians 5:24
*Now as the church submits to Christ, so also wives should submit to their husbands.*
A wife's response to her husband should reflect how believers love and respond to Christ.

Ephesians 5:25
*Husbands, love your wives, just as Christ loved the church and gave himself up for her.*
A husband's response to his wife should reflect the very essence of love and the gospel of grace that Jesus demonstrated at the cross.

## God uses family to tell His story.

The New Testament suggests that every husband, wife, and child has a unique role in portraying God's love to each other. The family exists, even in its imperfection, to display the heart of God to every generation.

I used to wonder why so much genealogy was included in the Old Testament; those Scripture passages don't contain a lot of profound revelations or much that seems relevant to my daily issues. However, I realize now that these lists display family after family and generation after generation to show that every family and every generation was connected to God's story. You can see the continuation of God's redemptive plan as it unfolds in the Hebrew family tree from Adam to Jesus, from Genesis to Matthew. Maybe these lists are there to remind us that God is actively using families to link the past to the future so that they might broadcast His love to every generation. The family was and is God's primary conduit. It is interesting that He used families—mothers and fathers, daughters and sons—as a timeless platform throughout history to put His glory on display. In the Old Testament, God's promises and commandments were passed from one generation

THE HEART OF GOD
WAS COMMUNICATED
PRIMARILY THROUGH THE
HEART OF THE FAMILY.

to the next through the conduit of the family. The heart of God was communicated primarily through the heart of the family.

Although the concept of family has had different expressions in every generation, it has always been significant to our existence. Governments are organized, walls are built, and battles are fought for the sake of families. It is the core of civilization and a primary influence on the human condition. Family has shaped the fabric of the social, religious, and political structures of every civilization. The heart of the family affects the direction of every child and the future of every nation. For centuries, kings and queens, presidents and senates, pastors and priests have attempted to address and resolve issues concerning families, because every wise leader knows that whatever happens in the family makes an impression on the world.

Later in the book we'll address five major things church leaders need to know about partnering with the family, but here I think it is important to discuss some things families need to know about partnering with the church. As you think about church, you are probably thinking about church in the context of a certain way of thinking about family. We like to mix it all up. We'd like to help you think Orange. Not just red. Not just yellow.

## LEAVING A LEGACY

There is a famous story about a leader who was appointed to govern an entire race of people who had been severely oppressed. The people had suffered hundreds of years of persecution; their identity as a race had been threatened, their will crushed, and their faith assaulted. In a legendary rescue attempt, this leader became the strategic influence that saved the entire nation from probable genocide. He helped them rediscover their distinctiveness as a people and rebuild their faith. Their transition to healing and recovery took them through several decades, hundreds of miles, and countless challenges. The entire race endured an agonizing process in preparation for redeeming its heritage.

After years of waiting, the day approached when the people would reclaim their homeland and settle their families in their native country. Suddenly, rumors spread throughout the nation that their leader was stepping down. The people were aghast, thinking he had come too far not to complete the journey with them. He had become the patriarch of their race, a hero to their children. He had rescued and revived their destiny as a people. This was their pivotal moment. They were on the brink of their most promising days.

They gathered tentatively to listen to his farewell speech. He began by recounting their journey and reminding them of the covenants they had made with their God. They had heard all this before, and for a while it seemed as if he was simply reviewing what they already knew. Then he subtly began to shift his message. In his voice and words, they could hear concern about their future they had not anticipated. They had been ecstatic about finally arriving at their promised destination, yet he seemed anxious about how their newfound blessings might affect their faith. More specifically, he seemed intent on addressing how they would transfer their faith to their children and the generations to come. Too much was at stake to let this fall by the wayside. It had taken a long time to get to this point, and he wanted to ensure they didn't make the same mistakes many of their parents had made.

Then he said something profoundly different from anything he had ever said before, challenging the hearts of every family:

*Hear, O Israel: The LORD our God, the LORD is one. Love the LORD your God with all your heart and with all your soul and with all your strength.*

*These commandments that I give you today are to be upon your hearts.*

*Impress them on your children. Talk about them when you sit at home and when you walk along the road, when you lie down and when you get up. Tie them as symbols on your hands and bind them on your foreheads. Write them on the doorframes of your houses and on your gates.*

*When the LORD your God brings you into the land he swore to your fathers, to Abraham, Isaac and Jacob, to give you—a land with large, flourishing cities you did not build, houses filled with all kinds of good things you did not provide, wells you did not dig, and vineyards and olive groves you did not plant—then when you eat and are satisfied, be careful that you do not forget the LORD, who brought you out of Egypt, out of the land of slavery.*[14]

Deuteronomy documents the message Moses gave to the Israelites before he died, just before they took possession of

Canaan. He is transitioning his leadership to Joshua, giving his farewell address regarding the critical issues facing Israel's future. As a seasoned, 120-year-old leader, Moses warns the Hebrew people against the danger of becoming spoiled by the wealth of Canaan. He admonishes them to "be careful" not to forget God, because he knows how easy it will be for them to get distracted by prosperity and riches. He gives them a plan to guard their heritage and transfer their faith to the next generation. The reason this text is so important is that it's his final challenge. As their leader, he leverages the historical context of the Hebrew people and an understanding of their potential future into a carefully crafted exhortation. His words are deliberate and strategic for anyone interested in leaving a legacy.

These verses from Deuteronomy 6 are some of the most frequently referenced by churches to explain the importance of family. In this pivotal moment in Israel's history, Moses is speaking to the entire nation and calling everyone to be responsible for how the next generation is raised. His comments have incredible insights for all parents about their role to influence their children's relationships with God. Although we shouldn't assume that the context of the family *then* was anything close to the family concept *now*, there are some critical principles contained in this passage that transcend every culture.

RETHINKING FAMILY VALUES

Just like the debate on which church style is the most effective, some engage in an ongoing controversy about how family should be defined. The purpose of this chapter is *not* to resolve that issue. Instead, I want to tap into some of the values Moses highlighted about transferring a legacy of faith to the next generation. I hope you will consider what these verses suggest to us today as parents and leaders when it comes to the value of family.

Please don't get this confused—this is not a debate about family values. Many leaders are fighting for their definitions of family values, but often they have forgotten what it means to actually value their families. Have you ever considered the possibility that how families treat each other may have far greater consequences on children than where we draw the line on issues of sex education, gay marriage, or stem cell research? It's one thing to stand up for what you believe, but it's easy to lose sight of the root issues that genuinely affect a family. While numerous organizations have waged a war for family values, family relationships continue to break down. In the United States alone,

- divorce still affects almost half of all marriages;
- nearly a million children are abused every year;
- the second-highest cause of death for teenagers is suicide;
- one-third of single parents live below the poverty line;
- twenty-two percent of women have experienced domestic violence.

I am hopeful that we will honestly ask ourselves as Christian leaders, Are we so focused on fighting for "family values" that we are not being effective at fighting for the relationships we should value in our families? It's amazing how transferable the words spoken over thirty-five hundred years ago are to families in our culture. I believe they can help us *rethink* our family relationships and establish a new set of values that can transform how we do family.

FAMILY VALUE #1
IMAGINE THE END

*The LORD our God, the LORD is one.*

In one phrase Moses establishes a frame of reference for everything—God. He begins the passage by reminding Israel about the centrality of the nation's faith. He says, "Hear, O Israel [meaning listen and don't forget this]: The LORD our God, the LORD is one." As you lead, do it from a perspective that everything is connected to God. It is as if Moses was saying, "Everything I have said and everything I will say hinges on one essential truth that trumps everything: Our God is God." It's all about Him. It's not really about nations. It's not really about church. It's not even about family. Everything is really about God. If we don't start with God, we may end up in the wrong place.

There is a reason this passage is recited frequently in Judaism. It is referred to as the *Shema*, and it is a basic credo and cornerstone for the Jewish faith. Moses seems to be making the point that *it really doesn't matter what our kids know if they don't know what really matters*. It will be heartbreaking if your children enjoy the benefits and the prosperity of a better lifestyle, live in a land flowing with milk and honey, and become experientially rich, but never really know God. The shift from trusting in God to trusting in stuff is gradual, but when it happens everything hangs in the balance. It was for this reason God met Moses on the mountain and gave him the first commandment and warned him about the dangers of idolatry. When it comes to the battle for the heart, what is temporary has a way of crowding out what is eternal. Moses is simply saying, "Stay focused. Don't forget who your God is."

## IT'S ALL ABOUT FOCUS

When Moses encouraged the Hebrew nation to remember "the LORD our God is one," he wasn't concerned about the danger of the people becoming atheists. He was warning them about the risk of losing their focus and shifting their priorities. Practically speaking, when families intentionally and consistently embrace the value that God is God, it means they strive to parent from a single-minded perspective. The more they remember this is really all about God, the easier it is for them to focus their priorities on what matters most.

The power of the *Shema* is that it establishes God as the central character of a story that connects every generation, every family, and every individual to God's goodness. When we can trace His infinite love through time and space, through countless genealogies, it gives us a reason to pause in the middle of our chaos and get clarity. A clear view of God's character forces us to come to grips with our smallness and His magnitude. Isn't it true that we have a predisposition to lose focus because of our limited human perspective? As a parent, I am quick to pick up the yardstick that culture hands me and measure success for my children by a superficial standard. Over time I start thinking the most important thing is for them to attend the right college and find the right career. I want my children to marry the right partners, live in the right neighborhoods, and have the right friends. I expend enormous energy to make sure I instill the right values. These things are all important; it's just that they are not what's *most* important. Imagining the end is about focusing my priorities on what matters most.

## A TANGIBLE REMINDER

Since the time of Moses, those who live in the Hebrew community recite the *Shema* twice a day. They hang it on their doors as a visual reminder of God's role in their daily lives. It is always there, ever ready to help realign the family's value system when it gets distracted. The practice is not a routine in the Hebrew home designed to add pressure to the role of the parent. It is there to help them keep perspective. *When you remind yourself frequently that God is God, it doesn't cause you to stress* more; it causes you to trust more. Regardless of what is happening at any unpredictable moment, the character of God provides a predictable context for your story.

Every family has an opportunity to create a physical environment that is leveraged as a frequent reminder that "the LORD our God is one." This is so important because of the nature of what is spiritual—it can't be seen, touched, or felt. Therefore whatever can be seen, touched, or felt gets more attention. We must make a conscious effort to remind ourselves that there is a bigger story, and God is at the center of it.

When I was a teenager, someone challenged me to find an object in my daily routine that could be leveraged as a reminder that God loved me. For some reason, I picked an antique clock that had been given to us by an aunt who raised my mom. It sat in our den, just around the corner from my bedroom, chiming the exact time every hour and once every half hour. For several years I had a built-in alarm to God's faithfulness and presence.

I would hear it when
I woke up in the morning,
I had an argument with my parents,
I was stressed about school,
I was watching TV,
I came in from a date,
I couldn't sleep at night.

Day after day, it just kept chiming, reminding me of something bigger. Whenever the immediate details of life would distract me, the old clock would give me a cue. It would nudge me back onto the right mental track and steer my thinking in the direction of what was eternal. If I became too absorbed with my own problems, started throwing a pity party, or was tempted to think the world should revolve around me, it would sound at a strategic moment.

When Moses stood before the people that day, he was ringing a bell. He was showing us how important it is to recalibrate the heart and to give it something to focus on. As a leader, he was modeling to every parent the need to constantly guide those they love back to what is core, to what is most valuable. Moses knew that keeping the Hebrew family's focus on God would affirm its identity and shape its destiny.

I have learned that some things are beyond my capacity. As a father of almost-grown children, I have lived through several stages of parenting. I remember walking into my office one day and looking at the rows of books I had collected on family issues. One of my daughters had been through an extremely difficult situation, and I was panicked and frustrated. As I grabbed books off the shelf, I recall saying out loud, "The problem I'm dealing with right now is not in any of these books!" That day I was overwhelmed with the kind of uncertainty and fear that sometimes paralyzes parents. I am embarrassed to acknowledge that my lack of faith arose because I had lost focus. The only way I got any clarity was when I realized that my only comfort, my only hope, my only source for direction was God. Until I surrendered to the idea that God had a bigger story, one in which He desired to demonstrate His love and grace, there was no resolution.

Sometimes I don't have an explicit revelation from God that tells me immediately what I'm supposed to do. Sometimes there are no simple solutions, no clear paths of action, no quick fixes; there is just God. Somewhere along the way I have learned to lean on a principle I refer to as "imagine the end."

The fog usually begins to lift when I mentally fast-forward to the final chapter of my children's lives and ask a pointed question: Who do I really want them to become? I know that in the middle of that answer is an understanding of who God is. Then I imagine the end and remember that God is writing His narrative. When it comes to my children, the most difficult thing I have ever done is to trust God to show up and do what only He can do. *Did I mention I have control issues?* Some days I just needed to be reminded that my family is a part of a bigger picture and that God desires to demonstrate His redemptive power through us. He even leverages the most frustrating conflicts in my family life to remind me that He is God. That day in my office, it was if He seemed to say,

I am not trying to make them happy;
I want them to really live.

In the middle of their pain,
I can be a better friend than anyone,
even you.

I am the only one who can really
*love* them unconditionally,
*forgive* them forever,
and be a *perfect* Father.

So maybe you just need to trust Me
enough so they can see Me.

Besides …
with all your issues,
I think it's probably better
for them to trust Me more
than they trust you.

Isn't it more important for them
to love Me more
than they love you?

I can heal their hearts;
you can't.

I can give them eternal life;
you can't.

I am God;
you're not.

## YOU CAN'T COMPETE WITH GOD

As strange as it sounds, I think I have made the mistake of sometimes trying to compete with God. Instead of pointing to Him, I tried to be the hero. There is a critical difference between being an influence or leader in my kids' lives and trying to be everything to them. I have always believed wise leaders in the church work hard to keep God in the spotlight, and the same principle applies to parents. Smart parents will strive to make sure they are not trying to become a substitute for God. I am learning how important it is to fast-forward to who I want them to become. When I imagine the end, it enables me to distinguish more clearly between what matters and what matters *most*. And as much as I want my relationship with my children to be everything it should be, it's much more important that they are pursuing a right relationship with God.

If I could go back in time, I would take the antique clock from my house as a teenager and make it an integral part of my home as a parent. I have to be as strategic and deliberate as I can to make sure that my family stays focused on the bigger picture. It is critical for every family to establish the home as a place where God is central.

## FAMILY VALUE #2
## FIGHT FOR THE HEART

*Love the L*ORD *your God with all your heart
and with all your soul and with all your strength.*

Moses is challenging the entire Hebrew nation as the people are about to move into Canaan. He recounts their story over the past forty years and then reminds them of their covenant with God. At a pivotal moment He reestablishes the cornerstone principle of their nation when he says, *"Hear O Israel: The L*ORD *our God, the L*ORD *is one."* Until this point, there had not been anything too novel about his words. It had been a healthy review of God's activity through the years and the commandments He had given them. Then Moses says something that grips their attention, something that is recorded for the first time in Scripture, something Jesus Himself would repeat and amplify fifteen hundred years later.

*Love the L*ORD *your God with all your heart
and with all your soul and with all your strength.*

Forty years earlier, Moses had stepped off Mount Sinai with the commandments God wanted him to deliver to His people. Tucked away in the middle of those commandments was a short reference so brief in comparison to the rest of the law that it almost went unnoticed. In Exodus 20, after God had explained His commandment against worshipping other gods or idols, He touched on the core issue that separates a system of religion from a faith that is relational. In verse 6, God says He will show His love *"to a thousand [generations] of those who love me and keep my commandments."* The reference seems almost insignificant in the body of text, but it makes an important connection between love and obedience.

Prior to this passage there are few, if any, references in the Old Testament that point to a person's expressed love for God or to the relationship of that love to His commandments. There are passages about God loving people and about human love for each other, but not a person's love for God. Most of the text until this point suggests the need for people to worship, respect, and fear God. That's why the words Moses speaks in Deuteronomy 6 are so pivotal for Hebrew culture. Here, he is standing in front the Israelites as a veteran leader who has a comprehensive perspective of their history, culture, practices, and faith. He has been on the mountain with God, lived their story, and has a frame of reference like no one else. In one sentence he connects the dots in an attempt to give them an even better understanding of the big picture. What he says in this one phrase changes the conversations that the Jewish people will have for thousands of years beyond this day. He explains the missing link that so often occurs when we allow our faith to become a system of rules.

The only thing that separates a living faith
from a ritualistic orthodoxy
is one word,
one idea,
one compelling force:
Love.

Not only does Moses clearly connect the idea of obeying God's commandments to the issue of love, he takes the concept of loving God to a much deeper level. He puts a cornerstone in place that Jesus will later use to build an entire kingdom. Over the next several chapters Moses will restate this command more than a dozen times.

*Love the L*ORD *your God with all your heart
and with all your soul and with all your strength.*

Moses is fighting for something that is more important than lifestyle or practice. He is fighting for the heart. As a seasoned patriarch he knows that faith in God is not the result of anything external. It's internal. He's suggesting this issue is primarily about the heart, and it is a critical point that shouldn't be missed in the text. Moses is warning about the danger of a generation losing their faith. If you want to pass on a legacy to the next generation, it has to be transferred relationally. Anytime you pass down rules, practices, or truths outside of the context of a genuine, compelling love, you establish an empty religion. You promote an orthodoxy that will ultimately die, become abusive, or even incite rebellion among its followers. Moses was drawing a circle around the entire faith of his people, and it centers on loving God.

## A NEW RULE

Then, as the Israelites approach the Promised Land, Moses reminds them of this critical truth once again. Don't forget the context of Moses' speech—the Israelites' past was colliding with their future. Everything had been leading up to this moment. It wasn't just that Moses was setting them up for what he wanted to say that day; God had been setting them up for decades for what He wanted to seal in their hearts forever. What Moses does in his presentation is genius. In one hand, he is holding the chapter that outlined their history up to this point, reminding them of their disobedience and of God's faithfulness. In the other, he is holding a new chapter that describes the reality of Canaan.

The contrast is amazing. Before, there was the wilderness; now there is Canaan. Before, there were the inconsistencies of a nation's faith; now there is the ultimate demonstration of God's faithfulness. It's as if Moses was saying, "God is doing what He promised: You are about to taste the honey and take a walk on the beach. It's settled now! God did what He has been saying He would do." As Moses stands there, he connects the past chapters of their heritage to their future with one pivotal statement:

*Love the* LORD *your God with all your heart*
*and with all your soul and with all your strength.*

But why? How is this relevant to the legacy? Why now? They are about to realize the blessings of Canaan—what

does that have to do with enduring in faith and loving God? Besides, how can you *command* people to love? It seems that Moses was saying, "From now on everything should be different. Based on what you have seen and what you know now, you should stop thinking of God only as someone you fear, but as someone you can love. What is about to happen should settle what you believe about the character of God forever. God keeps His promises. God can be trusted with your heart, your soul, and your strength. He is giving you Canaan not because you deserve it, not because of who you are, but because He is God. He has no reason to do what He is doing for you except that He wants to make a lasting impression on you about His nature. Your story is about to transition to a new chapter; from now on the story will be told differently. It will have a climax it never had, a resolution that will establish a different frame of reference. From this point on you should transition from a people who simply obey rules to a people who pursue a love relationship with their Creator God. And remember: There is a generation behind you watching your response to your God."

Moses is establishing a new commandment that supersedes all commandments. This new rule implies that something is more important than the rules. It elevates the significance of a relationship with God above everything else, indicating that our motive for obedience should mature beyond our fear or reverence. Moses was warning the people about the danger of passing down rules without the context of a loving relationship.

This is so relevant for parents. Most parents buy into the myth that what is most important is to pass down the reasons for the rules. If they simply explain *why* they have the rule, it will result in a different response and behavior from their children, right? If it makes sense, if it's logical, then they will behave. If Webster's Dictionary, the Bible, and Dr. Phil all agree, certainly there should be a consensus in the home.

Truthfully, though, I don't recall a time when I gave such a wonderful explanation of the rules that my children agreed and said in unison, "Oh, now we understand, Father! You have explained it so well, we will do exactly what you say." The problem with reasons is that you can debate them; you can't debate a trusted relationship. Unfortunately, some of us parents are better skilled at fighting to win the argument than we are at fighting to win the heart.

It's not that parents shouldn't give answers when their children ask "Why?" It's just that the answers never carry more weight than a healthy relationship. One of the most powerful things a parent can do is to learn to communicate in a style that values the relationship. Parents thousands of years ago faced the same family issues that we do today. Moses told the Hebrew families a day would come when their kids would question the rules. In Deuteronomy 6:20, he says, "In the future, when your son asks you, 'What is the meaning of the stipulations, decrees and laws the LORD our God has commanded you?'"

Now stop for just a second. If you're a parent, does that resemble any of your conversations with your kids? I'm not sure about the age of the son in this verse, but let's say he was somewhere around thirteen years old. I can imagine a Jewish parent sitting with Moses in therapy saying, "I don't know what went wrong. I let him have the reins to the camel. He has access to the oasis in the backyard. He had his own private tent. Now he's complaining about the rules. He doesn't want to show up for any of the feast days, and he's asking questions about Passover. What am I supposed to do?"

In my home, I overreacted many times when one of my kids would ask "Why?" I would pull out the whiteboard, draw a line down the middle, and begin: "On this side of the line is what will happen if you do what is wrong, and on the other side are the benefits of doing what is right. As your father I have thirty years of experience, plus

your mother and God agree with me on this. Besides, if you don't do this, you'll be grounded for a month. Any questions?" (Maybe it wasn't that extreme, but that's how my kids remember it.)

Moses gives the people interesting advice in this situation. He advises them that whenever their child asks the meaning of the stipulations and the laws, "tell him: 'We were slaves of Pharaoh in Egypt [translated: You think you feel like a slave because of these rules? You have no idea. Let me tell you what real slavery is like.], but the LORD brought us out of Egypt with a mighty hand. Before our eyes the LORD sent miraculous signs and wonders—great and terrible—upon Egypt and Pharaoh and his whole household. But he brought us out from there to bring us in and give us the land that he promised on oath to our forefathers. The LORD commanded us to obey all these decrees and to fear the LORD our God, so that we might always prosper and be kept alive, as is the case today.'"[15]

It's interesting that Moses' response doesn't really sound like an answer to the child's question. It sounds more like he's telling a story about how great God has been. Moses is not giving a lot of practical reasons here, except for the fact that God can be trusted. He wants children to understand they are part of a story in which God is actively involved, and God has proven how much He loves them since the beginning of time. Moses wanted future generations to see how they were linked to a bigger picture, how they fit into a master plan, and how they were connected to a relationship with their Creator. Instead of encouraging parents to assume the role of attorneys who build a logical case for why the law should be followed, Moses prompted them to focus on the character of the Lawgiver. Moses knew that respect for the rules is a by-product of a trust.

The most important way you fight for the heart is to build a relationship that is trustworthy. This is a crucial parenting principle modeled in God's relationship with the children of Israel. The story of the Hebrew race is a story that documents the actions of a Father who is unchanging in His devotion. The main point of the epic is that God can *always* be trusted.

He miraculously delivered the Israelites from a horrific existence as slaves.

He continued loving them when they ignored His instructions.

He never stopped leading them throughout their wilderness experience.

He refused to disown them in spite of their skeptical and rebellious behavior.

The point that echoes through time and generations is that God will always fight for the hearts of the people He loves. That's why Moses can stand at the crossroads of generations and say, "You can give God your heart and soul. You should love Him with everything, because you can trust Him forever."

The immaturity and inconsistency of Israel's behavior actually became an effective backdrop to highlight God's faithfulness. In a similar way, the unpredictable and rebellious actions of children provide an opportunity for parents to demonstrate a consistent message. Parents need to understand the significance of this principle as they attempt to fight for the hearts of their children. Too often they drift into a parenting style that suggests their primary goal is to get their children to follow the rules. One of the greatest gifts parents can give to their children is simply to prove that the parent can be trusted over the long haul. During the formative and teenage years, it is actually more essential for the parents to earn trust with the child than it is for the child to earn trust with the parents.

Chap Clark has been a speaker at our Orange Conference, and he offers some strong insights about creating a healthy structure for adolescents when he challenges parents with the following advice: "[Moms and dads] need to see their parental role as a marathon, recognizing that building a relationship in which their child trusts them is even more important than whether they can trust their child regarding the immediate issues of the day."[16]

I wish someone had given me that challenge when I started out as a parent. Although it may seem intuitive, intentionality is required for consistency in my actions and relationships with my kids. It's ironic that sometimes my reaction to what I see as broken trust on their part can affect their confidence in me. The truth is that their trust in me is affected when I …

discipline in anger,
use words that communicate rejection,
ignore their voices,
don't try to understand who they really are,
break my core promises.

It's easier to get hyperfocused on the child's need to earn trust and measure up than to actively pursue my need to build trust as their parent. It's somewhat counterintuitive, since I often think of myself as the mature one, and they are the ones in development. I tend to get so absorbed with molding them into what they should be that I forget my need to develop consistency in how I respond to them. It took me a long time as a father to realize the impact it made when any degree of trust was breached on my part with my kids. How trustworthy I am at this stage is much more important for their growth than how trustworthy they are.

In interviews with hundreds of teenagers and college students, the wounds that go deepest are those connected to the issue of trust. When I fight for the hearts of my children, I establish a lifestyle of proving I can be trusted. Parents need to recognize how important it is to build trust with each child individually—it is the relational glue that seals intimacy and love.

The key to all this begins when parents love the Lord their God with all their heart, soul, and strength. Moses knew a secret about obedience—it starts when you really believe that God can be trusted. He knew that if the generation of parents and leaders he was speaking to would choose to love God with all of their hearts and souls, it would show up in their lifestyle. As a result, those who trust God would be trusted by the next generation, and the legacy would continue.

FAMILY VALUE #3
MAKE IT PERSONAL

*These commandments that I give you today are to be upon your hearts.*

The principle of legacy is connected to a contagious quality of love. Moses says you are to "love the LORD your God with all your heart" and that "these commandments" should be in your hearts. Moses is setting up the adult population of Israel to understand how to pass their faith on to the next generation. We know this particularly because he goes on to teach them to "impress" these commands on their children. First, he establishes God as the cornerstone of their identity. Then, he challenges them to pursue a love relationship with God as the basis for how they live. Then, to make sure they don't miss the contagious nature of their legacy, he reminds the Israelites that these things have to be in *their* hearts before they can hand them off to their children. If you are a parent or a leader, you understand the basic principle that it has to be in *you* before it can be in *them*.

Moses is implying that before I can ask who my children are becoming, I have to examine who *I* am becoming. As church leaders, it would fundamentally change the way we look at our ministries if we really believed the greatest thing that could happen in the heart of a child would be what happened in the heart of a parent. Again, it is counterintuitive: In a ministry where the target is to pass a personal faith along to children, one of the priorities should be to convince parents to make faith personal in their own lives. Although we claim to understand this principle, a closer look at the programs or processes in our churches seems to indicate that we rarely make this connection.

Please don't confuse this with the overused phrase, "Some things can't be taught; they just have to be caught." I have heard this cliché for twenty years, and it sounds so catchy that some ministries actually teach it. These ministries claim that the issues of faith are contagious, yet they set up classroom-style venues to teach what they say can only be caught. Though they say they believe in the principle of coaching and the concept of modeling, they don't really practice it. I believe the role of the parent should be championed in a number of ways, but at some point, parents need to be coached on how to coach, and they need real models that help them model. Another problem is that few churches know exactly what they are trying to get kids to "catch." When you start asking specific questions about what they are trying to transfer to their kids, it's vague. We know it's in the Bible and it has to do with God, but beyond that it gets fuzzy.

It is possible to mishandle this value in a way that can be more discouraging than encouraging to parents. Some things are in me that I don't want my kids to catch. What am I supposed to do about those things? I have this dilemma: On one hand, I don't think I am ready for my children to pick up even my virtues. I'm just not finished learning yet. My faith is not quite strong enough, and my character isn't as spotless as it should be. On the other hand, I am nervous because there is this list of other quirky issues I have that I don't want to hand down. So in both ways, I struggle. Truthfully, I have never met a parent who claimed to be ready to parent when the first child was born. The National Center for Health Statistics reports the average age of first-time moms is twenty-five.[17] That's how old I was when we had our first child. I am speaking for myself and not my wife when I say I learned by trial and error, and there were a lot of errors.

Admit it: If you're middle-aged, you probably cringe when you think about what you were like in your twenties. My wife and I grew as parents by practicing parenting. We were not experts before we started; we essentially tested our theories on our kids.

This is different from anything else you do. You can find a dancing instructor before you two-step in public, a coach for baseball before you play an official game, and a degree or training before you start a career, but no university offers a major in parenting. You don't get to go to a room somewhere and practice parenting before you really have to do it; there is not even a dress rehearsal. You're just supposed to know how to be a parent. The assumption is that your parents parented you, so now you should be able to parent your kids, and they will parent their kids based on your example.

The sobering fact is that parents *will* have influence on their children. It can be negative or positive, but what you do will make an impact on your kids. How I pursue God, how I love my wife, how I treat others, how I respond to authority, how I spend your money, how I work, and how I communicate will all affect their values and perspectives in life. The dilemma most parents face is that they don't have the margin or luxury to get all of those things right before they start parenting. Their only viable solution is to do with their weaknesses what all wise and loving parents do—cover them up! Bury them so deep that the kids will never find them. But sooner or later, they will surface. The parents' attempts to bury what's wrong in their lives may spotlight it in a damaging way, because it's actually a form of excusing or justifying their sin.

Parents, you must never try to impress your kids with who you want them to think you are. Trust me, you can only fool them for so long. What's more, when they grow up, they will despise you for trying to trick them. Or rather they will be disappointed that you were never able to admit your struggles and weaknesses; either way, you and your children both lose. It's a funny thing about my weaknesses; after mentioning something I struggle with, I have never heard my wife and kids say, "Oh really? I didn't know that." They know. They watch me every day, so I might as well admit the weaknesses I am asking God to work on in my life. It's okay for my kids to see who I really am, especially if I want them to see the difference God is making in my life.

Moses was not suggesting that parents live a perfect example or model. He was not implying that they couldn't expect to pass on their faith until they obeyed all the commandments. He was saying that these truths need to be upon their hearts. This is about desire and passion. Everything doesn't have to be right in parents or about them before they can be a positive influence in their children's lives. To be that positive influence, parents need to make it personal, letting their kids see faith in action by putting themselves first when it comes to personal growth.

Kids already have a front-row seat to their parents' lives; the question is, what are they watching? Is it just show? Or is it a real-life adventure where they see courage and passion to overcome personal obstacles? Parents must show them what it is like to pursue a better relationship with God. Show them what a committed, loving marriage looks like. Show them how it looks to prioritize Jesus above anything else. Show them what it is like to reject the materialism and consumerism of this world. If parents want their children to have it in them, they have to see it demonstrated.

Kids need to see their parents
struggle with answers,
face their weaknesses,
deal with real problems,
admit when they are wrong,
fight for their marriage,
resolve personal conflict.

Children need to see their parents make relational, emotional, and spiritual growth a priority. If parents don't make it personal, it may never be personal for their kids. Some of my favorite stories through the years have been told by children of single parents who watched their moms or dads overcome difficult obstacles. Don't forget that God is writing a story in the hearts of parents, a story of redemption and restoration. One of the most powerful things that children can see is God at work in the lives of their parents, but they can't see who their parents are becoming if they never see who they were in the first place. Otherwise, how will they know the difference God has made and continues to make in their parents' lives? It is the firsthand look at that difference that will give them hope for their future and faith in what God can do in them.

FAMILY VALUE #4
CREATE A RHYTHM

*Impress them on your children. Talk about them when you sit at home and when you walk along the road, when you lie down and when you get up. Tie them as symbols on your hands and bind them on your foreheads. Write them on the doorframes of your houses and on your gates.*

What Moses says about family seems so commonsense that, at a first glance, you wonder why he even said it. Then you realize it's a remarkably futuristic statement; you would almost think he had a divine revelation about what was coming. Actually, he did. His statement transcends every generation and taps into future families represented by a variety of cultures. In some ways, what he said about the role of the family has more meaning to us today than it did to the Hebrew people then. I'm sure some of the parents in that crowd thought, "Isn't that what we have been doing? We have already been talking about this in the morning, through the day, and at night."

It's not like they had much of a choice; there were a few powerful and tangible object lessons God had already put in place to systematically remind them of Himself. There was the manna they depended on *every day* to eat. The cloud of smoke that hovered over them *every day* to lead the way. The pillar of fire that was there *every night* when they went to sleep. They were nomadic people with a God who was present in their *everyday* experience. There were no fast-food restaurants, no computers, no cell phones, no movie theaters, no televisions, no video games, no concerts, no iTunes, iPods, iPhones, digital photography, Jet Skis, Monday Night Football, indoor plumbing, air-conditioned buildings, or even Starbucks. I mean, they really needed God, and He was obviously present. But Moses was aware that their current existence would not be their future reality.

My translation of what he was saying would go like this: "If you are going to impress these truths in the hearts of your children, you will have to be more deliberate about *creating a rhythm* within your home. In the future, there will be a host of things that will distract you, and it will be easy to drift away from the importance of having an *everyday* kind of faith."

I believe Moses knew that in Canaan, families would have to be
more conscious about creating a rhythm
that transferred an everyday faith,
more deliberate about establishing visual reminders
of God's power and presence,
more innovative about how and when
they told God's story.

What was instinctive for the Hebrew family in its past experience had to become more intentional for the family in its new reality.

Moses recognized the danger of a compartmentalized faith—that over time the daily relationship with God would be marginalized to a part of the day, then the week, then the month. He anticipated the people's tendency to segment God into an isolated category instead of viewing Him as the integrating force that influences all of life. He was concerned that society might one day view God as only a smaller part of culture and life.

It's characteristic of humans to create an image of God that is so narrowly defined that it separates Him completely from culture. Instead of seeing everything as somehow connected to God's story, we love to categorize and segment our faith. Leaders draw man-made lines to separate what is spiritual from what is secular. They create terms and labels to quantify and qualify how God works and how He doesn't. It's almost as if they share the same anxiety that Moses had about Canaan.

God will somehow be forgotten.
Eternal truths will be diluted.
The faith of a generation will die.

These are real tensions and legitimate concerns, but as leaders we should be extremely careful about how we approach and confront this danger. Notice what the seasoned patriarch of Israel did *not* do: Moses never once said, "For the sake of our faith, maybe we should stay isolated in the wilderness. Our faith is safer here." Instead, he pushed ahead to invade Canaan with a plan. What he handed them that day was a strategy to create a rhythm that would help keep their faith alive. The rhythm would break down the walls of every culture to reveal a God whose story transcends time and space. The role of the family was being strategically positioned as the primary platform to display God's message of restoration to the hearts of every generation.

Don't miss what happened: Moses glued the words of God to a core relational entity and sent them into a foreign culture. God has always been on a mission to redeem the world.

Moses makes a passionate plea to impress on the hearts of children core truths that relate to God's character. Some translations use the phrase "teach diligently." I once heard someone claim that the Hebrew concept of "teach" means "to cause to learn."[18] In other words, it is different from the lecture- or classroom-based education in which a teacher's responsibility ends once the material has been presented to a child. Moses is promoting a systematic teaching process that persists until the core truth is understood and embraced. In other words, he expects parents and leaders to refine and adapt their presentations until there is actual learning.

There is a sobering revelation here about who is ultimately responsible for the stewardship of eternal truth. It's not Moses or the child, but the parents who are ultimately responsible for what should be learned.

Family has always been an integral part of God's design.

What Moses set in motion for the Hebrew people was very strategic. He tapped into the design of creation and leveraged it to nurture a lasting faith. It's so obvious, it's genius. This principle of rhythm is transferable to every culture throughout all time. Generally speaking, all people groups get up with the sun, move around in the day, share a meal, and sleep through the night. It's just the way things naturally flow. It's the transcendent pattern of life, this rhythm that establishes a consistent process to challenge the mind and inspire the heart. If the *Shema* provides a focus for your relationship, these instructions for daily life provide the structure that enables your relationships to flourish. Moses clearly highlighted certain patterns or times throughout a day that were opportune for teaching.

Look closer at what he said:

Talk about them when you **sit** at home
and when you **walk** along the road,
when you **lie down**
and when you **get up**.

It is important for parents and leaders to cooperate with the way life naturally happens. It is important for parents to create a rhythm that works for their family.

It's why a newborn is put on a schedule.
It's why teachers establish structure for their classes.
It's why a student is required to keep an agenda.
It's why families establish traditions.

Children learn best through routine, and when families create the right rhythm it helps to accentuate learning and development. Although every family should look for the patterns that work best for them in light of their schedules, four specific times are listed in this passage that any family can leverage to build the faith of their children. Each time seems to suggest a different style or approach to learning, and, interestingly enough, each time also presents the chance for a parent to play a different role. It's almost as if Moses had studied human behavior and earned a master's degree in child development.

Consider the following ideas:

**Eating meals together** is an optimal time to have a focused discussion. It gives parents a specific time to assume the role of a facilitator or teacher to target a specific truth in an interactive and relational context. Mealtime can be effective as an environment to systematically establish core principles. (I could list a lot of overused stats here, like the ones that claim the more meals families eat together, the better chance their children have of never taking drugs or going to prison. But I won't do that.)[19]

**Walking or traveling together** seems to provide a unique opportunity as well. It is a convenient time to stimulate the kind of informal dialogue that allows kids to drive their own agendas. These times give parents an opportunity to build a relationship through nonthreatening experiences. At some level the parent can actually function as a friend or companion and interpret life together with their children. (Today's cultural mirror to this can be drive time. It has a few "enemies," like video games, cell phones, and music, even though creative parents may actually use some of these enemies to generate interesting questions or dialogue.)

**Tucking children into bed** can also be a meaningful time for families. Too many parents miss the potential of this time because they have a habit of sending their kids to bed rather than taking them. There is something about the private domain of a child's room that gives the parent a chance to have an intimate conversation and become the kind of counselor who listens to the heart of a child. (Have you ever seen a child get mad and go to her room and shut the door? It's like she is saying, "I am upset with you and closing you out." The door to a child's room is an important metaphorical door to keep open.)

**Getting up in the morning** provides a blank page for the family to start fresh relationally. Whether you eat breakfast together or just interact for a brief moment, morning has the potential of planting an important emotional seed in the heart of a child. Just a few *encouraging words* carefully spoken or written can give your children a sense of value and *instill purpose*. Imagine parents as coaches, sending their kids into an important game. Parents should ask themselves the question, What can I say or do to give them fuel for dealing with whatever they have to face today? (Most teachers will tell you they can sense if things went well at home by a child's demeanor when he arrives at school.)

If families decided to take advantage of the times already built into their routine, the effort required to initiate interaction during some of these times would be minimal. The return could be potentially enormous. The ancient culture of the Hebrew people recognized not only a rhythm to their day, but the rhythm of their week and year as well. They set aside Sabbath once a week for honoring and worshipping God. They set feast days like Passover on the calendar to reflect and celebrate God's faithfulness. It developed a culture rich with the kinds of traditions that gave context to their story and identity as a people. Most of all it gave families an opportunity to establish their faith and relationships as a priority.

A priority is a simple pre-decision about your time. That's what it means to create a rhythm—to determine in advance how you will spend your time. It's important that this principle not be confused with the idea of simply spending time together as a family. Rhythm requires two primary components—intentionality and constancy—and can be defined as a strong, repeated pattern. In music, rhythm requires an intentional sound happening constantly within a frame of time; otherwise, there is no rhythm.

The point Moses is making in this passage parallels the idea of rhythm as he emphasizes two important things.

First, there must be an effort to make an impression or to communicate what is core and important. Second, the effort should happen repeatedly and establish a pattern over time.

The time families spend together should be both interactive and intentional. Consider the following finding: "There is nothing to suggest [in research] that time in and of itself is what is beneficial to children. What is beneficial is time that is spent in healthy and satisfying interaction."[20]

For years we have debated over which is more important, the quantity or the quality of the time families spend together. What Moses is suggesting in this passage of Deuteronomy is that it takes both quantity and quality times working together. When families increase the quantity of quality time they spend together, they leverage their ability to positively impact their children's faith.

It reminds me of my relationship with our community YMCA. I have a membership. Our offices are next door. I can see it from my window. I am near it every day. It's hard to explain, but sometimes I feel like I stand a better chance of getting in shape because I pay monthly dues and spend a lot of time in close proximity to people who are working out. They have a great lobby and sitting area where I have actually spent time hanging out and working on the computer. The problem is that spending time near the YMCA doesn't make me healthier. That's the myth of *quantity time.*

Several years ago, I was feeling guilty because months had passed and I had not done any kind of exercise. So I got up early one morning and actually went to the YMCA to work out. I wanted to make up for lost time. It felt so positive to finally be doing something productive and to be working out that I became energized. So when I finished doing reps on all the machines, I started over again. I spent several really good hours putting a lot of effort into the routines and left feeling better about myself. The next morning I woke up in excruciating pain. My damaged muscles had locked up, and I couldn't move. It took a few weeks of therapy before I was normal again. That's the myth of *quality time.*

Now, YMCAs have a program called Fit Link. When you enter, you log in at a main computer terminal before you start your workout. That computer is linked to a monitor at every station that records the weight and the number of reps that you lift. It beeps at you if you go too fast or too slow. On your next visit, it calculates what your progress should be based on your last workout and automatically assigns a heavier weight and updated routine to every station. If you skip your workout, it sends a cue to a personal trainer who will e-mail or call you to get you back in your routine. Why? Because someone at the YMCA believes that the only way you can get in shape is to have a good workout on a consistent basis. That what *quantity of quality time* means.

It's not enough to spend time together as a family if a family's time together is never meaningful or strategic. It's not just about quantity, and families can't make up for frequently missed opportunities by going on a nice vacation once a year or by spending several days together during the holidays. And it's not just about quality—families have to be both intentional about how they spend time together and consistent about how often they spend time together. In short, they need to create a rhythm. As leaders, we should act like Moses and encourage families to get in sync with the natural patterns that already exist in life. We need to help them find their beat and see their time as an opportunity to celebrate God's story.

| TIMES | COMMUNICATION | ROLE | GOAL |
|-------|---------------|------|------|
| MEAL TIME | FORMAL DISCUSSION | TEACHER | ESTABLISH VALUES |
| DRIVE TIME | INFORMAL DIALOGUE | FRIEND | INTERPRET LIFE |
| BED TIME | INTIMATE CONVERSATION | COUNSELOR | BUILD INTIMACY |
| MORNING TIME | ENCOURAGING WORDS | COACH | INSTILL PURPOSE |

FAMILY VALUE #5
WIDEN THE CIRCLE
*Hear, O Israel …*

As we wrap up these five family values, let's go back to the text. There is something right at the beginning that we may have rushed past. It's the phrase *"Hear, O Israel."* According to the sequence of the passage, we should have started with this part of the verse, but I wanted to save it for last.

Whenever I hear people talk about Deuteronomy 6, the covert context of the passage seems to get left out. Don't forget that Moses is speaking to all of Israel about the importance of families passing on their faith to the next generation. In other words, he was talking to every parent *and* every leader. As important as the monologue was for parents, it was not only for them; Moses was speaking to all of Israel. The culture of the Israelites was that of a community, and not only were parents listening, but so were other relatives in the crowd—siblings, aunts, uncles, grandparents, cousins, and probably even some extra wives.

Okay … strike that last one. But the family unit then was not always as neatly defined as we sometimes think. Regardless of how you would describe that ancient system, there was significant multigenerational support for parents. I think the reason Moses would say things about "you, your children and your children after them"[21] is that all those generations were represented in the crowd. We read in Deuteronomy 5 that Moses "summoned all Israel." It is clear in his language that he was challenging the entire nation with this principle. These values were intended to be practiced at every level of Hebrew society. More specifically, the strategic role of the family was valued and supported by everyone. These were tribes of families in relationship with other families who believed in the role of family to nurture the hearts of a generation to trust God.

When Moses was delivering the message, he was making this a national issue, a tribal issue, and a family issue.

Certainly every smart leader knows that in most of our multicultural, racially mixed, religiously diverse communities we should not try to re-create the Hebrew cultural model. That was a past reality that is not a present possibility. Although it is important to understand the Hebrew model for context, don't confuse customs with the principles that drove them. Society has evolved, and in many ways for the better. If anyone suggests that we should reestablish the exact practices from the Old Testament, remind him of some of those strange commandments pastors never discuss.[22] The real question is, how do we rediscover the *principle* of community that existed in the Hebrew story? How do we rally leaders and parents to see how strategic it is to support the family in its role to nurture the hearts of children? How can we motivate parents to "widen the circle," as we say at reThink, and invite other leaders into their kids' lives and broaden the range of influence?

If you are a leader, Moses is suggesting that you recognize why it's important to support the role of the family. If you are a parent, he is implying that the issue of your kids' relationship with God is not your concern alone. You are not alone in your effort, nor should you try to do this alone. Parents of younger children will often buy into the myth that they are the only adult influence their children need. But parents of teenagers often realize that their children are hungry for approval and advice from someone who is not their parent. So there are really only a couple of options:

Kids will either seek out another adult's validation
on their own, or
the parent can be a part of the process
and pursue strategic relationships for them.

In a culture where community is not automatic and role models are limited, parents should become intentional about finding spiritual leaders and mentors for their kids.

MEAL TIME
DRIVE TIME
BED TIME
MORNING TIME

# Family Times

Based on Deuteronomy 6:7, we believe these are the four key times all families can leverage to build the faith of their children.

"Impress [these commands] on your children. Talk about them when you sit at home and when you walk along the road, when you lie down and when you get up."

MEAL TIME **When You Sit at Home**
Focused discussion as a teacher to establish core values

DRIVE TIME **When You Walk along the Road**
Informal dialogue as a friend to help your child interpret life

BED TIME **When You Lie Down**
Intimate conversation as a counselor to listen to the heart of your child

MORNING TIME **When You Get Up**
Encouraging words as a coach who gives a sense of value and instills purpose

Every son and daughter needs other adult voices in their lives who will say things a Christian parent would say. One of the smartest things a church leader can do for a family is provide a system where kids and teenagers can be connected to that kind of adult influence. One of the smartest things moms and dads can do is to participate in a ministry where they can find the right kind of adult influences for their kids.

I frequently make random visits to senior pastors because I love to see what God is doing in various places. I am not hired to do it, and it's not official in any way; it is just something I am really passionate about doing. The part I look forward to is the opportunity for personal time with the pastor. I am not even a "quality time" type of person, but I look forward to talking about the things that are important to them. For most of my ministry I have worked next to senior pastors, and I have had the privilege of watching them up close. I guess that's one of the reasons I have so much respect for the demands and pressures they face. What is interesting is that many of the conversations I have with these leaders revolve around their families. It's so refreshing to see firsthand that most senior pastors have a burning passion and desire to be the right kind of husbands and dads.

Recently I was in another city visiting with a senior pastor who had a positive reputation as a leader, husband, and dad. He is pastoring a handful of young multisite churches that reach quite a few twentysomethings. The area of the city he lives in does not have a lot of families so his son, who is in middle school, doesn't have a lot of community with kids his age. As a dad, this pastor has been very intentional about spending time with his son, and he told me stories about what they had done together to build his son's faith. I actually found myself thinking, I wish I had thought of doing that with my son. Then he asked me if there was any advice I would give him before his son went to high school. My first impulse was to say, "No, not at all.

We need to video your relationship and train other leaders so they can know how to do this."

Then I had this thought, and I told him, "If you want your teenage son to keeping growing in his love for God, you should help him develop other adult leaders in his life besides you, other leaders who also love God."

I am not an expert on the family, but I have observed a lot of teenagers. From the time they hit middle school, they start moving away from home. They are not doing anything wrong; it's just the way they are made. They are becoming independent, and they begin redefining themselves through the eyes of other people who are not in their immediate family. The older they get, the more important it is to have other voices in their lives saying the same things but in a different way. Teenage sons and daughters need to have other voices speaking into their worlds. Parents who do not understand this principle have forgotten what it was like to be a teenager. I cannot count the times my kids would quote something our pastor, our student pastor, or a small-group leader had said. They would act like it was the first time they had ever heard it. At times I wanted to blurt out, "I have been telling you that for sixteen years!" The point is they were hearing it in a different way because they were at a different stage, and they just needed a different voice.

We need to make it easier for parents to widen the circle. This is an important value for families to embrace. Even though it doesn't seem important when children are young, it's more important than it feels. Establishing the principle of community early in their lives can potentially prevent a lot of unnecessary strife later. When you widen the circle, the goal is to have other trusted adults in the lives of children *before* they need them so they will be there *when* they need them. Moses passed these values along to the entire community because he knew it would take multiple influences to guard the faith of a generation.

No other passage in the Bible defines the family's role as clearly as Deuteronomy 6. Moses stands before the entire nation as a grandfather and leader to position the family as God's primary conduit to tell His story of redemption and restoration. During this time of critical transition, Moses highlights values that should transcend time and culture. I believe he is challenging leaders and parents to …

*Imagine the end* in order to stay focused on the big picture.
*Fight for the heart* of their families by loving God with all of their hearts.
*Make it personal* and let kids see what God is doing in their parents.
*Create a rhythm* so time together as a family will nurture an everyday faith.
*Widen the circle* and make sure kids have additional influences to guide them.

As leaders we need to remind all parents of their calling to highlight a divine drama. We have to be intentional in telling children about the ongoing love story between God's people and Himself. We should understand that the primary purpose of the family is to show them God's love through that relationship.

Imagine the end …
It is an *infinite* love that is linked to His character.

Fight for the heart …
It is a *compelling* love that moves us to trust with our hearts.

Make it personal …
It is a *contagious* love that we demonstrate personally.

Create a rhythm …
It is an *everyday* love that is developed in the rhythm of families' lives.

Widen the circle …
It is an *authentic* love that connects us in wider circles with others.

*At the heart of every family is a primary calling to lead a generation to the heart of a perfect, loving God.*

CREATE

RHYTHM

FIGHT FOR THE HEART

IMAGINE

WIDEN THE CIRCLE

MAKE IT PERSONAL

A RHYTHM

FIGHT

FIGHT FO

IMAGINE THE

AGINE

END

CREATE IMAGINE THE END

IMAGINE THE END
FIGHT FOR THE HEART
MAKE IT PERSONAL
CREATE A RHYTHM
WIDEN THE CIRCLE

# Family Values

Many leaders are fighting for their definitions of "family values," but often they have forgotten what it means to value their families. A closer look at Deuteronomy 6:4–7 reminds us to stay focused and keep trying.

**IMAGINE THE END**
Focus your priorities on what matters most.

**FIGHT FOR THE HEART**
Communicate in a style that gives the relationship value.

**MAKE IT PERSONAL**
Put yourself first when it comes to personal growth.

**CREATE A RHYTHM**
Increase the quantity of quality time you spend together.

**WIDEN THE CIRCLE**
Pursue strategic relationship for your kids.

# 4

## ORANGE GLOW

Okay, so enough about Moses for a while, except to remind you that God used two combined influences in Deuteronomy to make a greater impact, much like yellow and red combine to create orange: Moses and family.

Make sure you don't miss what Moses did—he was God's leader in communicating a strategy to God's people, and he challenged parents to leverage the family to nurture their kids' faith.

Moses did other things too.

- He grew up at Pharaoh's house.
- He talked to a burning bush.
- He picked up a snake by the tail.
- He parted the Red Sea.

After this book, I hope there's something else you will always remember about Moses:

- Moses was called to *light* the way for God's followers.
- Moses encouraged parents to nurture a generation's *heart* for God.

Light + heart.
Yellow + red.
What does that give you?
Orange.
Moses was an *Orange leader*.

**Orange Leader:** *any leader who connects other leaders and parents in order to synchronize their efforts to build faith in the next generation.*

Moses was probably one of the first people to think Orange. There is a good chance if you are reading this book that you are an Orange leader too. As far as some of us are concerned, you don't have to purchase, subscribe, download, log in, or wear anything specific to be an Orange leader. You can even be an Orange leader and not know it. As long as you are working to combine the efforts of the church and the home to make a greater impact, to some degree you are leading an Orange cause.

**Let's review for a minute.**
If you have read up to this point, you have heard us explain the following: (*If you haven't read up to this point, you've just saved an enormous amount of time.*)

- God has designed the *church* to shine a *light* to show every generation the glory of God's Son.
- God has designed the *family* to nurture the *hearts* of a generation to love God.

They are both primary influences designed by God for a purpose, and when they work together, they are Orange. Both the church and the family are systems comprised of imperfect people—that's why God desires to use them as a platform to tell His story of restoration and redemption to the world.

**We're learning to dance together.**
Every once in a while I meet leaders who think in terms of yellow so much they seem to have an aversion to the family. They think what happens at church is much more important than anything else on the planet. Likewise, sometimes I meet parents who have thought red for so long they think the church is not that important. They seem to believe their family is the center of the universe.

But since God made the planets and the universe, and God made the church and the family, they are all important. Jesus gave His life for the church. When you consider that, coupled with the fact that the Bible implies the love a dad has for his family should reflect that same quality of sacrifice, both are high on God's list of important things.

So, to recap, when it comes to entities that God has created specifically to make disciples and accomplish His mission, there is the church … the family … and … nothing else.

Sometimes we fight about the church as if the church is sacred, or we fight for the family as if the family is sacred. In reality, it's God who is sacred. Our fights should really be for the mission of the church and the mission of the family instead of trying to have bigger churches or better families. What we should really be concerned about is our collective ability to influence a generation to have a stronger, deeper, and more authentic relationship with God. The church and home are critical platforms for that mission, but they are both losing ground; both entities are struggling to be effective. They both need each other more than ever, but they're too skeptical of each other to make a real commitment. They have tried to dance a few times, but it was just a little awkward. Neither partner is sure who should take the lead. So instead of working on their steps together, they just sit quietly in the corner as the music keeps playing.

What would happen if …
… churches started believing in the potential of the family to influence their own kids?
… families started believing in the potential of the church to influence their sons and daughters?

Better yet, what if both churches and families started believing in the potential of combining their influences to accomplish the same mission?

What if churches decided to leverage their influence with families and rally them around a synchronized plan to influence a generation's faith? What if they started programming as if they believed parents play a critical role in the moral and spiritual development of children? What if the church decided to treat families, every family, as if they played a significant role in the future of a generation? Maybe families would begin to believe in the potential of the church as a trusted partner. Perhaps the reason a lot of families ignore the church is that they honestly don't think the church has their best interests at heart. The truth is that a lot of families are coming back to give the church a second chance, but they are walking away disillusioned.

That's why we need more leaders thinking Orange.
It's happening—the conversations are changing. The level of dialogue is picking up. Publishers are going to press. Everybody is getting in the game. Everyone is putting their unique spin on what Orange thinking looks like in their style of

church or in their community. The point, however, is that someone has to lead this effort. But please don't get confused; I am not talking about one individual who "champions the movement."[23] It's important to recognize that we need more than one person to champion this issue. The true champions are those who lead and serve in local churches every week, engaging parents and families in a better strategy. This is not a cause that is unique to one type of church—this kind of thinking has the potential to transcend every version of church and to impact multiple definitions of the family.

## Don't mistake practices for principles.

It is vitally important that we don't get confused between the practice of a specific local church and the principles that transcend those practices. I believe in best practices and the honest evaluation of what is really working—as stewards of our ministries and churches we should constantly tweak and upgrade to improve what we are doing—but it's important that we hold the *principle* tighter than the *practice* of it. Why?

*Sometimes we push a specific practice for so long that it gets old and becomes less relevant.* Then, when it stops working as effectively as it once did, there is a tendency to abandon the principle. *At other times, we promote a practice so passionately that it drowns out the core principle.* This may result in a number of problems wherein some people wholeheartedly buy into the practice but never fully understand what is driving it. Therefore, they don't have a reference point to effectively evaluate how the practice should morph and change. Overselling the practice may also push good leaders to discard the key principle. If a leader has a practical or philosophical reason for not embracing a specific practice, it may result in the rejection of an important principle. That is why it is very critical to clarify the principles before you debate the practices.

While I was on the Orange Tour in Oregon, a young student pastor asked a question that I hear multiple times every week: "How do I get my pastor to buy into this vision?"

My immediate response was, "The answer depends on what exactly you are trying to get him to buy into. If you try to get him to embrace decisions regarding practices before you have agreed on principles, you have just complicated the process. You should always begin

**CLARIFY THE PRINCIPLES BEFORE YOU DEBATE THE PRACTICES.**

the process by making sure everyone gets on the same page regarding the principles."

I haven't met a senior pastor yet who doesn't think Orange to some degree, so I am confident that most leaders would agree with a few basic assumptions. These are the primary principles we have established as the basis for our approach to family ministry (later in this chapter we will further explain the term "family ministry"):

- Nothing is more important than someone's relationship with God.
- No one has more potential to influence a child's relationship with God than a parent.
- No one has more potential to influence the parent than the church.
- The church's potential to influence a child dramatically increases when it partners with a parent.
- The parent's potential to influence a child dramatically increases when that parent partners with the church.

There are a lot of different voices communicating a host of conflicting information about how the church and family should partner. These statements clarify the primary issues I believe most of us agree on, establishing a point of reference for why we believe it is important to think Orange. I know of a number of situations where passionate leaders have hastily implemented programs in their churches without carefully connecting them to the reasons behind their actions. They often hit a wall when other leaders or parents don't understand the core principles. It is also possible to start with the same premise yet end up in some very different places in the application. I think it is a good thing for a church to find its own rhythm with the principles. If any partnership is going to work effectively between a church and a parent, there needs to be a degree of customization; it should fit your culture and your community. The one thing that is usually missing is a cohesive plan that everyone understands and embraces.

The landscape, however, is varied when it comes to how different churches approach their responsibility to family. For those focused more on programs than processes, family ministry can mean different things, including the following:

- Creating annual events to celebrate faith or development milestones
- Designing a church built around families who homeschool
- Challenging all departments to do something for the family

- Adding supplements to existing age-graded curriculum
- Doing church in homes with a few families
- Requiring teenagers to sit with parents in church

Although I would apply the principles in a somewhat different way than most of the examples above, I am grateful for the renewed emphasis so many churches are giving family. I guess, technically, anything that a ministry does for the family could be called family ministry, but that's actually part of the problem.How you define family ministry is definitely an important issue. There is a difference between doing something *for* the family and doing something *with* the family. Most churches are characterized by random acts of ministry to the family. What some churches call family ministry can involve everything from a counseling center for families to a recreation program in a family life center to a list of books for families to read to seminars or workshops for the family. Various departments in the church may schedule a sermon series on family, a mother-daughter tea, a father-son camping trip, a fall festival, or a host of other things in an attempt to be family-friendly. The reality is that all those things can actually overload a church's schedule and create competing systems. Over time, the hectic schedule they cause may even compete with the family relationships you are trying to encourage.

Family ministry should not be another program you *add* to your list of programs. It should be the filter you use to create and evaluate what you do to influence children and teenagers.

**Family ministry:** *an effort to synchronize church leaders and parents around a master plan to build faith and character in their sons and daughters.*

A family ministry should develop the process that drives how both the church *and* the home combine their efforts to influence the next generation. If we really believe that nothing is more important than someone's relationship with God, it makes sense to combine the influences of the home and church. This is what motivated Moses to rally the Hebrew nation around the *Shema* in Deuteronomy 6. It's why Jesus stepped on the planet and went to the cross. It's the reason the leaders and volunteers I know give the best years of their lives to ministry. There are a number of things we could argue—predestination, modes of baptism, symbolism in Revelation—but we're not going to figure out who's

THERE IS A DIFFERENCE BETWEEN DOING SOMETHING FOR THE FAMILY AND DOING SOMETHING WITH THE FAMILY.

right about any of those things until we get to heaven. We keep arguing about the things we can't know for sure, even though most of us really do believe that a hundred years from now the only thing that will matter is someone's relationship with God. And we can do something about that.

To combat this, I go by a simplistic doctrinal statement. I know it lacks a lot of detail, but I have this one memorized:

Jesus is who He said He was.
What the Bible says is true is true.
Everybody is going to be somewhere forever.

If those three things are true, I have a compelling mission both as a leader and as a parent to *lead people into a growing relationship with Jesus Christ.*

Basically it is just another way of asking you to think Orange.

Several years ago I was invited by a friend of mine, Sue Miller, to speak at the Promiseland Conference at Willow Creek Community Church in Chicago. She asked me to explain to children's pastors what I wanted them to know about family ministry. I remember thinking there were dozens of things I wanted children's pastors to know and that it would be difficult to condense them into a thirty-minute talk. As I thought about it further, these three ideas seemed to arise over and over.

**1.** *Kids need parents* **who will help them advance in their relationships with God.** Again, if you really believe nothing is more important than a child's relationship with God, then you know how important the next phrase is:

*No one has more potential to* **influence**
*a child's relationship with God than parents.*

As we have said, parents *will* have spiritual influence in their kids' lives. Parents are spiritual leaders whether they want to be or not—that is their role. They will teach their kids about a relationship with God through their *own* relationship with God. They will have an effect on their children's experience with God because of how they connect with their children. Kids will form their opinions about who God is and how He works by how their parents treat them. God knows this—that is why He uses the image of a Father to describe how He wants to relate to us. Your relationship with your parents affects your picture of God. If your earthly father was strong, accepting, and loving, you'll probably have an easier time seeing God that way. If your earthly father was distant, uninterested, or demanding, you might have difficulty understanding some aspects of God's character.

*No one has more potential to **monitor** a child's relationship with God than parents.*

There will never be a church pastor, leader, volunteer, or teacher who will have as much potential to observe what is happening in a child's life as a parent. Parents are in a unique position to answer questions about where their children are spiritually and what the next steps should be. The reason for that is simple—time.

Soon after we started North Point Community Church, a few of us who were working with kids and teenagers were wrestling with how to prioritize our programming with children and students. As we sat a table evaluating attendance and playing around with calculators, we realized something very sobering. At best, with those who attended our church consistently, we would only have about forty hours in a given year to influence a child. When we calculated holidays, sick days, custody issues, sports, vacations, and other factors, we realized how limited our time with children really was. The same fourth-grader who would spend nearly four hundred hours playing video games and studying math would spend forty hours in our environments with our leaders and teachers. That same day we calculated another number that shocked us: the amount of time the average parent had to spend with their children. It was three thousand hours in a single year. For the next decade, we consistently reminded our leaders and parents of the 3,000/40 principle. It forced us to begin thinking in terms of ministry style driven by Orange thinking. Every time we would train leaders, parents, or other churches, we would come up with a creative new way to demonstrate the time difference.

When I spoke at Willow Creek, there was a basket of forty plastic balls on the table I used as a podium. When it was time to demonstrate how much time a parent had, dozens of grocery carts came from every corner of the auditorium filled with three thousand plastic balls. They kept rolling them up on the stage until the contrast between the small basket and carts was astounding. I spoke for the rest of the time explaining from a practical point of view why we shouldn't spend one hundred percent of our time and resources on the forty hours spent inside the church. As leaders, we had to learn to spend some of our energy leveraging the three thousand. Over the past few years, a number of organizations and churches have used several different versions of the illustration to demonstrate the need to partner with family. The church simply cannot compare with the amount of time that the family has, most of it unplanned, to influence the heart of a child.

**2. *Parents need churches* that will help them know how to be spiritual leaders.** The vast majority of parents already believe they are responsible for the moral and spiritual development of their own children. It is intuitive to both non-Christian and Christian parents alike. Countless surveys show they are wired to feel a sense of concern and commitment to how their children are growing in character and faith. Every church is filled with parents who desire to raise their own kids the best way they can. Here are some statistics the Barna Group released a few years ago:

- 85 percent of parents believe they have the primary responsibility for teaching their children about religious beliefs.
- 96 percent of parents contend that they have the primary responsibility for teaching their children values.[24]

Another interesting statistic suggests that the majority of adults in the United States do not attend religious services. The exception to that statistic is parents who have children under the age of eighteen. Nearly two-thirds of these parents attend church at least once a month. Forty-three percent attend church at least weekly.[25] These are the parents who need—and are seeking—guidance in how to engage in dialogue with their kids about faith.

*Even though two out of three parents of children under the age of eighteen attend religious services at least once a month, the **majority** of parents do not spend any time during a typical week discussing spiritual issues.*

So parents of school-age children are attending church at a much higher rate than other adults. Why? I believe they are at a stage where they feel a heightened sense of responsibility for the spiritual and moral development of their children. It's like they are waving their arms and saying, "Here we are. We have kids and a family.

The average church only has
40 hours in a given year to
influence a life

The average parent has 3,000
hours per year to influence
a life

It feels like this is what we are supposed to do. We don't want to mess up as parents, so we are coming to church." The parents who live in the neighborhoods around your church have a high felt need to be a better parent. And it doesn't seem to take a lot to get them to come to church. But here's the problem …

*Only **one** out of **five** say they have ever been contacted by their church to discuss their responsibility to influence their children spiritually.*[26]

Why is it that so many parents who are coming back to church claim that the church has not really helped them lead their kids spiritually? Maybe it's because the church has been programmed to only think in terms of the color yellow. We don't really know how to partner with parents. Our programming and resources are built around the forty hours we have with kids. Some churches have unintentionally discouraged parents from becoming the spiritual leaders in their homes—they have believed that parents probably won't assume responsibility for their own children's spiritual growth, so they have tried to become a parent substitute.

It's a logical assumption; a lot of parents don't take on that responsibility. So we feel that if they don't assume the responsibility, we should. Why? Because too much is at stake, right? If nothing is more important than a child's relationship with God, and if parents are not going to make their children's faith a priority, shouldn't the church step in and take over? We do what feels like the right thing to do—we implement programs to replace the parents who should be the spiritual leaders. We gradually create a mindset that allows parents to believe that the church should assume responsibility for the spiritual growth of their kids. Then parents, over time, adopt a "drop-off" mentality. They decide that the church, not the family, is primarily responsible for the spiritual growth of their children.

It's hard to decide which issue is more problematic. Is it that the church is trying to assume a parent's responsibility because parents are not? Or is the bigger issue that parents stop assuming responsibility because the church makes them feel like the church should assume it?

We must believe that God would not give parents the responsibility to do something He has not equipped them to do. He doesn't work that way. We are the ones who orient our programming as if parents are not capable of doing what God has created them to do. Maybe the greatest gift a church can give parents

CHURCH LEADERS ARE
IN A GREAT POSITION
TO REDEFINE SPIRITUAL
LEADERSHIP IN TERMS
THAT ARE PRACTICAL AND
POSSIBLE.

is the confidence and courage to do what God has wired them to do. We should do exactly what Moses was doing for the Hebrew parents in Deuteronomy 6—we should challenge them to lead their own children spiritually.

Some leaders ask, "But what if parents don't do what they should?" I have never met a parent walking out of a delivery room holding a baby who said, "I can't wait to ruin this kid's life!" I'm sure there are parents who don't care, but those are a rare exception, not the rule. In my experience, most parents want to do this right, they are just not sure how.

When parents show up at church, they are often asking silent questions that we must answer, questions they don't even know they're asking. To begin looking at parents through a different filter, imagine that every time a parent walks through the door, he or she is asking you to do three things:

1. *Give me the plan.* Most parents are parenting reactively, yet many of them desire to be proactive. They want a plan that will give them a system of support, consistent influence, and a steady flow of relevant information.
2. *Show me how it works.* Parents need influence as much as children do, and they desire to be engaged in the process in a way that prompts them to take the best next step.
3. *Tell me what to do today.* If we are going to truly partner with parents, we have to give them specific instructions.

If you're going to help a parent know how to be a "spiritual leader," consider telling the parent what that phrase actually means. Church leaders are notorious for using passed-down phrases while never stopping to ask what those phrases mean exactly. If you were to send me an e-mail with a clear definition of spiritual leadership, what would it be? Have you ever written such a definition? Church leaders are in a great position to redefine spiritual leadership in terms that are practical and possible. I am convinced that most parents feel inadequate when they hear the term, and as a result they are not sure it's something they can do.

Several years ago I was invited to a meeting by the leaders of a national ministry to brainstorm ideas for partnering with parents. When the meeting started, the facilitator walked to the whiteboard and wrote 2 Timothy 3:17 on it: "So that the man of God may be thoroughly equipped for every good work." He took his marker and wrote the words "THOROUGHLY EQUIPPED MAN OF GOD" in huge letters. Then he said that if we can get every man in our country to become a "thoroughly equipped man of God," we will solve the family crisis in America.

As he continued explaining that the purpose of our meeting was to come up with ideas to help men become the standard-bearers of that passage, I started getting uneasy. The letters on the board seemed huge. I felt like they were just staring at me. It seemed like he just kept repeating them over and over. I remember thinking at some point, *I don't believe I can recall my wife ever using the words "thoroughly equipped," "man of God," and my name in the same sentence. I have middle-schoolers; by the time I become a "thoroughly equipped man of God" they will be parents themselves. I'm not sure I can ever be whatever that is, and I am not even sure what it means.* Sometimes I think many parents feel that way when they attend the typical church. It is possible to create an expectation that is so lofty and unattainable that they walk away discouraged.

Several years ago we presented parents with the following definition:

**Spiritual leadership:** *assuming the primary responsibility to help kids advance in their spiritual growth.*

Spiritual leadership means that parents become involved in helping their kids take the next step in their spiritual growth. The problem arises when we make parents feel like they are not qualified to do this, so let's make this practical and possible. It is really no different from what a parent would do to help children with schoolwork or when they are sick. No parent is going to say, "I can't help you with your homework; I didn't get an education degree," or, "I can't make sure you take your medicine; I'm not a doctor." Churches can give parents the tools, the ideas, the words, and the encouragement so they will have the confidence to lead and do what God has designed them to do as parents.

3. *Churches need leaders* to do less for kids and more for families.
The big question we should ask is, "If the church doesn't do this, who will?" Where will the leadership come from to partner with parents and encourage them to assume responsibility for spiritual leadership in their homes? What entity is the most logical one to help parents have a positive influence in their children's lives?

MAYBE THE MOST
STRATEGIC AND
EFFECTIVE THING YOU
COULD DO FOR YOUR
FAMILIES IS TO *STOP*
DOING SOMETHING.

Public or private schools? The government? When we talk about combining two influences, we are implying that influence goes both ways. It means the church is going to have to *rethink* what it does and how it can possibly synchronize with the family.

Some leaders will read this and immediately think, "But you don't understand—there is no margin in our ministry to do more than we are already doing. There is no more staff, no more resources, no more volunteers. There is definitely no way we could fit anything else on our church calendar." I agree.

One of the greatest Orange moments you could have in reading this book could be right now. Maybe the most strategic and effective thing you could do for your families is to *stop* doing something. Doing more for the family may mean that you actually do *fewer* programs for kids. A book I coauthored a few years ago, *The Seven Practices of Effective Ministry,* has a chapter called "Narrow the Focus" that describes the importance of doing less so you can make a greater impact.[27] In that chapter, we provided a long list of things we decided not to do so we could do a few things really well. As a result, North Point Community Church has demonstrated enormous growth by staying simple and focused. One of your greatest enemies is complexity. A lot of us who were mentored in ministry were told that the more programs you have, the more people you will reach. I talk to church leaders every week who admit that if they were to stop doing something, another part of their ministry would probably thrive.

During an Orange Leaders meeting in Minnesota, a student pastor asked me a great question: "If we start being more intentional about partnering with parents, won't that distract us from doing our student ministry with excellence?" At this point, it becomes necessary to begin thinking with the business side of our minds. You have forty hours in a given year to spend with students. Parents have three thousand hours. What would happen if you reduced the amount of time and resources you were spending on the forty hours down to 80 percent? And what if you took that extra 20 percent and invested it into the three thousand hours? The potential of having a more excellent student ministry is fifteen times greater. Let's say that only 50 percent of your parents actually respond and engage with their kids an hour a week. You have potentially doubled your influence with half of your kids. Do the math; partnering with parents is one of the best ways to have greater influence with students.

It doesn't take leadership to kill something that is not working. That's easy; it's already dead. All you have to do is take it to your deacons and elders, kick it a few times, get a consensus, and go bury it. What really takes courageous leadership is to kill something that is working. The thing that usually gets in the way of what would work best is something that is already working pretty well. According to the pruning lesson Jesus gave in the Gospels, you have to cut off what is living so another part can thrive.

Doing more for the family is the best way the church can have consistent influence in the heart of a child. As a leader, you will have a limited amount of influence in the lives of those who come through your ministry. One day, inevitably, they are going to walk away. You may stay connected to a few for a while but not most. On the other hand, parents will have lifelong influence. They will be there for birthdays, graduations, weddings, and holidays. They will be the ones who show up at the hospital to celebrate the cycle starting over again with a new baby. Parents, by default, have lifelong influence. So when you influence parents, when you merge with them, you influence the relationships that will impact the child the most.

Doing more for the family requires the church to make an intentional shift from a yellow mindset to an Orange ministry mindset. When you think Orange, a different kind of conversation starts—there has to be a shift in the way you see things. Once you get in the habit of looking through an Orange filter you will be amazed how quickly the creativity and new perspective will change how you view everything.

*If you think yellow,*
You invest most of your time and resources creating programs for kids.
*When you think Orange,*
You invest quality time and resources creating programs for parents *and* kids.

*If you think yellow,*
You are consumed with answering the question, "What are we going to teach kids?"
*When you think Orange,*
You are consumed with answering the question, "How can we get parents to also teach what we are teaching their kids?"

WHAT REALLY TAKES COURAGEOUS LEADERSHIP IS TO KILL SOMETHING THAT IS WORKING.

*If you think yellow,*
You promote what you want parents to know about your programs.
*When you think Orange,*
You focus on what you want parents to do at home.

*If you think yellow,*
You think what happens at church is more important than what happens at home.
*When you think Orange,*
You believe what happens at home is as important as what happens at church.

There are reasons that church leaders sometimes don't do well at partnering with families. And there are reasons parents don't do well at partnering with the church.

They are each preoccupied with their own self-interests.
They don't really think it's that important to work together.
They have a hard time thinking a different way.
They are preoccupied with individual goals.
They tend to see the other entity as relevant only if it can further their own goals.

If leaders who think *yellow* are deciding how to participate with *red*, *yellow* will always be the priority. Their ultimate goal will be to preserve and promote the *yellow* cause over the *red* cause. And if things go wrong, they will tend to point their *yellow* fingers at all of those who are *red* and blame them for the way things are. And those who are *yellow* will only see the significance of *red* in terms of how it highlights or supports their *yellow* happenings.

In the same way, if parents who think *red* are only participating with *yellow* for the sake of their *red* issues, then they will only support *yellow's* role whenever it is beneficial to help them become a deeper *red* or when they are having a *red* crisis. And if things go wrong in their *red* world they will tend to point their *red* fingers of blame at everyone *yellow*.

The needs of *red* will never really be
a priority to *yellow* thinkers over the needs of *yellow*.

The needs of *yellow* will never really be
a priority to *red* thinkers over the needs of *red*.

**It's not either/or; it's both/and.**
Both red and yellow need to recognize there is a polarity to be managed. It's easy to drift toward an either/or mindset, but it's a tension that is normal and can be leveraged for a powerful partnership if they start believing in the possibility of both/and. Churches have a tendency to point their fingers at parents and say, "The problem with the world is that we need to fix the family." And parents have a tendency to drop their kids off at the church. When it doesn't change the kids' behavior, parents will point their fingers at the church and say, "The problem with the world is that we need to fix the church."

Here's a news flash: *We are the church. We are the family.* We are pointing at ourselves. If something needs to be fixed, it probably has a little or a lot to do with both. It's a dilemma, and it's hard to figure out sometimes. Even in my own mind as a parent and leader, it creates a double-minded way of thinking.

If you were to ask me as a *leader* if I trust the average family to be primarily responsible for a child's spiritual growth, I might honestly say no.

If you were to ask me as a *parent* if I trust the average church to be primarily responsible for my children's spiritual growth, again I would say no.

If I put on the church leader's hat (that's the yellow one), I want to say to churches, "You change whatever you have to change, regardless of what the family does, to encourage a child's relationship with God." Why? There is too much at stake.

If I wear the parent's hat (that's the red one), I want to say to parents, "You should change whatever you have to change, regardless of what the church does, to encourage your children's relationship with God." Why? There is too much at stake.

But when I put on the Orange hat, I can see that both are possible.

Both are right. Both are important. Both can complement or both can become competing systems. You can either attempt to manage each one separately with little regard to how it affects the other, or you decide to enter into an honest debate to make changes to both in order to achieve an effective partnership and a more desirable outcome.

**Things Every Kid Needs**

A REALLY BIG GOD
SOMEONE ELSE
ANOTHER VOICE
UNCOMMON SENSE
NOSY PARENTS

# Things Every Kid Needs

**A REALLY BIG GOD they can trust no matter what**
Kids should grow up knowing that God is big enough to handle whatever they may face.

**SOMEONE ELSE who believes what they believe**
Kids need friends who will encourage them to grow in their faith.

**ANOTHER VOICE saying the same things parents say**
As children grow older it becomes more important to have other adults in their lives as spiritual mentors and leaders.

**UNCOMMON SENSE to help them make wise choices**
God's point of view and His truth should become the filter for how kids view life and make decisions.

**NOSY PARENTS who know where their kids are spiritually**
Kids need parents who will be intentional about spending time together as a family and staying actively involved in their children's spiritual growth.

# 5

## SKEEPLES AND LOMES

*Some of us have become a little fanatical about what thinking Orange could possibly do for children. So it seems logical to explain the concept in a way that maybe the child in all of us could appreciate. You may think you are too sophisticated and decide to skip over this next section. But don't do it. If you do, it may be an indicator that you are just too yellow to engage in an Orange revolution.*

*Thanks to some really creative minds and the talented writing of Greg Payne, here's a story that should inspire your imagination about how the right amount of Orange could change the world.*

The Skeeples were yellow, no doubt about that,
From the points of their Gil-boots to the lights on their Sill-hats,
But amazing Crelunkers when it came down to that,
And they loved to help anyone stuck in a Cravat.

No matter how dark or how terrible the plight
The big yellow lamps on their Sill-hats burned bright,
Illuming the corners with yellow spotlights.
They were born to do rescues and set things aright.

But the Skeeples were aloof, often kept to themselves.
They lived up on Mount Tilley, slept on yellow shelves.
They kept rescue equipment for whate'er befell.
They trained daily for rescues and rang alarm bells.

The Lomes were world famous as huggers and reachers.
At the foot of Mount Tilley they lived and they played, sure.
The first thing you noticed when you saw these fine creatures
Was their red-colored bodies and red-colored features.

The next thing you noticed if you were standing quite close
Was a cozy tucked feeling, like warm buttered toast.
It made everything warmer, but they wouldn't boast,
For this gift put inside them inspired their utmost.

The Lomes all lived close at the base of Mount Tilley.
The Skeeples on the mountain, and the reason was silly.
They each got along, although sometimes ill-will-y.
They'd lived close for years, but relations were chilly.

Even so, that grand mount was an idyllic spot;
Everyone was so thankful for the things that they'd got.
Both the Skeeples and Lomes would agree on this spot,
That they were most thankful for the Eph-lip-i-tots.

Eph-lip-i-tots were all cuddly and cute.
When they grinned or they giggled everyone "Awwwed" and said, "Shoot,
I love Eph-lip-i-tots. I love watching them grow.
I love their tiny red hands and their wrinkly red toes."

Mostly, life on that mountain was exciting and fun.
The Lomes played in the shade. Skeeples warmed in the sun.
They'd say all of their problems boiled down to just one:
Eph-lip-i-tots tended to wander and run.

See, Eph-lip-i-tots were young. They had lots to learn.
To walk and to wander their tiny hearts yearned,
But often they'd tumble as teeny feet turned
Toward the Cave of Cravats (and some didn't return).

I could tell a thousand stories of the 'Tots and their beauty!
The most famous is about Tinkit Potten—that cutie!
She shared and she sang, and she was never, ever snooty.
She was all charm and all red, from her head to her booties.

Like every Eph-lip-i-tot she was made for a reason,
A treasure we hold, but just for a season.
To suggest any different would sound just like treason,
And this is one thing that red and yellow both agrees in.

So surprised were the Lomes the day Tinkit walked out,
They mumbled, "She's walking toward the cave. What's that about?"
At first they just whispered, then it turned to a shout,
"Tinkit Potten, come back! Please don't … Look out!"

The Lomes fell behind, crying, "Please, Tinkit, come back!"
But little Tinkit kept tottering her dangerous track.
Then the Skeeples' bells rang, and they loaded their packs.
"To the rescue!" they called and ran down switchbacks.

"GORP!" lurped the Cravat as little Tinkit tumbled in
And turned her bright glow of red to a black gucky ruin.
As quick as a wink the glop grabbed to her skin.
(I wish she'd never found the evil cave with the goo in.)

Then the two warmest Lomes darted into the cave
Headed straight toward poor Tinkit (more determined than brave),
But it was so black and dark, the situation was grave,
And they both thunk a thought, "Can our Tinkit be saved?"

They planned to pull Tinkit all free from the harm
By filling the cave with the Lomes' special warm.
Then the goo would get melty, release her red arms,
She'd get out of the pit, and they'd end the alarms!

But the Lomes had a problem right from the start.
No matter how warm the love poured from their hearts,
They couldn't see Tinkit. The cave was too dark!
The two Lomes were forced from the cave to depart.

"We need some more help!" said a voice from the crowd.
And a heavy, dark silence came down like a cloud.

They all knew who to call, but now were they too proud?
Why, the Lomes call the Skeeples? It's hardly allowed.

The Lomes stood in silence outside the Cravat.
They looked at their feet, and some held their red hats,
And right then, uninvited, a Crelunk rope went "Splat!"
And from over a rock appeared a bright yellow hat.

Yes, the Skeeples came down from their Skeeply inclines
With their Sill-hats in place and all ready to shine.
They took charge and set up some bright yellow tapelines.
Finally, oh, finally, things might work out fine!

But one group of the Lomes just weren't ready for this.
"Just where have you been? You're too late!" they all hissed.
And some Skeeples were ready to cease and desist,
Until they thought about the child stuck inside the abyss.

So the Skeeples kept working, although taken aback,
Setting up lights without being sidetracked.
"Just leave it to us. Please, take one step back.
We'll get the child out. We've observed her whole track."

The Skeeples all worked with their confidence sure.
Their methods were proven, and their motives were pure.
All their lights lit the cave with no corner obscured.
In the dark cave they knew Tinkit couldn't endure.

Little Tinkit was stuck, and that fact was plain,
So the Skeeples mapped out the deadly terrain.
With the cave brightened up, they could see everything.
"We'll simply lift the child out, and success is attained!"

The rescue sounded so easy and quick,
'Til they found that the goo was especially thick.
The red Lome child was caught in a Cravat dirty trick.
One Skeeple came out looking solemn, sad, and sick.

"We've assessed our assessment," he announced to the crowd,
"But it looks rather grim," he said not so loud.
"We can see that she's caught. She's stuck even now.
And we can't get her loose. We just aren't sure how."

Some Lomes' lips trembled. No one knew what to do.
Then through all the mumbled prayers, one voice sounded through.
"But, well, what if we try it as one team, not two?
Let's all work together and get her out of that goo."

No one's sure who shouted, "But we can't do that!"
But a Skeeple looked away and then pulled down his hat.
"It's just not tradition," and he turned, and he spat.
"Mix red and mix yellow? Beside a Cravat?"

Just then Grandpaw Lome spoke, "Now that's about enough!
I've heard red and heard yellow and all that old stuff.
We're going to save Tinkit. Don't give me no guff!
So, now who's on the team? Or do I have to get rough?"

And with that Grandpaw Lome marched his way right back in.
Then the quiet got thick, but pride started to thin.
Everyone stood still waiting till one Skeeple joined him.
Why, he followed the Lome, and by golly he grinned!

Red and yellow filled the cave, coming in two by two.
The task was too important not to try something new.
The Lomes warmed their hearts, and their special heat grew,
While the Skeeples lit the cave up like sunshine at noon.

But Red Lomes and Yellow Skeeples? How could this be?
Could this be the way Tinkit might become free?
The Cravat slowly warmed, and the Lomes now could see.
It had taken an Eph-lip-i-tot to make them agree.

Then Grandpaw stepped up and took Tinkit's red hand.
The Chief Skeeple stood by, and then right on command
The two pulled on her arms and something wondrous began.
Tinkit's skin glowed orange, so bright and so grand!

Then almost at once that dark cave changed its mood.
Orange glow moved up Grandpaw, and the Skeeples approved.
The Chief Skeeple glowed orange, and all the Lomes "Oooooo'd!"
The Cravat goo turned orange, and Tinkit Potten … moved!

The orange Skeeple on one side, and Grandpaw on the other;
They lifted Tinkit out, and handed her to her mother.
As the tiny one was hugged until she nearly was smothered,
The orange glow spread to aunts, cousins, and brothers.

The cave filled with orange on that wonderful day,
Then it covered Mount Tilley with bright orange rays.
The Cravat Cave then brightened its other passageways,
And more Cravats were revealed with 'Tots trapped and afraid.

Chief Skeeple then ordered, "Men, roll up your sleeves."
And rescues began like you wouldn't believe.
Eph-lip-i-tots were unstuck and parents relieved.
It was a day that no Skeeple or Lome could conceive.

Just outside the cave's mouth a party blossomed,
And as each 'Tot was freed, not a one went straight home.
They danced and they sang under an orange Lome-dome,
Had orange punch, orange cookies, and orange ice-cream-foam.

Red and yellow high-fived and stopped being so rotten.
They named that fine day "The Day of Freed Eph-lip-i-tot-en."
The Skeeples and Lomes were so glad that they'd gotten
The importance of Orange. Just ask Tinkit Potten.

# Part Two
## Five Orange Essentials

Design a strategy that combines the family with the faith community to demonstrate the message of God's story, in order to influence the next generation.

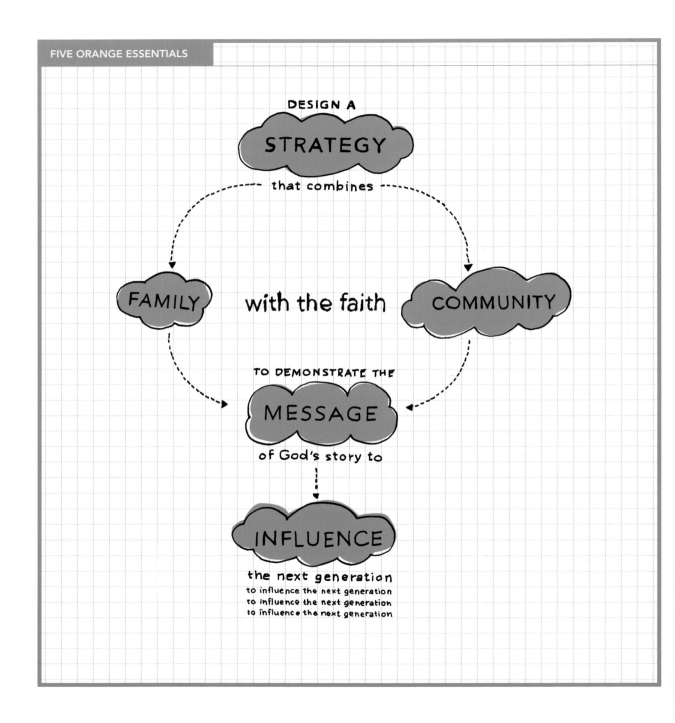

DESIGN A

STRATEGY

that combines

FAMILY          with the faith          COMMUNITY

TO DEMONSTRATE THE

MESSAGE

of God's story to

INFLUENCE

the next generation
to influence the next generation
to influence the next generation
to influence the next generation

There are two primary influences responsible for the spiritual formation of a generation:
The church.
The family.

When you combine these two influences, you make a greater impact than either of these influences will make individually.

Regardless of your model or style of church, there are key principles that are critical to helping you create a culture that will think Orange.

Your ability to synchronize the church and the family
is intricately connected to how you …
… meet and work together as leaders
… craft and present truth
… enlist parents to actively participate
… recruit leaders to mentor or coach
… mobilize kids and teenagers to serve

These issues have an interdependent relationship. Collectively, they provide a core framework for combining the influence of the home and church. During the rest of the book we will explore the Five Orange Essentials:

INTEGRATE STRATEGY *to create synergy.*
REFINE THE MESSAGE *to amplify what's important.*
REACTIVATE THE FAMILY *to build an everyday faith.*
ELEVATE COMMUNITY *to increase the odds.*
LEVERAGE INFLUENCE *to mobilize generations.*

Although there will be a variety of illustrations and practices discussed in the rest of the book, be careful. Don't miss the transferability these principles have to any size or style of church or ministry. Spend time with your team customizing these concepts so you can retrofit them into your model.

Just in case you don't read the rest of the book, let me give you the idea in one sentence:

Design a **strategy** that combines the **family** with the faith **community** to demonstrate the **message** of God's story, in order to **influence** the next generation.

ESSENTIAL #1

# INTEGRATE STRATEGY

**WHEN** YOU
**COMBINE 2**
INFLUENCES, YOU

## CREATE SYNERGY

# 6

## INTEGRATE STRATEGY
### ALIGN LEADERS AND PARENTS TO LEAD WITH THE SAME END IN MIND

Did you know …

When Ronald Reagan was running for president, Nancy Reagan started a tradition many politicians still practice of rolling a good-luck orange down the aisle of the campaign plane (and later Air Force One) as soon as it took off.

In 1968, young rock hopeful Clifford Cooper built his own guitar amps using tube technology and basic wooden boxes covered with orange vinyl. When his ironically named band (the Millionaires) went broke, Cooper put the amps in the window of the practice studio to sell for extra cash. Today, artists like U2, Alanis Morissette, Madonna, and Kid Rock still use Orange Amps. (Even Blue Man Group uses Orange!)

Ice cream entrepreneur Howard Deering Johnson decided to open a chain of restaurants in the 1930s with a friendly feel for travelers on the new interstate highway system. The orange-roofed, Cape Cod-style houses became national landmarks for those looking for a good meal and a safe place along the lonely road.

I know what you are thinking. All this seems kind of random. What does it really have to do with anything about churches and homes, or Deuteronomy and Revelation, or Skeeples and Lomes?

Are you making the connection?

Randomness … leadership … orange …

Leaders who have a passion for Orange will sort through the present randomness so they can guide people to a clearer path. If you're a leader, it's your job to make sense out of this for your world.

**YOU NEED TO MAKE SURE THAT EVERYONE WHO LEADS WITH YOU IS LEADING IN THE SAME DIRECTION.**

You probably have Orange leaders in your church who are already doing this. They work every week turning chaos into order. They invest in a style of critical hands-on ministry. They make the initial connections with dozens of people who show up in your church. These leaders meet people at important intersections in their lives and give purposeful direction. Have you noticed them? Do you know who they are? They are the men and women who push through countless situations and the stormy weather of life to lead others. They rise earlier than most so they can prepare to communicate a critical message to everyone.

Is it your senior pastor? No.
Is it your worship leader? No.
Is it your teachers? No.
Is it your preschool leaders? No.

They are the individuals who greet you in the *parking lot* every Sunday.
They have mastered one primary tool …
an *orange* safety cone.

Yes, we are talking about those things used in your parking lot to help direct traffic and show people where to go. A lot of research has been done to determine why they should be orange. There's even a Manual on Uniform Traffic Control Devices. It's really amazing how a few pounds of orange thermoplastic and rubber can control the direction of a two-ton car. Hundreds of automobiles are guided every day by the strategic placement of those orange cones.

It's kind of like your leadership. If you're a church leader, you have been put in a position to lead families in a specific direction, and it's probably a good idea to spend some time figuring out where you want to lead them. Whether you like it or not, a few misplaced parking cones can confuse a lot of people and lead to some nasty wrecks. You need to make sure that everyone who leads with you is leading in the same direction.

Nothing can cause havoc like multiple parking cones scattered across the pavement by independent leaders pointing people in different directions. Frequent communication between all those in charge is essential to avoid potential collisions. If we are going to be effective at creating synergy, we have to sometimes think like the guys who wear orange and know how to handle those orange traffic cones. They have embraced a couple of basic principles:

Traffic cones exist primarily to show people where they should go.
Traffic cones were designed to work together to have greater influence.

They have bought into the idea of *integrated strategy*.

I know the word *strategy* bothers some leaders who have an aversion to any term that is not in the Bible. The word may not be there, but I think the concept is. Some leaders would caution, "What does a word that is used in a military or business context have to do with building a better bridge between church and family?" Before you write the idea off too quickly, consider the following definition.

A strategy is a plan of action with an end in mind.
That means you have identified what you want something (or someone) to be, and you have used your creativity and intellect to devise a way to get it there. *You have figured out where to place the cones so you can lead people where you want them to be.*

When we use the phrase *integrate strategy,* we are suggesting that your plan of action should synchronize with that of others. It implies you are combining multiple influences, primarily those in the home and church, working off the same page for the sake of what you want to accomplish in the hearts of the next generation. An integrated strategy means that *leaders and parents are leading with the same end in mind.*

Without an integrated strategy,
parents struggle over how to partner with the church,
programming tends to be isolated in impact,
there is no consistent forum to evaluate and improve what you are doing,
volunteers become disillusioned with the lack of direction,
leaders and staff drift toward silo thinking,
overprogramming and competing systems dilute your influence.

I remember distinctly the day I became convinced that our church should become more intentional about partnering with parents. We were brainstorming ideas,

**WE CAN'T REALLY EXPECT PARENTS TO GET ON THE SAME PAGE WITH THE CHURCH UNTIL WE GET ON THE SAME PAGE AS LEADERS.**

and I experienced a moment of revelation, realizing that a lot of our leaders were not in sync. I thought, We can't really expect parents to get on the same page with the church until we get on the same page as leaders. When age-group ministries that are characterized by competing systems and disconnected staffs try to enlist families to participate with their programs, there will always be limited success.

When it comes to thinking Orange, you need to constantly work on five different areas as a team. In these next several chapters, we will talk about these concepts and give ideas about how to implement them. Regardless of your size or style of church, you can identify ways to combine your influence with that of the family.

There is another Orange leader who will help us illustrate the concept of integrating strategy. It's someone who is almost as famous as Ronald Reagan. See if you can guess from this list of characteristics:

- a prestigious job and political influence
- ability to raise a lot of money
- great respect and appreciation for military leverage
- mobilized one the largest volunteer efforts in history
- a well-known community organizer
- knew how to inspire millions of people

No, it's not Barack Obama.
It's Nehemiah!

Think about his story: His hometown is in trouble. The next generation is disillusioned and at risk because an entire community has lost vision. Very real enemies threaten their survival. According to his journal, the Hebrew nation is living "in disgrace."[28] Nehemiah appeals to the king, enlists support, and secures funding to rebuild Jerusalem. Then he takes a leave of absence and travels to the broken-down city. After he carefully evaluates the situation, this leader challenges the people to implement his plan to renovate the city. In spite of a threatening enemy and impossible odds, the people rally and rebuild the walls in only fifty-two days.

A number of things are evident in his story and are important to keep in mind, especially if you hope to restore your influence as a church.

- Nehemiah developed a clear plan.
- He was driven by a passion for God's story to be demonstrated.
- He inspired leaders to get involved.
- He recognized the need to rally the family.
- He demonstrated the value of influence.

I want to focus on a few applications from Nehemiah for those of us who are trying to rebuild our homes and churches. When you read Nehemiah's journal, one of the first things you notice is that he thinks in terms of strategy. He appeals to the king, estimates how much time and money it will take, and anticipates various other details. He has an end in mind, a vision of rebuilt walls and a restored city. When he arrives, he secretly evaluates the condition of the wall and determines a plan of action. The work begins and it's obvious that different groups have been assigned to specific gates. Detailed instructions have been given to various leaders. Nehemiah was not just on a mission—he had a strategy. I even like to say he had an *integrated strategy.*

There was a plan.
There was a target.
There was coordination.
There was synchronization.

There were orange cones everywhere. Everyone knew where to go and what to do. People were using their skills and gifts. Every generation was engaged. There was a buzz inside and outside the town. The walls began to go up.

Nehemiah knew something critical needed to happen if he was going to accomplish God's mission. When you think in terms of your mission to influence the next generation, always remember …

*It's the effectiveness of your strategy,*
*not the scope of your mission,*
*that ultimately determines your success.*

When I stress the importance of strategy I am by no means implying that you shouldn't depend on God. Even more so, you and I have a responsibility to prepare and manage the mission that God gives us. Nehemiah said, "Our God will fight for us,"[29] but the Israelites still worked on the wall with a tool in one hand and a weapon in the other. So, who exactly was supposed to fight? Both God and the Israelites. God expected them to be prepared, to work the plan, and to fight for themselves. Just because God is backing the mission doesn't mean we have permission to be lazy or unintentional with the strategy. At reThink, we work with thousands of churches that participate in the vision to reach the next generation. I am sure they have all crafted a mission statement that everyone understands. It probably hangs on their walls and is stated publicly every week. But trust me on this, the fact that you have a mission, even if it is the most incredible mission on the planet, doesn't mean you will accomplish it.

Before Nehemiah showed up, the Hebrew leaders just sat around, surrounded by broken-down walls. They realized the walls needed to be built, and I'm sure they had a desire for the city to be protected. So what was the problem? The task seemed daunting. No one had arranged it into a specific plan. There was no strategy. This is one of the reasons that volunteers are sometimes not clear about what to do, or the reason parents don't seem to engage or participate, or the reason well-meaning organizations spin their wheels. They need a Nehemiah to speak order into the chaos, clarity into the confusion.

The notion that any church is somehow exempt from integrating a strategy is tragic.

Personally, I believe Nehemiah knew the stakes were high. He saw the next generation standing in the wings, watching its leaders passively continue in their state of disgrace. He was personally burdened about the fact that families and children were unprotected and vulnerable, and he knew it would ultimately affect their perception of God. So Nehemiah aggressively pursued a strategic solution. Sure he prayed, and he listened to God. But he didn't only pray; he acted. He evaluated, rallied, recruited, and implemented. He had an integrated strategy. He figured out what God wanted him to do then challenged every leader and worker and parent to do it. There is no excuse for churches full of wise and savvy men and women who believe in God and know the stakes are high to remain immobile while the walls of the home and church are broken down. We need modern-day Nehemiahs who are willing to take risks and lead a revolution. With

God's help and an integrated strategy, they will become an active part of God's story to restore and redeem what has been broken. Everyone will have clarity and focus. Leaders and families will be on the same page. Everyone will be able to do together far more than they could have done alone.

**When you integrate strategy, it magnifies everyone's focus.**
Nehemiah rallied an entire nation to hyperfocus on a clear mission. The strategy he communicated connected every leader and parent, every tribe and family, to their role in building the wall. What would it be like if we could create a strategy so clear that leaders and families would understand exactly how they connect to the mission?

Several years ago, I got the urge to purchase a motorcycle. Something just happened to me when I was looking at them at our local motor sports superstore. It's hard to explain. During high school and college, I had driven a small Honda street bike. As a starter bike for my middle-age years, I gave myself a 650-pound Yamaha V Star. When the manager handed me the keys, my common sense kicked in and I realized I should probably practice driving it before I actually went out on the road. So my dad put the new Yamaha on a trailer and delivered it to the church parking lot that afternoon. I made him wait until I was sure most of the staff had gone home. My plan was to get acquainted with it in the safe environment of our after-hours church parking lot before I headed out to the north Georgia mountains. I hadn't ridden a motorcycle in more than twenty years, and it was more difficult than I remembered. I just couldn't get comfortable on it. I put five hundred miles on the bike in the church parking lot in those first few weeks.

Little did I realize that some of my family and friends on the church staff would get together and watch me attempt to maneuver it around parking cones at the church. One day a few people confessed to spying on me, and they gave me an ultimatum. "We have all talked, and we are not going to let you take the motorcycle to the mountains until you actually take lessons from someone who is certified. You are not very good at this."

My wife signed me up for a class, and the first thing the instructor did was a skill test to see how well I could drive. He arranged six cones in a pattern along a hundred-foot-long stretch of pavement. The object was to start at one end and drive to the other, weaving in and out of the cones, without knocking any of them over. It seemed easy enough. I started moving, doing what seemed intuitive. I carefully made my way around the first cone. When I cleared it, I turned to look at the second cone. That's when I realized I was farther away from the second cone than I had anticipated. I overcompensated and barely made it around the second cone. Knowing I was drifting off course, I turned as quickly as I could to make it around the next one, but by the time I spotted the third cone I was running into it.

The instructor motioned for me to begin again, so I stopped and went back to the starting line. I was convinced I had not anticipated the angles of the cones very well and had been tricked by some kind of optical illusion. Starting again, I concentrated hard on the first cone and estimated the angle and distance to the second cone, easing up on the gas. I repeated the same errors almost identically, barely getting past the second cone and plowing over the third one. The instructor began walking over to me.

As he came closer, I started explaining what I thought I was doing wrong and implied that this time I was going to slow it down some.

He smiled and said, "The only thing you are doing wrong is looking at the cones."

I was confused. I asked, "So then where am I supposed to look?"

He said, "At me."

I thought, *That doesn't make sense at all. I am supposed to drive around something and somehow not look at it?*

Then he explained, "The object is to focus on the end point and keep your head pointed in the same direction. Then, with your peripheral vision, you will see all the cones at the same time, but in the context of where you are going. That's the only way you can really judge their relationship to each other."

So I started again. What happened was kind of hard to believe. By adjusting my focus, it changed everything. Although it felt counterintuitive, the result was amazing. When I focused on him, I could actually see everything in the context of where I was going and I *could* navigate around each cone perfectly—the first time

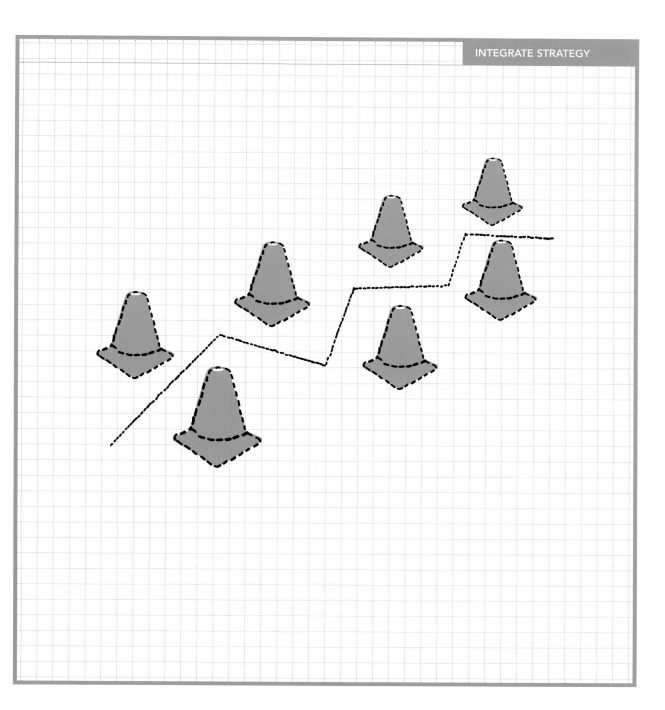

I tried. It worked because I was able to evaluate the relationship of everything in front of me in connection to my ultimate destination.

For a long time, I did ministry the way I first drove a motorcycle. I had a tendency to get so focused on what was in front of me that I didn't see two things:

- where it is ultimately supposed to lead
- how everything should be connected

I'd simply work on one project until I was finished with it, then I'd look around for what was next. It would usually be coming at me much faster than I anticipated. At some point, you get disillusioned and burned out. How does all this fit together for you and your ministry context?

One of the most critical discussions you can have as a team is to decide where you really want to lead people. Where do you want them to end up? What do you want the students or the children who come through your ministry to ultimately become? Back up and look at everything else in the light of that one focus. What if all your ministries and all your families agreed about the focus? How would that change what you do?

Jesus was always clarifying the end, keeping the focus. He had a way of zeroing in on what really mattered. I wish I could have been there when the Pharisees showed up and started asking questions. (Sometimes it reminds me of the bloggers I read. I think the Pharisees would have loved blogging. I am not suggesting that all bloggers are Pharisees; I just think they would have loved the potential it provides to stir something up, then back away and watch the chain reactions.) The Pharisees loved to flex their spiritual muscles and theological intellect. Anytime they got an opportunity to discredit someone who threatened their identity, they would take their shots. This happens specifically in Matthew 22, after Jesus had silenced the Sadducees, and the Pharisees got together to try to trip Him up.

"One of them, an expert in the law, tested him with this question: 'Teacher, which is the greatest commandment in the Law?'"[30]

Just think about the situation from God's point of view. Here is Jesus, God in the flesh, being asked a trick question by a Pharisee who was known to be an expert about God. Maybe he had no idea he was *talking* to God. Jesus pulls out a commandment, something He had actually said to Moses on the mountain fifteen hundred years earlier. It had been given a new meaning in Deuteronomy, and now Jesus is about to elevate this passage to an even more significant level: "Love the Lord your God with all your heart and with all your soul and with all your mind. This is the first and greatest commandment."

Did you see what happened? Jesus just pulled a Moses on the Pharisees. Now they are in a tough spot. Not only did He bring up the *Shema*, He just promoted it to another level.

I'm not sure what happened next, but here's how I imagine it. Maybe a few people clapped. The disciples breathed a sigh of relief. The Pharisees were visibly uncomfortable. There was a dramatic pause.

And then Jesus said, "And."

Thomas panicked. He was already nervous. He probably thought, "What? There is no 'and' after the *Shema*. I really wish Jesus would stop messing with what Moses said. Somebody is going to get really mad."

But Jesus continues. He wants to make a point, especially to the Pharisees. "The second is like it," He says. "'Love your neighbor as yourself.' All the Law and the Prophets hang on these two commandments." Jesus basically adds a piece of Scripture to the sacred *Shema*. He establishes three important relationships as priorities: God, others, and self. He suggests to everyone listening how their relationships with God affect everything else. It's as if He is suggesting, *When your focus is on God, you will be able to see the rest of God's commandments with your peripheral vision.*

In the next chapter, we will talk more specifically about how this principle applies to what and how we teach. At this point, it's just important to recognize a more subtle point that is made through this passage: Not all truth is created equal. When you integrate everyone on the team, including parents and leaders, you are able to narrow the area of focus, bringing what really matters into sharp clarity. It gives parents and leaders a powerful tool to use in

ONE OF THE MOST CRITICAL DISCUSSIONS YOU CAN HAVE AS A TEAM IS TO DECIDE WHERE YOU REALLY WANT TO LEAD PEOPLE.

effectively evaluating how everything should connect together. It establishes a clear "end in mind" that keeps everyone on the same page.

**When you integrate strategy it synchronizes everyone's effort.**
I grew up in a model of church that fueled competing systems. In order to understand the complexity of how the system worked, you should draw a grid. First draw three vertical lines parallel to each other and write "preschool," "children," and "youth" at the top of each column. That's a picture of the age-group departments.

Then, draw four horizontal lines parallel to each other that cross each of the vertical lines. At the left end of the lines, write "music," "education," "missions," and "recreation." (Note: It's important that music goes at the top, because it was always the priority when it came to space or budget. There was also an entirely separate grid that represented the music department staff.)

Now, you have seven lines forming a grid, representing seven different departments. There was a minister of education who managed all the age-group programs, and age-group programming was heavily influenced by four other departments. In a large church like ours, each of the seven lines represented a full-time or part-time staff member. In some smaller churches, the top horizontal line would represent the only paid full-time staff (which, again, is the minister of music). Everyone else would be part-time or volunteer staff. It is also important to note that the roles represented by horizontal lines were higher in the organizational chart than those represented by the vertical lines.

In staffing this way, every department that worked with children or teenagers was controlled or affected by departments that had more value in the eyes of the overall church. And in every place where two lines crossed, there was the potential for a competing system. With twelve intersections in all, it seemed that everyone was competing for the same children, parents, volunteers, budget, calendar, and facilities. Those who were responsible for age-group ministries could be easily trumped for something that was deemed a higher priority. The executive staff even created a system for calendar meetings in which activities on the calendar were labeled A, B, or C to give greater weight to horizontal events than those that were vertical.

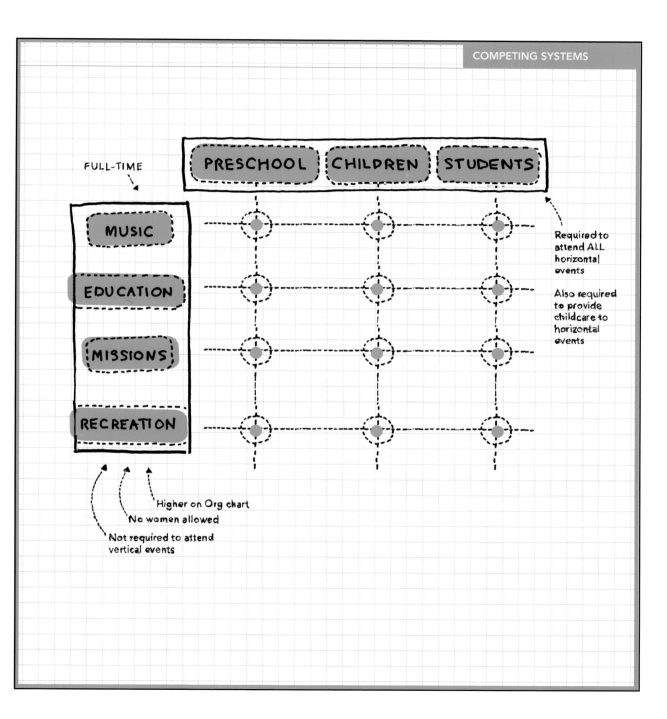

**THE PROBLEM ISN'T THAT CHURCHES ARE NOT DOING PROGRAMMING FOR FAMILIES; THE PROBLEM IS THEIR LACK OF STRATEGIC PROGRAMMING FOR FAMILIES.**

There were also a few other unwritten "policies":

No one on a *horizontal* line was expected to attend a *vertical* event.

Everyone on a *vertical* line was required to attend every *horizontal* event,

as well as provide child care.

And women were not allowed to fill a role *anywhere* on a *horizontal* line.

One of the most common struggles with churches attempting to partner with families is complexity. As we stated in the last chapter, sometimes you have to deliberately decide to do less in order to do more. If you go back to the grid mindset, you realize that one of the problems in a silo-driven model of church is overprogramming. We are competing not only with each other but with the family unit itself. Whenever I hear a church or leader say, "We challenge all our leaders to think of ways to impact the family," I cringe. What they will probably do is encourage a lot of leaders to create more programs that will dilute the family. The problem isn't that churches are not doing programming for families; the problem is their lack of *strategic* programming for families.

Think about the grid above with horizontal and vertical silos. It may be exaggerated, but the truth is it is easier to drift toward a style with a lot of random activity for families than to develop a ministry team that actually complements the role of the family.

*See Concentrate 6.1*

Several years ago, I spent a couple of days with a large church that wanted to do more for families. After two days of discussing a variety of ideas, it became apparent this church's system had become too complex through the years. The calendar collected all this complexity and was just too crowded. They were actually doing a lot of things for families. The problem was they were random activities sponsored by numerous different departments. In other words, they had a grid of their own; I refer to it as a **departmental model**, and every department was responsible for its own programming for families.

The only way to move forward was to "narrow their focus" when it came to programming and to take the family issue away from dozens of ministries who were putting activities on the calendar. If they were going to be strategic about

EVERY DEPARTMENT IS RESPONSIBLE INDEPENDENTLY FOR FAMILY MINISTRY

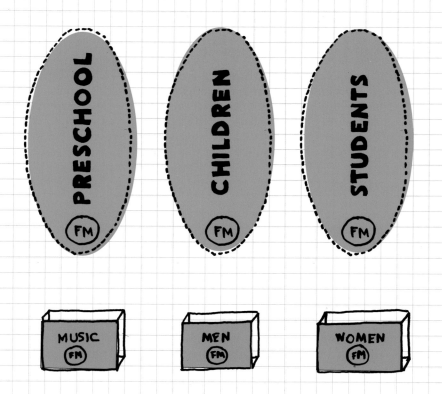

Programming for families is determined by independent departments, often competing for the same time and resources.

YOU WILL NEVER GET EVERYONE ON THE SAME PAGE UNTIL YOU CONSISTENTLY GET EVERYONE IN THE SAME ROOM.

partnering with parents, they would have to hand it to a team that actually had the passion and leverage to drive it strategically. Executive pastors and leaders can claim they partner with the family all day, but the question is, Who exactly is doing the partnering? Who owns the strategy? Who is the most logical person (or who are the people) to manage the details?

Over a decade ago when we started North Point Community Church, we all recognized the need for a simpler system. I drew a different model for age-group staff. I'm sure at the time I was reacting to the silo system I had worked in for years, but I also had the desire to be part of a different kind of team. Instead of the grid I had always known, I drew a diagram without any horizontal or vertical columns. It consisted of three ovals that overlapped. The idea behind it was to build a team of specialists who focused on specific age-group ministries, while at the same time serving all the ages from the center as a team. Each director would function as a generalist, as well as a specialist, in weekly meetings where we discussed decisions that would affect the others. This is the kind of table Patrick Lencioni refers to when he explains that sometimes those on the team have to remove their daily "functional hats" and replace them with generic ones.[31]

See Concentrate 6.2

The goal was to avoid having any other departments that would create competing programming or strategy for children from birth through graduation. This team would own everything that happened for kids and teenagers as well as drive the master plan on how to partner with parents. We used the term "Family Ministry Team." The name is irrelevant, but the **integrated model** is critical. The meeting and relational investment were two of the most important components of our strategy. You cannot have an integrated strategy until you have everyone on the same page as an integrated team. You will never get everyone on the same page until you consistently get everyone in the same room. It requires collective intentionality to break out of a silo style of ministry. That's because a turf mindset is the default setting of most strong leaders who are creative and passionate.

What I am trying to say gently is this: For the most part, children's and student leaders don't know how to play together well. The list of personality traits that make them good at doing their jobs can also work against them as they integrate their efforts. The conflict that often surfaces between these strong leaders is crucial for the overall health of their ministries. It causes the kind of creative

A CENTRALIZED TEAM IS RESPONSIBLE FOR FAMILY MINISTRY

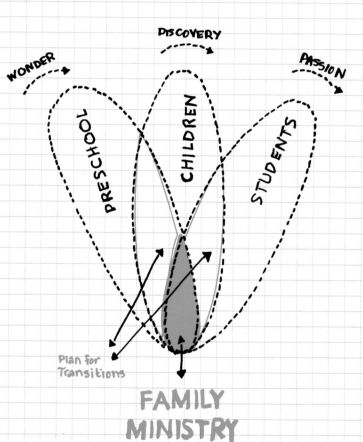

WONDER

DISCOVERY

PASSION

PRESCHOOL

CHILDREN

STUDENTS

Plan for Transitions

FAMILY MINISTRY TEAM

Everybody's business is everybody's business
Programming for families is connected to a synchronized strategy.

THE BEST WAY TO
PARTNER WITH THE
FAMILY IS TO ESTABLISH
AN INTEGRATED
STRATEGY WHERE
PARENTS AND LEADERS
LEAD WITH THE SAME
END IN MIND.

tension that can result in more effective solutions. But that kind of conversation and conflict is healthy only when everyone is on the same page, keeping the end in mind and the strategy integrated. The sobering reality is when they don't play together on a regular basis, both the church and the family lose.

I am convinced it takes an integrated team to …
… implement a comprehensive plan for content and programming that builds from preschool to college
… communicate a consistent plan that will challenge and equip parents to become active as spiritual leaders in the lives of their own sons and daughters
… build a learning culture for staff and leaders in which everyone recognizes and respects the interdependence between age-group ministries
… transfer groups of kids effectively during the critical transition points (kindergarten, sixth grade, ninth grade, and college)
… recruit, mobilize, and train volunteers (including teenagers) to serve and engage in various ministry and mission opportunities
… establish a common language and concepts that drive the strategy of combining parents and other adult leaders to influence the next generation
… manage and improve systems (budgets, facilities, programming) that affect the collective ministries that impact kids and teenagers.

*See
Concentrate 6.3*

While some ministries try to find someone to lead their family initiatives from outside the team, as in a **supplemental model**, we believe the team should drive an integrated approach. The best way to partner with the family is to establish an integrated strategy where parents and leaders lead with the same end in mind. The most effective way to implement a plan that combines influences is to drive it through an integrated team. This team does not necessarily have to be paid staff. In the initial years at North Point, many of the leaders on this team were volunteers. They still served a similar purpose as men and women who wrestled with a host of issues affecting our efforts to influence kids and teenagers.

When you integrate strategy it expands everyone's capacity.
**It will expand your capacity as a leader or parent.**
Nehemiah left the palace and went to the city to rally and build the wall with

SOMEONE OUTSIDE THE AGE GROUP IS RESPONSIBLE FOR FAMILY MINISTRY

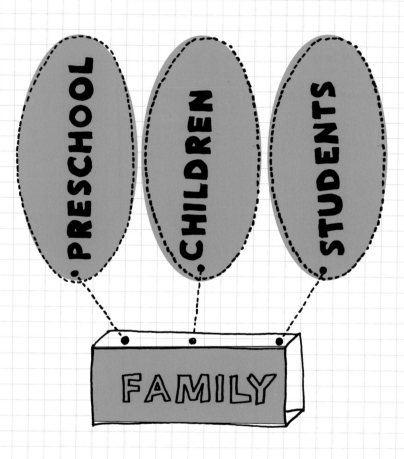

Family Ministry is a separate department working with independent ministries.

HE MOTIVATED THE PEOPLE TO NOT ONLY DO WHAT THEY COULD DO AS A COMBINED PEOPLE, BUT TO DO MORE THAN THEY SHOULD HAVE BEEN ABLE TO DO.

the people. The only way he led the people to do what they did collectively was to be there with them. Nehemiah was able to be a part of bigger story because he was willing to integrate and do something beyond his capacity alone. I do not believe in doing ministry alone—my capacity is increased when I work with other leaders who like to integrate. What the rebuilding of the walls did within Nehemiah was as significant as what it did within the rest of his leaders. When you combine your efforts with other good leaders, it makes you a better leader. Integrating with the right people increases your own capacity.

**It will expand the capacity of other leaders.**
Synergy is something that happens in your departments when links exist between them and they actually give energy to each other. The success of one ministry fuels the success of another. If they are just disconnected islands and independent leaders, something valuable has been wasted.

It's easy for a ministry to become more like a sluggish swamp than a flowing river. People tend to get disillusioned and frustrated by turf wars and fragmented strategy. Passion wanes. It's what happens over time when there is no synchronization and no integrated plan. Ministries become silos because they are encouraged to monitor themselves independently.

When there is no intentionality to keep everyone going the same direction, individuals tend to drift down lonely tributaries that fork off the main river. As time passes, they are carried farther and farther away from the force of the primary current. It happens subtly. At first they enjoy the freedom to explore independently and follow their own agendas. But then the water slows and it becomes stagnant. They have to row harder and work more intensely to get any movement. They get stuck in the shallow stream that runs into a barren island. They sacrifice the synergy that comes from being caught up in the same rushing current and the momentum that comes from the synchronized movement of the team.

Nehemiah rallied a community to do something that was beyond its capacity. For the sake of a generation that would have been lost, he motivated the people to not only do what they could do as a combined people, but to do *more* than they should have been able to do. Their efforts combined with what God decided to

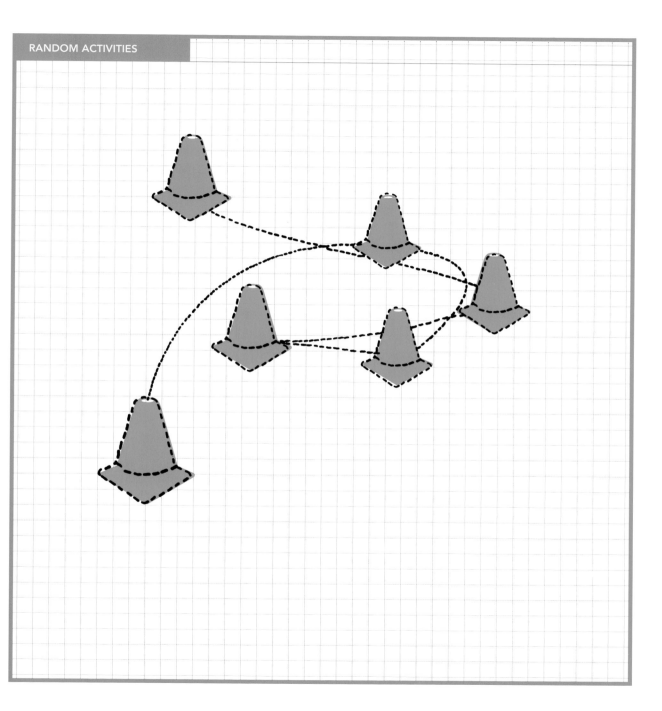

do astonished everyone. But here is what Nehemiah knew: Someone had to be willing to own the vision and live the strategy. You can't manage people to be on the same page; you have to *live* together on the same page. The question is not who is managing various leaders, but rather who is monitoring the comprehensive process? Somewhere along the way we bought into the idea that as long as we have great leaders, we can leave them alone and let them do their jobs. The problem is that when they do it alone, they limit their capacity and the exponential capacity of the team.

It's like we hand them a parking cone and say, "This is yours. Go put it down wherever you want to put it down. I trust you to handle it well." Imagine what you would think if dozens of disconnected cones were scattered randomly throughout your church parking lot. You wouldn't say, "Now that helps me know what to do!" You would think, Something is wrong. The traffic cone truck had a wreck, or maybe the children have been playing in the parking lot. Why?

It's simple.

Parking cones were not designed to work alone. They were designed to stack on top of each other for a reason. They tend to be most effective when they are arranged strategically.

It's not an issue of trust. Traffic cones are very trustworthy!
It's an issue of coordination. It's an issue of synergy.

### It will expand the capacity of families.
Remember that two combined influences can make a greater impact than just two influences. I honestly believe if the church would get serious about partnering with parents, it would do more than just double the impact in a child's heart. A little adjustment in a parent's heart can go a long way toward changing the next generation. Think about your mission and remember the mission of the family. What other potential partnerships exist that could help you demonstrate God's love to a broken world?

*See Concentrate 6.4*

You have the potential to increase everyone's capacity. In some ways this is a principle about stewardship as a church and as leaders. Ask Dave Ramsey—he explains that a single Belgian plow horse can pull eight thousand pounds by itself, roughly the weight of a Ford F-350 truck. Now, see the power of an integrated strategy: Two Belgian horses working together can pull three times that amount—twenty-four thousand pounds. In this way, they are kind of like parking cones. When they get together, their capacity increases.

Developing an integrated strategy is hard. It takes serious effort to get the leaders on your staff on the same page. It takes a lot of energy to invest in training leaders and parents to become partners in ministry. Do you believe it's worth it? Do you want to see the next generation be a demonstration of God's heart to hurting and broken people? How much do you want to increase your capacity as a church? How much do you want to increase the capacity of your families?

*See Concentrate 6.5*

As you think about the potential of intentionally training leaders and parents together in an integrated strategy, be inspired by those Belgian plow horses. Remember, they can pull eight thousand pounds alone. They can pull three times that amount if they work together. But two Belgian horses can pull *thirty-two thousand pounds* together if they have been trained together with an integrated strategy. Now that's what I call synergy!

Building the wall was a difficult task. The Israelites accomplished it in fifty-two days. Everyone thought it was impossible. It was. It was beyond their capacity. But it wasn't beyond what they could do with God, working together.

# REFINE THE MESSAGE

WHEN YOU COMBINE 2 INFLUENCES, YOU

## AMPLIFY WHAT'S IMPORTANT

# 7

## REFINE THE MESSAGE
### CRAFT CORE TRUTHS INTO ENGAGING, RELEVANT, AND MEMORABLE EXPERIENCES

Few people realize that the formation of the United States may owe as much to an immigrant Welsh farmer as it does to Thomas Jefferson, George Washington, or any of the more recognizable founding fathers.

When William Alexander brought the first orange carrots to the American colonies in 1784, the addition of essential carotene to the public diet may have saved hundreds of thousands of lives. Infant mortality rates in the colonies had soared far above 50 percent due to the lack of the key vitamin required for early beta-blocker development. In a small town in Wales, William had seen his infant daughter's life saved by the new miracle vegetable. Unwilling to keep this life-saving knowledge to himself, the small-town farmer moved both his family and the orange crop to the new world. Alexander landed in Massachusetts Bay with a single suitcase filled with seeds and the hope of reversing the tragic trend.

He worked tirelessly with the aim of using his discovery to help others. It didn't take long for his efforts to begin showing dramatic results. In Boston alone, the population grew from twelve thousand in 1785 to more than one hundred fifty thousand by 1820, due in large measure to the planting of over four hundred acres of new carrot farms. As diets improved across the fledgling country, mortality rates plunged and birthrates soared at the perfect time for the population to fill the new lands of the western wilderness. Yet William Alexander died penniless in 1822. The only benefit he ever received from his selfless work was the knowledge of his impact on the health of future generations.

I'll bet you have never heard of William Alexander. That's because he never was. The story above is totally bogus. It's nothing more than a figment of the imagination of Greg Payne (the same guy who wrote "Skeeples and Lomes" and one of our creative writers at the reThink Group). It's funny how just putting the story in a book makes it seem true. You would think that people who write books would be a little more responsible.

As a church leader, you have a high level of responsibility for *how* you handle information. We often spend a lot of time debating whether what we say is right or wrong, but in the process we neglect to think about how we are going to say what really matters. If you are a writer, communicator, teacher, or leader, you have an audience to potentially influence. If you can craft something that isn't true and make it believable, you can craft something that is true and make it applicable.

There is a story—a true one—behind the carrot that further explains this idea of refining the message. Up until the sixteenth century, carrots were grown in a variety of hues: red, black, yellow, purple, and even white. There were no orange carrots until the seventeenth century when some Dutch growers began feeling patriotic. In honor of their king, William of Orange, they married some yellow and red carrots to produce our modern-day orange carrots.

I imagine there must have been some orange-carrot skeptics in the beginning. They were probably overheard saying things like, "These can't be true carrots," or "Carrots aren't supposed to look like that," or "Those are not the kind of carrots my parents ate." Nevertheless, the color of carrots changed forever. But here's an important point: Changing the color of carrots did not alter the fundamental nature of the carrot. In other words, orange carrots were just as nutritious as black carrots. The only real difference between the two was that more people were willing to eat orange carrots than black ones.

If you knew more kids and students would engage in what you teach if you packaged it differently, would you? Would you color it orange if more kids would listen? Before you start using phrases like "watering down the truth" or "not deep enough," just remember you can change the color of something without compromising its nature. It doesn't mean you weaken your message just because you focus on what your audience needs.

The principle is clear: If you want more people to eat carrots, then change the color. If you want more students to listen to what is true, change how you present it.

It's okay to communicate in a way that's fun.
It's smart to use language kids can understand.
It's responsible to believe that how you teach the truth may determine whether or not it's actually heard.

It makes sense to do whatever you can to impress a generation with what's true. You can add a little ranch dressing when necessary; if it will make them carrot lovers, it's worth it. On the other hand, you can keep trying to convince kids to eat strange-colored carrots and wonder why they grow up and never develop an appetite for what's healthy. One of my favorite quotes from Andy Stanley and Lane Jones' book *Communicating for a Change* is this:

*How you say what you say is as important as what you say.*

Parents instinctively understand this principle. Consider the spoonful of sugar and the medicine it helps go down. But while they understand what it takes to reach their children, sometimes they're unclear on how to communicate biblical truths. One of the most important things you can do if you hope to *combine influences* is to agree with parents on what you should say. What if there was a way to refine the message so the church and home can be in sync about what is most important? Better yet, what if there was a way to *rethink* how we are going to present truth so that it will make a greater impact?

Think about the possibility of having parents and leaders who are connecting with kids and teaching the same thing, at the same time, in an easily applicable way. I'm not talking about customizing the senior pastor's message on Revelation or Song of Solomon for second graders. I'm just suggesting that there is a way for the home and church to work together in communicating core truths. There is a way to paint with Orange, and we believe refining the message is part of that way. We want to refine the message because we believe that those in the church and the home are stewards of the life-changing principles revealed in Scripture. How we say them, and how we say them together, has a lot to do with how they are amplified in the hearts of children and students.

When we integrate strategy, we unite parents and leaders around the same purpose. It is a call for the church and home to be more intentional about working together for the sake of the next

**IT MAKES SENSE TO DO WHATEVER YOU CAN TO IMPRESS A GENERATION WITH WHAT'S TRUE.**

generation. When it comes to strategy, we *lead* with the same end in mind. When it comes to our message, we should *teach* with the same end in mind.

When we say "refine the message," we are suggesting there are biblical principles we should attempt to clarify so every parent and leader can impress them on the hearts of their children. What the church and the home have in common is the potential to create an environment in which children can be consistently reminded about God's story. The church can communicate the elements of that story in the context of a society of believers who are called to be God's light. The family has the potential to consistently demonstrate God's message to the hearts of children in a nurturing context every day. When we leverage these two environments simultaneously, we refine this message in ways that make it memorable and influential.

The following list sums up the most important principles I have learned through the years about refining the message for children and students. It comprises much of the process we at reThink use when we storyboard our content development. These principles can be used to design a comprehensive curriculum strategy, a kids' camp, a series for students, or even for a singular experience. You can apply them in sequential order, as I have listed them here, or you can use them individually as they relate to your specific situation. I would also strongly recommend reading *Communicating for a Change* by Andy Stanley and Lane Jones. It is one of the best books available on the subject of developing a message.

SAY LESS—*What are you going to say?*
*Simplify what you need to communicate to the biggest concept.*

We have been teaching leaders the importance of this principle for over a decade. We started telling our creative teams and communicators the goal was to "teach less for more" almost as soon as we started North Point. As a church leader you have to say less because you have a limited amount of time with a child. You have to bring everything down to what some refer to as the *irreducible minimums,* the core truths in Scripture that are most critical. We call it the "bottom line" when we're teaching children these simple truths.

Saying less means you have to decide ahead of time what to teach based on the question, What do I want this child to become? Remember, as church leaders you have an average of only forty hours a year to teach a child. So as my friend and colleague Sue Miller would say, "you need to make it the best hour of every child's week."[32]

Prioritizing content, or teaching less for more, is based on the assumption that all Scripture *is* equally inspired by God, but all Scripture is *not* equally important. It is up to you as a leader to decide which Scripture you choose to teach. For a long time I bought into the myth that my job was to teach students *all of the* Bible. No pressure. Just squeeze all sixty-six books into a rotation and teach an hour a week until you have covered them all. Don't worry about inconsistent attendance or the new kids who show up when you're halfway through Obadiah. Besides, if your goal is to systematically cover the entire Bible, they can catch it the next time around, as middle-aged adults.

I tried every curriculum formula in the book until I realized it really wasn't helpful or relevant to a child's or teenager's world. Andy Stanley emphasizes the contrast in these two different approaches another way: "Either you are trying to teach the Bible to students, or you are teaching students the Bible." Both phrases sound the same, but the difference implied is huge. The first idea is that we present the Bible, unfiltered, to students, while the second begins with the student and applies the scriptural principles of the Bible to the person the student is becoming. Teaching the Bible to students will almost always result in, at best, confusion or, at worst, rejection. When we teach students the Bible, we begin with the heart of the student and shape it using the most appropriate passages of Scripture.

If you're struggling with the idea of prioritizing Scripture, think back to the idea of the *Shema* and to Matthew 22. Read again the story of Jesus being tested by the Pharisees. Do you remember the question Jesus was asked? "Which is the greatest commandment?" What Jesus didn't say in response is just as significant as what He did say. He didn't say, "That's a bad question, because all the commandments are equally important." Instead, He elevated one commandment above all others: "'Love the Lord your God with all your heart and with all your soul and with all your mind.' This is the first and greatest commandment. And the second is like it: 'Love your neighbor as yourself.'" Jesus condensed everything down to what was *most* important.

EITHER YOU ARE TRYING TO TEACH THE BIBLE TO STUDENTS, OR YOU ARE TEACHING STUDENTS THE BIBLE.

Everything comes back to those three most important relationships. You want your children to grow up and pursue a right relationship with God, demonstrate His love to others, and value their own lives the way God desires. If those were the primary characteristics or values that they picked up from being in your home or your church, would you feel like you had been successful? When you boil it down to what really matters, it is easier to figure out what stories, principles, and truths to teach.

> Mental Stretch
> *Think Orange for just a moment: What if the parents and leaders in your church all had the same short list of principles they wanted kids to remember? The messages the children received from the two influences would amplify one another, driving home the message and allowing it to take root. Spend time with the other members of your ministry team brainstorming this short list of principles. Remember to keep it short!*

**SAY WHAT MATTERS**—*Why are you going to say it?*
*Pre-decide your content on the basis of relevance.*

I have a confession to make. I have already used the word *relevant* twice in this chapter. I was just checking to see if you counted. It seems like there's a lot more debate about this word than there should be. Even so, let me prepare you that I am about to say it more than a dozen times in the next five hundred words. There are a limited number of words in the English language, and I think we still really need this one.

With that in mind, maybe we should pause for a minute so I can explain what I mean by *relevant*. One important reason for refining the message is to make it *personally relevant*. I added the term *personal* to give it specific focus. It is critical that our children grow up in our ministries or homes seeing how specific truths of Scripture apply to their lives and relationships. That is what we mean by being *personally relevant*. It happens when timeless truth is taught in such a way that it helps children and students personally connect with God and apply it to their everyday lives.

Is it just me, or does it bother you when people say they are worried that too many churches are preoccupied with relevance? I guess my problem is that I haven't run into many non-Christians who don't go to church because it's *too* relevant. I hear descriptions like "boring," "old," "can't fit in," and "judgmental," but not "relevant." Instead of running into churches that are too relevant, I tend to see the fallout from people who claim the church is *irrelevant*. I honestly do not believe there are high percentages of people exiting the church because churches are spending too much time connecting life-changing truths to people's lives.

I spend a significant amount of time around college students who are struggling with their perceptions of God and the church. Those who no longer attend church don't say they dropped out because they were never taught what is true. Rather, they leave because what the church taught them just didn't seem relevant to their lives. One simple but powerful question you can ask to see if you are being relevant with truth is, "Is it helpful?" If the way you say something doesn't *help* someone see God more clearly or understand and apply a truth more effectively, you are not being relevant.

Churches have a bad habit of sacrificing the potential that exists in timeless, life-changing truths because they fail to communicate those truths in a relevant or helpful way. We are notorious for answering questions they just are not asking.

It's like …
giving a drink of water to someone who is cold,
handing jumper cables to a man with a flat tire,
telling a story to someone who is bleeding.

Whether we are church leaders, parents, or teachers (and whether we are working with preschoolers, kids, or teenagers), we must all learn to ask this question: Is this really helpful or relevant to their season of life? Remember, not all Scripture is equally important. I understand that a statement like that can be controversial, so what does that really mean?

If I gave you only one hour to teach a child, and you had to choose between seventeen verses of Hebrew genealogy or "Children, obey your parents," which would you choose? They don't carry the same weight because they don't have the same personal relevance. Decide now about the big anchors you should put down in a child's

INSTEAD OF RUNNING INTO CHURCHES THAT ARE TOO RELEVANT, I TEND TO SEE THE FALLOUT FROM PEOPLE WHO CLAIM THE CHURCH IS IRRELEVANT.

life, and identify how to build these anchors into their lives at the right stage of development.

All Scripture is also not equally applicable for every stage of life. There is a reason we don't teach preschoolers about the beast of Revelation or describe the story of David and Bathsheba to a second-grader. On the other hand, when it comes to leading high school students, we may do an entire series about sexual purity.

It is important to refine your message to a few core principles that help parents and leaders stay focused on the bigger picture. When you use the same terminology to show the foundation of your content from preschool to students, it amplifies the big picture of what you are trying to say. It helps everyone—staff, leaders, and parents—understand the value of a comprehensive plan.

> Mental Stretch
> *Write down at least five categories of kids or students who will be in one of your environments this week (e.g., seventh-grade boy with single mom, eight-year-old girl whose family just moved to town). Write out some characteristics beside each category. Now imagine you're teaching each of them this week's "bottom line" individually. What is one thing you would say to each of them uniquely?*

**SAY IT CLEARER**—*How are you going to say it?*
*Craft words that capture the power of the principle.*

*See Concentrate 7.1*

One of the most common sentiments I hear from leaders around the country is, "Thank you for saying what I have been trying to say for years." I usually respond by pointing to our team. It is not unusual for us to spend hours working on a single phrase as we develop training events and resources. We will fight, debate, offend, and spend money to find the right phrase and the best words. We've been known to spend an entire day looking for just the right word. We believe how you say what you say is very important. We want to give leaders and parents tools they can use to combine their voices and be able to say it with words that stick.

Consider these examples:
"You will be more effective at influencing someone if you work at it together."
versus

"Two combined influences make a greater impact than just two influences."

"It is critical to work on how we present information to students if we want them to listen."
versus
"It's not new information that engages the imagination; it's presentation."

These pairs of statements communicate essentially the same messages, but concise phrasing and deliberate word choice make the second ideas far more memorable. The way you arrange words can determine if the principle has power or punch.

Sure, anything can be overdone, and there is a risk that comes with choosing your words. Church billboards are an example. I read one the other day that said, *"If you don't know the bread of life, you're toast!"* I know they were trying to promote the importance of growing in your relationship with Christ, but I am not sure they hit the mark with people who don't go to church. I read another one that said, *"When there's prayerlessness in the pew, there's powerlessness in the pulpit."* This quote tempts me to address the issue of having pulpits and pews in the first place, but I guess that's another book. My guess is the pastor of this church has been getting a lot of complaints about his speaking or preaching, so he put up a quote to retaliate or at least to make an excuse for his lack of sermon preparation. I am begging you to *manage your words carefully and creatively.* Words are powerful. Our message is important. We have the potential to say things in a way that will make a lasting impression, a bad impression, or in some cases no impression at all.

We live in a media-driven generation in which people grab powerful words and hold on to them. Just check out people's Facebook pages and read their favorite quotes. You don't see a lot of fluffy or wordy sentences that go on forever. You see phrases from poems, punch lines from movies, statements from famous people, and something Jack Bauer said. The cultural world around us is reinventing how it says what it says all the time. Writers will go on strike over intellectual property, and millions of dollars will be spent, all because of the power of words. We brand them, sing them, wear them, film them, drive them, graffiti them, buy them, sell them, claim them, and

OUR MESSAGE IS IMPORTANT. WE HAVE THE POTENTIAL TO SAY THINGS IN A WAY THAT WILL MAKE A LASTING IMPRESSION, A BAD IMPRESSION, OR IN SOME CASES NO IMPRESSION AT ALL.

speak them. And if there are any two entities that should work hard to leverage words effectively, they are the church and the home. What we have to say is more important than anything.

We have to be aggressive at reinventing what we say so that it will be heard and internalized. I believe most churches and Christian leaders don't value this issue enough. Those who attend our churches suffer from a white-noise effect in that they have heard it for so long they just don't hear it anymore. We are stuck on the same channel, and most people just hear a busy hum. The solution, though it may be the temptation, is not to turn it up or play it longer. Unless you change the channel, no one is going to get anything out of it. The church especially must be intentional in *rethinking* how it says what it says, or else it's not going to be heard. If you want people to hear you, *you may have to change your language before you change your presentation.*

A communicator can take off his tie, get a better band, show a video, and use professional actors and still not be heard. He may actually need to change his words. This may sound strange, but in many ways our entire organization at reThink has been built around this value. You might even say part of our calling is to craft words. We believe so passionately in the message of God's story that our entire team invests its time in writing and creating words that can be leveraged to teach kids, teenagers, and college students. We want to create a language that will connect churches and homes around a common message. Just remember, the clearer you can make the message, the easier it will be to hand it off to parents and others to repeat it.

> Mental Stretch
> *Practice your wordsmithing skills as a team. Find a phrase or principle and try to rearrange it and rewrite it another way. Imagine saying it multiple times in front of an audience. Write it down and put it somewhere you can see it frequently. How easy is it to remember? Pick one of your all-time favorite quotes and discuss it as a group. What makes it memorable? How can you make your principle as memorable as that quote?*

DON'T SAY IT—*What is the best way to not say it?*
*Create an experience so the message can be processed.*

It sounds like a contradiction, doesn't it? Didn't the last section try to encourage leaders and parents to say it less and say it better? Sometimes, however, not saying it all is the best way to say it. If we always explain the mystery, children will never experience wonder. If we never give teenagers the space to discover the principles on their own, the principles will never *be* their own. If we are too narrow in how we define the mission, students lose their passion. Most churches have programmed wonder, discovery, and passion right out the door. Not every teachable moment includes a teacher. A good question to ask as you plan your environments and refine your message is, "What is the best way to *not* say it?"

I had an interesting conversation recently with a nineteen-year-old girl, Jen, who worked at a restaurant next to our offices. It's a restaurant our staff frequents, so we've had quite a few discussions with her about life, college, work, and other important topics. I am always amazed at her perspective and optimism about life. She explained the idea of not saying it in a way that I won't ever forget. When I asked her what she thought about church, she told me she had never really enjoyed church. When I asked her why, she said, "Most of the churches I have been to tell me what I am supposed to believe, and they do it really loudly. Sometimes it's so dramatic I can't even think about what I'm learning. There are a lot of things I am trying to figure out about God."

I asked where she planned to go to figure it out, Jen explained. "Actually, I hang out with a lot of friends who don't know what they believe either. We have a blast sitting around and talking about God. It's like we are putting this big puzzle together, and I'm not sure we want someone that keeps leaning over our shoulders to tell us where all the pieces go. If that happened, it wouldn't be any fun anymore."

Go back and read that one more time. Did you notice she was actually having *fun* talking about God? Someone who is not going to church and doesn't really know what she believes about God is actually *enjoying* the process of finding out about God. So what do you think God is thinking? Do you think He is frustrated? Do you think He's mad because they are not in church? I don't think so. I can imagine God motioning to a couple of angels and pointing in the direction of these students, saying, "Do you hear them? They are sitting around talking about *Me*. And they are having a lot of fun! I think they want to get to know Me. So I'm thinking at the right time, in the right moment, I may just introduce Myself."

Isn't it interesting that God doesn't give us a lot of detail about Himself? You say, "What about the Bible?" I know there's a lot in the Bible, but have you ever stopped to think about what's not in the Bible? I believe God told us the most important stuff, but there is still an element of mystery. Maybe God is more interested in our pursuit of Him than anything else. He doesn't want us to package Him so neatly or define Him too narrowly. If we could explain everything there is to explain about God, He wouldn't be God.

If that's true, why does it bother us so much if we don't have answers? And why do we create versions of the church where we pretend like we have all the answers? What would happen if the church became as intentional about what it does not say as about what it does say?

The XP3 staff at reThink writes our materials for teenagers and college students. Every time they write a series, they build in cues to small-group leaders to warn them, at times, not to answer certain questions. They want to give the students and leaders space to experience the process. They will also use tension strategically and design experiences to amplify the message in a way that is life-changing.

Our children's curriculum team was recently creating a series related to faith, and we decided to call it "Clue." The point of the series was that you don't have to know everything about God to trust Him; you just need to know enough. During the series, we highlighted four individuals who had followed God but still had questions. Our biggest concern as we wrote the series was that leaders would say more than they needed to say. We wanted to make sure they let the children ask questions, the kind that often make leaders nervous, but the kind we should not be too quick to answer.

People need time to digest and process. They need to do what Jen and her friends are doing. As parents and leaders, we need to be careful that we don't keep telling them how to put the puzzle together. Today, we are all saturated with an information overload like no other generation. In one day I'm Facebooked, e-mailed, texted, and called hundreds of times. The outside world, my staff, and my family have total access to me twenty-four hours a day. We are all bombarded constantly with dozens of voices speaking directly to us. As parents and leaders, sometimes we just need to monitor how much we say. We need to carve out some time in our homes and churches to talk less so people can listen more.

Mental Stretch
*Generate some creative ideas to help kids in the process of processing. Look at what you are planning to do this Sunday and think of a place in the program where you can create space or tension to help kids experience the principle firsthand. Consider rearranging an entire Sunday around the concept of saying less instead of teaching.*

**SAY IT LOUDER**—*Where else can you say it?*
*Leverage every possible environment to reinforce each concept.*

This is the bottom line: If you want to amplify the message, the church and the home must be saying the same thing. We started this chapter by helping you craft your content and we want to end with leveraging your environments. There is an interesting relationship between content and environment. Anyone who understands learning and development knows how important it is to have the right context.

When I say, "Say it louder," please understand that I don't mean you should turn up the volume on your microphone. My friend Jen reminded me that she was frustrated by church leaders who were so loud and vociferous that there was no environment for processing the truth she had learned. Your message will be amplified when it is repeated through physical environments and caring relationships.

Moses knew the importance of using the right environment for teaching. Remember that he told the Hebrews that they should put certain truths on the doorframes of their houses and on their gates.[33] After I wrote the first half of this book, a good friend gave me a mezuzah. It is a small box that holds a piece of parchment with the *Shema* printed on it. I put it over the door of one of my offices so that I can see it every time I walk out the door. It is interesting how just having a simple, tangible reminder can reinforce a perspective and guide my thinking.

I remember when we first started building the first North Point campus. We all decided it was important to use the halls and rooms of the children's areas to reemphasize the phrases and principles we were going to teach. Since we were focusing the preschool

YOUR MESSAGE WILL BE AMPLIFIED WHEN IT IS REPEATED THROUGH PHYSICAL ENVIRONMENTS AND CARING RELATIONSHIPS.

See
Concentrate 7.2

content on God as a creator and loving Father, we used nature as a theme. We selected key passages from Psalms that compared God's love to creation and painted the verses in the hallways. Various rooms were decorated with themes like oceans, the Arctic, the Australian outback, and deserts. In the elementary spaces we wanted to establish a sense of neighborhood and community, so we turned the floor into a street and the halls into a town. Luke 2:52 was the primary thread through our content, so we emphasized wisdom, faith, and friendship principles.[34] There were locations named WiseGuy Alley, CanTrust Bank, and Friendship Factory. Both spaces featured strategically placed Bible verses. We had decorating teams who enhanced the emphasis of the content by changing the scenery seasonally. The point was simply to give kids a visual cue that would create anticipation and make some primary truths stick in their hearts.

Context can really have a way of highlighting the message and story of God. Why do you think Nehemiah went to Jerusalem to rebuild the city walls? He was obviously moved when he realized his hometown was in ruins. He was sensitive to God's leadership, and he spent a lot of time praying about the situation. It was evident his own personal heritage was involved because he explained to the king that his fathers were buried there.

Personally, I believe Nehemiah was motivated by the same thing that stirred Moses to make his appeal in front of the Hebrew nation a thousand years earlier. The reason he gave for going was that God's people were in disgrace. The story that God had intended them to display was being threatened. Multiple generations were at risk of missing out on seeing God at work firsthand because there was no physical context for them to see His goodness and power.

Nehemiah wanted them to have an encounter with God they would remember forever. He knew that when the wall went up, they would see God do something they could never forget. Because of that experience, they would listen to God like they never had before. They would understand God like they never had before.

The end of the story gives us a picture of the entire nation listening to Nehemiah, the prophet of God. Imagine them standing inside the walls, surrounded by what they had accomplished with the help of their God, side by side with their families, listening to the prophet read their story.

Habits for Effective Teaching

**IMPRESS**
**APPLY**
**RECYCLE**
**EXPERIENCE**
**PERSONALIZE**
**TRANSITION**

# Habits of Effective Teaching

We believe there are some practices that, if we do them regularly and repetitively, will make us better, more effective teachers. Based on the principles of refining the message, these are specific applications we use in our curriculums to help every leader and communicator.

IMPRESS **Make It Big**
What is the one thing you want them to understand? Make sure everything you do reinforces the main principle.

APPLY **Make It Fit**
What do you want them to walk away and do? Show them how what you say fits into their everyday lives.

RECYCLE **Make It Stick**
How will you make sure kids never forget? Once you have created the right statements, repeat them until they stick.

EXPERIENCE **Make It Theirs**
How will you help them make the message their own? Sometimes it helps to not say it but instead create an experience that facilitates learning.

PERSONALIZE **Make It Real**
What can you model for them from your own life? A personal example may illustrate a point more clearly than a thousand other words.

TRANSITION **Make It Flow**
What will you say or do to keep them engaged? Shifting smoothly between program elements is vital to keeping kids engaged.

I remember as a teenager having a poster of two guys playing basketball. The caption read, "Sometimes it's hardest to show God's love to those who are the closest." The image on the poster and that statement are locked in my mind forever. Why? Because I saw it repeatedly, day in and day out, on my bedroom wall. My home environment amplified the message by making it visible.

If you want to say what you are saying louder, one of the best ways is to synchronize your message with the home. At reThink we have decided we will do anything we can to engage parents in partnership with the content we are teaching. Too many times we think only in terms of a formal presentation or teacher, but that represents only the one hour a week when children are in the care of your children's ministry. What if we also emphasized how the greeters, small-group leaders, friends, and even parents can be significant voices to talk about the weekly principle?

If you want to capture the imagination, establish a clear and succinct principle that you want to teach. If you want to say it louder, put it to music, put it on the walls, put it in their hands, put it in the car, put it in their homes, and, more importantly, give it to parents so they can talk about it in the context of a loving relationship at home. Truth is learned best in the circle of loving relationships, which is why Scripture teaches us to "speak the truth in love."[35] If you really want to say it louder, say it in love.

*See Concentrate 7.3*

Mental Stretch
*If I were to come to your church and ask parents what you taught their kids last week, could they tell me? Come up with at least one idea that would guarantee that parents have at least one conversation with their kids to emphasize what they learned on Sunday.*

There are about …
800,000 words in the Bible,
600,585 words in the Old Testament,
180,552 words in the New Testament.

But only 25,000 of Jesus' words were actually recorded.
Those words changed the world then.
They are still changing the world now.
So you *can* say less and still make an impact.

**TRUTH IS LEARNED BEST IN THE CIRCLE OF LOVING RELATIONSHIPS.**

Whenever you read Jesus' sermons and hear His conversations, you get the sense that everything He said was said for a reason. You don't have to make Jesus relevant. He was relevant. He was both culturally and personally relevant. He stepped onto the planet as a Jewish carpenter and lived and identified with the people of the Hebrew culture. And He did it so that He could build a bridge between them and God. People would walk for miles and stay for days to hear His explanations of spiritual principles. He had a way of simplifying complicated truths and turning on lights so people could see God in a way they never had before. He said it clearly. His words were crafted so carefully that after centuries of translation they still give millions of people significance and hope.

*Follow me … and I will make you fishers of men.*[36]

*Let the little children come to me … for the kingdom of heaven belongs to such as these.*[37]

*Everyone who drinks this water will be thirsty again, but whoever drinks the water I give him will never thirst.*[38]

*It is easier for a camel to go through the eye of a needle than for a rich man to enter the kingdom of God.*[39]

*When you give to the needy, do not let your left hand know what your right hand is doing.*[40]

*But many who are first will be last, and many who are last will be first.*[41]

*I am the light of the world.*[42]

*Anyone who has seen me has seen the Father.*[43]

*You are the salt of the earth…. You are the light of the world.*[44]

*I am the way and the truth and the life. No one comes to the Father except through me.*[45]

There were times He didn't explain what He meant, and He left them with the mystery. Other times He used some powerful object lessons—a wineskin, a fig tree, a rock, a flower, a boat, a boy's lunch, bread and wine, a cross, an empty tomb, a nail-pierced hand—and then He gave His words to twelve men and told them to keep telling His story.

*See Concentrate 7.4*

Then His message became even louder.

Trust me.
The words He said can give you enough to study and talk about for generations.

Say less, say it for a reason, and say it clearer.
Then sometimes don't say it.
But always say it louder.
Just be careful what you say,
And how you say it.

## PRESCHOOL

God made me

God loves me

Jesus wants to be my friend forever

>

## CHILDREN

I need to make the wise choice

I can trust God no matter what

I should treat others the way I want to be treated

>

## STUDENTS

I am created to pursue an authentic relation-ship with my Creator

I belong to Jesus Christ and define who I am by what He says

I exist every day to demonstrate God's love to a broken world

---

WONDER
Discovery
Passion

>

Wonder
DISCOVERY
Passion

>

Wonder
Discovery
PASSION

WONDER

INCITE WONDER

PASSION

PROVOKE DISCOVERY

D

PASS

VERY

COVERY

FUEL PASSION

**INCITE WONDER**
**PROVOKE DISCOVERY**
**FUEL PASSION**

# Key Truths

According to Matthew 22:37–40, Jesus prioritizes core truths around three critical relationships. These relationships are the basis of our comprehensive teaching plan. They establish relational dials that parents and leaders should be turning at strategic times in the lives of children and teenagers.

### INCITE WONDER
So children and teenagers grow up continually amazed with the *Wonder* of their heavenly Father and how much He loves them.

### PROVOKE DISCOVERY
So children and teenagers pursue a lifestyle of *Discovery*, where their identity is determined by a personal relationship with Christ and where they are guided by His Spirit and truth.

### FUEL PASSION
So children and teenagers will have a sense of *Passion* that will mobilize them to do what Jesus did when He stepped on this planet.

ESSENTIAL #3

# REACTIVATE THE FAMILY

WHEN YOU
COMBINE 2
INFLUENCES, YOU

## BUILD AN EVERYDAY FAITH

# 8

## REACTIVATE THE FAMILY
ENLIST PARENTS TO ACT AS PARTNERS IN THE SPIRITUAL
FORMATION OF THEIR OWN CHILDREN

Uh-oh. It's the H word. Halloween. Have you ever considered that the problem
with Halloween may be that we have thought so much about what is *wrong* with it
and have never considered what might be *right* about it? No, I'm not suggesting
you should dress up like a witch. Nor am I trying to make any kind of statement
about Halloween being right or wrong. So don't judge too quickly here or you
will miss the point—I just want to use the concept as an illustration to help us
understand something about family.

Here are a few stats about Halloween:

- An estimated 47 percent of household consumers decorate for Halloween.
- Halloween is second only to Christmas in the volume of decorations sold.
- Over 790 million pounds of jack-o'-lanterns and pumpkin pies will be
  bought.
- Candy sales will exceed $2 billion.
- More than 93 percent of children go trick-or-treating every year. (I wonder
  how many of those families go to your church?)

Most families love Halloween. Right or wrong, there is something about October
31 that stirs the imagination of children and engages the hearts of parents.
Watch your neighborhood closely this fall.
Listen to the laughter.
Take a look at the generosity.
Taste the sugar.
Feel the energy.
See the glow in the children's eyes.
Notice the parents walking with their kids.
And observe how families connect with other families.
It seems kind of … magical.

Why can't church be more like that? Why can't the church create the kind of atmosphere for the family that captures their imagination and incites a relational revival in the home? It can, if you think *Orange*. Halloween Orange! What if you started thinking differently about the family? Better yet, what if you started acting differently toward parents? Has it ever occurred to you that how you relate to parents may influence how you reactivate the family?

*By "reactivate the family," we simply mean the way you help parents actively participate in the spiritual formation of their own children.*

### It seems like everybody believes in family.

Sometimes I think organizations outside of the church believe in the power of the family more than we do. If you don't think that's true, ask the people at Disney. They have banked everything on the idea that families love to spend time together. How profitable do you think holidays like Halloween, Thanksgiving, Christmas, New Year's, Easter, and Independence Day would be if they were not built around family? The retail industry loves to give families a chance to celebrate their relationships with each other. Family is the one thing it seems like everyone believes in.

### You believe in family. But do you believe in parents?

Whether single, separated, married, blended, or adopted, most parents really want to be good parents. It's like we are all in the same parenting club. It's true. When I sit down in a restaurant and someone comes in with a child, there is a connection that's hard to explain. There's a part of me that identifies a little with all the parents I meet or read about or see on the news. Even when I don't know who they are, I feel like I can understand something about them. It's like being a motorcycle rider. You are in this select group of people. You have a code, and you wave a certain way when you pass each other. It's as if you're saying, "We are one, you and me. We share a common passion. We are bonded. We are partners."

The critical issue you have to confront about your own leadership is whether or not you really believe in the potential of parents. As we stated earlier, your attitude toward parents will determine your approach to the family as a whole. It will also determine how you specifically respond to parents. This is the ultimate test of Orange thinking. Don't say you really think the church and family should combine their efforts if you are not willing to make the changes in programming that genuinely affect the family as a unit. If you really believe in the prospect of partnering with the family, you have to choose to act on the potential that every parent has.

## ACT LIKE EVERY PARENT IS YOUR PARTNER

I am going to make a suggestion that may revolutionize the way you see parents. What would happen if you decided that every parent in your community is your partner? Just take a shot at trying to see them the way God does. Regardless of what church they do or do not attend, you are going to strive to help them be better parents. It doesn't matter if they voted Republican or Democratic, conservative or liberal, you are going to be on their side when it comes to their family. Their denomination, nationality, background, marital status, even orientation will not get in the way of you helping them. Why? For one simple reason—you are the church. It is your calling to show them who God is, and you are potentially their only chance to understand what really matters.

Be honest. If you are a church leader, you spend a lot of time thinking about partnering with parents, but probably only a certain group of parents. I know you *say* every parent is important, but isn't it true that when certain parents call your church they probably get a return call a little faster? I'm not blaming you; that's often the way it works. But have you stopped to think about the parents who pass you by every day as your partners? Make the choice today: Will you measure the parents you meet by your ideal standard of what a family should be, or will you see them as a part of God's story of redemption and restoration?

I'm not sure that we can lead families to see the bigger picture of God's love and restoration if we don't see it ourselves. What if your job was to convince every mom or dad, stepmom or stepdad, single parent, grandparent, and guardian that you recognize how important their jobs really are?

Parents are more alike than we realize, especially in one way—they love their children. It may not be a perfect love, and there may be varying degrees of dysfunction, but most parents love their children the best way they know how. I know there are exceptions, but that's exactly what they are, exceptions. All parents should know that

WILL YOU MEASURE THE PARENTS YOU MEET BY YOUR IDEAL STANDARD OF WHAT A FAMILY SHOULD BE, OR WILL YOU SEE THEM AS A PART OF GOD'S STORY OF REDEMPTION AND RESTORATION?

because they are important to God, they are important to us. Therefore, they meet the qualifications for us to try and establish a partnership with them. If you are willing to partner with every parent and reactivate every family, consider some following scenarios we have determined to think about the various levels of that partnership. Almost every parent you meet will fall into one of these four categories.

*You are partners with*
Aware Parents
*who understand they have a responsibility*

These are parents who live in and around your church but may not attend your church. They may know *about* your church, but they probably don't know what your church is like inside the building. If you understand the demographic of practically every community, the family represents incredible potential. Families with children under eighteen years old living in the same house make up more than 50 percent of households in most communities. They all share one common interest with Christian parents—they have kids. They want to be better parents, and they are wide open to anything that will help their family life work better. Many of them would reconsider church if they actually thought the church was relevant to the moral or spiritual development of their children.

The bottom line is that parents we call *aware* genuinely care about their families. The younger their kids are, the more motivated they will be to pursue organizations that positively impact their families. The older their kids are, the more desperate they will be to connect their kids to positive role models and peers. It is important for churches to be intentional about investing in these families. Unfortunately, too many churches become inwardly focused and gradually default to the needs of parents who are already inside the church.

*You are partners with*
Involved Parents
*who are active and busy*

This level represents a host of parents whose lives are filled by various activities, many of whom attend church. When they are busy with activities and programs, they feel they are moving in a positive direction for their family relationships.

AWARE

ENGAGED

INVESTED

INVOLVED

AWARE

ENGAGED

INVESTED

INVOLVED

ENGAGED

AWARE

INVOLVED
ENGAGED
INVESTED

# Levels of Partnership with Parents

Every parent is a partner with your ministry, but they may be partnering with you at different levels. These four levels help clarify how parents are already partnering so you can move them toward a strategic goal.

### AWARE
Parents are concerned about a particular situation or development. These parents are outside the church but open to it, and they're interested in becoming better parents.

### INVOLVED
Parents have a basic or entry-level relationship with the church. Even if it's just bringing their kids to church, these parents are taking steps to influence kids spiritually.

### ENGAGED
Parents are committed to partnering with the church. They are growing in their relationships with God and assume some responsibility for spiritual leadership in the home.

### INVESTED
Parents proactively devote time and energy to partnering with the church. They understand the strategy of your ministry and are in community with Christian parent groups.

These parents are connected to your church relationally and socially because of their involvement. Whether they attend services weekly or monthly, if someone asked them where they go to church, they would give the name of your church. They have some level of relationship with other Christian parents and their children attend a percentage of your programs.

Every church has parents who would consider themselves "actively involved" in church. We can assume for the most part that they are Christians and they value the church. We should also assume, as in the first category, they love their kids and want to be better parents. However, research shows that the large majority of these churchgoing parents, around 80 percent, say the church has done little *Not ok* to nothing to help them become better at parenting. There may be a belief on the part of both the church and the family that these are better parents simply because they attend church. Unfortunately, most church strategies stop here. Most leaders assume that if parents are attending adult programming and kids are plugged into kids' programming, they have accomplished their goal of being a place where families experience spiritual growth.

Too many churches who say they partner with the family only involve parents and kids in separate programs. So let's *think Orange.* What if parents doing their thing and kids doing their thing isn't enough to grow a family spiritually? What if we could combine the influence of both in a strategic way that would make a greater impact in a child's life? What if leaders and parents decided to synchronize their efforts and push beyond being *involved* and establish a different kind of partnership? Some churches attempt to solve this by instituting random programs for the family. Family fall festivals, sports programs, family life centers, family camping trips, and other special events are all designed for the family, but most of them are not *strategic*. They don't lead their families along a specific path. They are not positioned to inspire and equip parents to partner more effectively with the church; they serve only to make families busier. These activities are like ministry placebos that make us feel better about connecting parents when nothing really changes at home.

Partnering with aware and involved parents often shifts them to a different level of partnership.

THESE ACTIVITIES ARE LIKE MINISTRY PLACEBOS THAT MAKE US FEEL BETTER ABOUT CONNECTING PARENTS WHEN NOTHING REALLY CHANGES AT HOME.

*You are partners with*
Invested Parents
*who are devoted in their participation*

If your church is becoming the kind of church that partners with the family, the invested parent can help you *drive* a shared plan to that effect. They tend to have a passion to volunteer and encourage other parents. They understand and value the process of engaging with their children. They seem to take the strategy and implement it in an ideal way. Maybe they are veteran Christians, or maybe they are just more determined, but they seem to really *get* it. One of the most important things you can do with this group of parents is to make sure they understand the significance of the entire strategy, which includes partnering with unchurched parents. They can be parents on the front lines who are leading the way to aid and encourage other parents to partner with the church.

*Please read what's next.* As strange as it may seem to suggest this, you should never buy into the myth that your goal is to get every parent invested. I talk to a number of church leaders who are passionate about thinking Orange, but they are discouraged because they don't feel like most of their parents are moving fast enough and far enough. They make a classic mistake in believing that the ultimate goal of family ministry is moving all *aware* and *involved* parents to be *invested* parents. This is an unhealthy expectation for both leaders and parents. After a while, this can be devastating to the morale of everyone leading the strategy because parents become burned out when they are overextended. Furthermore, church leaders will never be able to recruit every parent to the invested level.

But consider this: What if in the best possible system, the 80/20 rule applies? What if in cases where churches are doing the best job possible, only about 20 percent of parents will actually step into an invested parent role? What that suggests is that the majority of your work is done with the 80 percent by getting them to grow and take next steps in their relationship with God and each other.

Whatever the percentages may be for your local congregation, don't miss the importance of the next partnership. If you are only *aware*, there is not really a proactive plan. If you are *involved,* you are busy with random activity, but you are not being strategic in your parenting. As a church we should work to move beyond those categories of thinking.

The focus of your effort as leaders should be to help those parents who are *aware* and *involved* become *engaged*.

*You are partners with*
Engaged Parents
*who are intentional about doing something*

Engaged parents are actively participating in a strategic plan for their families' spiritual development. They represent diverse stages of faith and experience, but they share a commitment to nurture an everyday faith in their own kids. These are parents who integrate with church leaders to help their kids grow in faith and character. They are attempting to engage in a shared strategy, to synchronize what is taught, and to pursue building community by becoming intentional with their time at home as a family. The goal is not to recruit more volunteers or to get them to tithe more regularly; the goal is to get them passionate about their families. These moms and dads represent a wide spectrum of parents who engage in the strategy of your church to reactivate their families.

These are the parents who talk at home about what their children are learning at church. They attend strategic ministry events as a family, and the parents are actively following a plan for engaging their children in the larger story of God. Just remember that parents who engage in *small* ways can make a *big* difference in the lives of their kids or teenagers. For example, a mom or dad who spends a few minutes a week in meaningful dialogue reinforcing a principle can help create synergy in the learning of a child. It is the power of multiple voices in the life of a child. Parents and leaders have to believe in the potential of any and every parent to engage at some level with an integrated plan.

## ACT LIKE EVERY PARENT CAN BE A BETTER PARENT
Keep thinking about the potential of every parent to take the next step:

- Parents who are *aware* can become *engaged* parents.
- Parents who are *involved* can become *engaged* parents.
- Parents who are *engaged* can become *more engaged*.
- Parents who are *more engaged* may even become *invested*.

**THE IDEA OF ENGAGING PARENTS INTO AN INTEGRATED STRATEGY OF THE CHURCH IS BUILT AROUND THE BELIEF THAT WHAT HAPPENS AT HOME IS AS IMPORTANT AS WHAT HAPPENS AT CHURCH.**

Never lose focus of the potential that so many parents have to engage with their kids. These are just terms to help you think of how parents can grow in their participation or partnership. Small changes in the lives of parents at other levels may actually be more significant than the changes that are happening in parents' lives who seem to be ideal. Don't let unmet expectations or unrealistic ideas keep you from celebrating what God is doing in the life of any parent. As important as your strategy is, God is still the one telling His story.

The idea of engaging parents into an integrated strategy of the church is built around the belief that *what happens at home is as important as what happens at church*. It means that church leaders start acting like they genuinely believe a little change in the rhythm of a family's time together can make a lasting impact on the heart of a child.

It is important as you attempt to engage parents that you don't create an unrealistic expectation. Instead, become a partner with all parents just where they are. Help them take the next step, no matter how small, in their potential to encourage an everyday faith. Most parents cannot do everything, but they can do something more. That "something" can make a huge difference in the life of the family and in the spiritual growth of a child.

It usually helps to think in terms of the various levels of partnerships because you realize as a leader that there will always be parents at every level. Your job is to make sure you understand parents outside and inside your church are willing to take a next step.

There is one more thing that is important to remember as you strive to get parents to engage with their children:

The goal is not to engage these parents to do everything,
but to engage them to do something more.

*If one dad who hasn't been praying with his ten-year-old daughter
starts praying with her …*

*If one mom who hasn't connected with her teenage son convinces him she really cares …*

*If one family who rarely discusses spiritual issues starts talking about God at dinner, even occasionally …*

*If anything changes in the rhythm of the home to remind everyone that God is telling a story through their family …*

*If one son or daughter sees God at work in the life of a mom or dad …*

*… it is more impacting than any leader or parent can imagine.*

I had a conversation with a woman on a plane who told me that her husband had attended a Christian men's conference a year earlier with some buddies and several thousand other men. One night in the middle of the conference, he drove home and woke her up at 3 a.m. He was emotional and broken. He apologized for being an irresponsible father and an insensitive husband. He asked her to forgive him for not making their family a priority. Then he drove back to finish the conference.

*See Concentrate 8.1*

As she continued to relate the story to me, she became emotional as she described that night. She explained that they had young children and there had been recent stress in their marriage. When he recommitted to her, telling her he wanted to start over, she knew it was an answer to prayer.

Then her voice quivered as she said, "That was over a year ago, and now I wish he had never gone."

I was stunned.

"Nothing ever happened," she said, "Nothing changed. I was hoping our marriage and family had turned a corner, but in a few months it was back to business as usual."

I said, "Assuming your husband was sincere and really did want to change, do you have any idea why he didn't?"

She answered, "I don't think he knows how to change. He never really had good models in his life." She asked if I thought he might have been sincere in his desire to change.

"Absolutely," I said. "I don't even know your husband, but when a man leaves his buddies to drive home at 3 a.m. to say to his wife, 'I was wrong,' then drives back to a conference to hear more sermons, I definitely believe he wants to change. If I were to ask your husband what he thinks you believe about him, what would he say?"

She was quiet for a few seconds, then said, "He knows I don't believe he will ever change, because that's what I told him."

I asked her what she thought might happen if she started acting like she really believed her husband could change, just to see if it made any difference. She agreed to try.

A few weeks later she called me and said, "You won't believe how much improvement has already happened in our marriage in the last few weeks. My husband wants to know if you will help us find a counselor." Within a year they were both *engaged* parents in our church, and today they are *invested* parents.

Here's the point: A husband tried and failed. Then his wife stopped believing, and he just quit trying. It was not her fault, but her belief in him had the potential to be a catalyst for change. There was also a very important next step—getting the influence he needed to change. He initially wanted to change. He might have even felt a measure of conviction. But ultimately, it was the combination of a desire to change, the strong and empowering influence of his wife, and relevant information about changing that actually enabled him to change.

Parents need these same things if they are to take the next step. They already have the desire, but it is up to us as the church to provide that empowering influence and relevant information. Like the wife I met, a lot of churches have stopped believing that parents can be better, and the parents understand this implicitly. As a result, a lot of parents have stopped trying to lead their kids spiritually. Something fundamentally changes in our approach to ministry when we start believing parents can improve.

## ACT LIKE EVERY PARENT WILL DO SOMETHING

I know what you are going to say. "It's one thing to say they can, but will they?"

Whether they do something is really up to you. What is your expectation? Too many parents walk away from conferences, workshops, Bible studies, and church services highly motivated but not equipped. At the end of the day they still don't know what to do. They still don't know exactly how to engage. *The church can change that.* We have the potential to give them a clear picture of what their kids can become when they partner with the church.

A lot of parents are stuck, and they need the right kind of catalyst to move them toward a different behavior. We can help free them by providing a clear next step that will change the rhythm in their homes so they can build an everyday faith.

As we said earlier in the book, we can imagine that every parent we meet is asking us to do three things. Consistently responding to these issues is a critical part of keeping parents in what we call the "loop of engagement."

### Give me the plan.

We developed the idea of the reThink Group well over a decade ago because we realized most parents did not have a plan when it came to the spiritual development of their kids. We choose to believe that parents desire to be more proactive and less reactive in raising their kids. Yet we recognize the tendency for families to live from day to day without a comprehensive strategy for spiritual matters. They need a support system, a consistent influence, and a steady flow of relevant information. In essence, what they need is the church as a partner. I am absolutely convinced that the local church is the key to implementing a lasting and effective strategy for parents.

That's why it is so important for an integrated staff to be responsible for the family getting on the same page. I have seen parents who were so hungry for a strategy they would implement even a bad plan, because at least it was better than no plan. When you integrate a strategy and refine the message, you have done your homework as a staff and are ready to partner more effectively with the parent. The first step is to present the big picture in terms that help parents understand the comprehensive plan of your ministry. You can do this by …

- using the "refine the message" process to craft a clear end in mind that you want to present to parents
- creating tools that explain the comprehensive plan from preschool to college
- making sure parents understand the basic truths and strategies for each age group
- involving parents in next steps so they stay engaged in the loop
- looking for ways to cast vision at every partner level, for example:
  - leveraging a churchwide series on family issues as an opportunity to explain strategy
  - using special family events or celebrations to communicate an overall plan
  - discovering creative ways to allow engaged and invested parents to network
  - establishing clear processes and information on an interactive Web site

You may be surprised at how important it is for parents to understand the plan. Giving them the vision is the first step in helping them engage with their kids. Then it's time to get a little more practical.

### Show me how it works.

Beyond just seeing the big picture, parents need to know how the strategy works. The reason we use the phrase "show me" is that it implies the need for *repeated influence* in their lives in order to be intentional parents. Even the best parents need consistent voices in their lives that encourage them to stay in sync with a strategy and to create a strong rhythm in their homes. Once again, the church offers the best opportunity for this kind of influence. It has the potential to provide parents with leadership to challenge them collectively and a network of families they can connect with personally.

Parents also need to know *how*. There has to be new information and a system to deliver it. Parents are like anyone else in that they need an occasional cue to remind them of the next phase of the strategy. When the church becomes more intentional about providing opportunities for families to connect, they can expect parents to become more intentional about engaging with their kids. There are a number of possibilities:

- Small-group studies. Design these around family values, season-of-life issues for parents, parents of preschoolers or teenagers, and other topics.

- Meetings for parents of students. Plan these during a strategic student series, at student event kickoffs, or during a special emphasis.
- Family celebrations. Build these around baby dedications, salvations, baptisms, graduations, and other life milestones.
- Shared family experiences. Create these opportunities for families to worship or learn together on a frequent basis (weekly or monthly) at home, in church, or off-campus.

Creating an excessive amount of random programming for families often has a negative effect. Keep it simple and strategic. As you create opportunities, they should synchronize with an overall strategy and make sense for those who attend your church as well as those who don't. The reason the church is so important in providing direction is that it is the natural part of a rhythm that complements the pattern of family life.

The goal is to establish a continual loop of engagement that incorporates updates and new information.

As you do this, you are intentionally helping parents reactivate as a family. It's much more effective to think in terms of partnering with the family from a looped approach than from a haphazard approach. Some churches will plan an annual conference or workshop, but parents don't parent annually or seasonally—they parent daily. Moms and dads can't wait for the next conference or workshop so they can learn the information they need to respond to their present situations. They need something more frequent and more consistent. The rhythm of Sabbath was designed so God's people could refuel and reactivate an everyday faith. In the same way, the church has the potential to help families nurture an everyday faith in the hearts and lives of their children.

I am convinced that one of the best ways to stimulate the rhythm of the family is to create frequent shared experiences for the family. Although this looks quite different when kids transition into their teenage years, the elementary years are a critical season to form the foundation for an everyday faith within the family.

Through the past several decades the church has drifted in and out of various versions of "assembling together." When I grew up in

**EVEN THE BEST PARENTS NEED CONSISTENT VOICES IN THEIR LIVES THAT ENCOURAGE THEM TO STAY IN SYNC WITH A STRATEGY AND TO CREATE A STRONG RHYTHM IN THEIR HOMES.**

**WE PUT ADULTS IN A SERVICE DESIGNED FOR KIDS SO WE COULD GET PARENTS EXCITED ABOUT WHAT WE WERE TEACHING THEIR CHILDREN.**

church, the age-group-focused concept dominated most churches. Families were segregated almost as soon as they went through the church doors, as kids went one way and parents went the other. Different versions of church have since continued to promote separating parents and kids. Although I am a strong advocate of designing adult services to be relevant for adults, most churches do not have any environments where kids and parents together can experience worship and learn faith principles.

The family as a whole needs a *repeated influence* to cue them. One way to establish a network and platform to systematically communicate to parents of elementary-age children is to create events for the family that serve as catalysts to spiritual growth and development. Sometimes we at reThink refer to them as "family experiences," or FX, and they can happen in a variety of ways. There are home versions designed to create an interactive evening for a small group of families by using video and creative activities. There are also large-scale productions or events designed for churches to host gatherings of multiple families, especially families in the community who are disconnected from church. Each FX has the specific purpose of stimulating the family to intentionally create rhythm as a family and to build an everyday faith.

Over a decade ago, I was on a team that created and started one of the first weekly family experiences in the country. The premise was simple. We felt like we needed to put parents and kids together in a shared environment on a frequent basis. Instead of putting children in a service designed for adults so we could get kids excited about what their parents believed, we flipped the concept. We put adults in a service designed for kids so we could get parents excited about what we were teaching their children. We hosted and produced this program, KidStuf, every week, and it became an integral part of our strategy. When we first brainstormed the idea and got advice from other children's directors around the country, they discouraged the idea. We were told that any environment that went from kindergarten to fifth grade and included parents would span too many ages.

We almost gave up on the idea until a movie came out that year that reinforced the concept for us—*The Lion King.* At the time, my children were eleven, nine, seven, and five, and as I sat with them I realized there were some pretty talented people who had mastered the art of creating a family experience. They were proving the church experts wrong. Halfway through the movie it was obvious that Disney's writers had included lines that would keep everyone in the audience engaged. I would chuckle at a one-liner from Whoopi Goldberg's laughing hyena character, and my five-year-old would eye me like she didn't understand what was funny. When she giggled at something Simba did, I rolled my eyes to tell her it was juvenile. My son was intrigued with the elephant graveyard. Everyone in my family responded to the part that had been designed for them, and in so doing, we shared an incredible experience together.

As we talked about our favorite scenes on the way home, I had an epiphany. I thought, *Why can't church be like this?* A few months later we started KidStuf in an elementary school cafeteria. We had a black backdrop painted with the KidStuf name, a couple of singers, two hosts, an actor, and a camcorder I purchased from Circuit City. Today, churches around the country are producing quarterly, monthly, and weekly family experiences. Some are production-driven, others are small-group-driven, but every FX is built on the same idea: It's not what happens during the family experiences that is most important, but what happens between them.

*See Concentrate 8.2*

Shortly after we began KidStuf, a CEO who had been attending with his daughter came to me at the end of the program and said, "I have been attending KidStuf for a few weeks, and it's really my first experience with a church. My daughter has started asking me questions about 'spiritual stuff' and I was wondering if I could meet with you so I can figure out what to tell her." It was that day I decided that I would look at all parents assuming they wanted to be better parents.

### Tell me what to do today.

When a husband wakes his wife in the middle of the night and admits he has failed, he is usually motivated by a desire to change. While lasting and radical change is certainly something that depends on God, many times behavior is directly related to the right instructions. When a child is young, if a parent tells him to clean up a room, the child may be so overwhelmed by the task that he becomes paralyzed. When children don't have clear enough instructions, they often don't know where to start. The same is true for parents. Sometimes the cause may be a lack of vision, but most of the time

**IT'S NOT WHAT HAPPENS DURING THE FAMILY EXPERIENCES THAT IS MOST IMPORTANT, BUT WHAT HAPPENS BETWEEN THEM.**

the parents just need repeated influence combined with specific instructions. This gives them a clear handle on how the information fits into their practical experience. If we are going to partner with parents and actually help them improve, we may need to be more specific.

In *The Tipping Point,* Malcolm Gladwell describes a 1960s experiment by social psychologist Howard Levanthal. He attempted to get seniors on the Yale University campus to get tetanus shots by distributing two different brochures. One brochure featured statistical information about the occurrence of tetanus and the vaccination's effectiveness in preventing it. The other was a more emotional plea that played on the reader's fear, using graphic images of tetanus victims to convince them to get the shot. After distributing the two brochures, he surveyed the students. Although the students who read the high-fear brochure were more concerned, only three percent of both groups of students actually went to the health clinic. The information they had learned did not translate into actions. Levanthal made one change to the brochures and redistributed them, and the percentage of students who got tetanus shots increased to twenty-eight percent. What did he do? He added a map showing where the health center was located in relationship to students' classes and a schedule of when the shots were being offered. When the students saw how the information fit into their lives, it changed their behavior.[46]

At reThink, we learned early on that one of the best things we could do to engage parents was to give them a map and schedule. So in every one of our curriculums, we have designed initiatives for the family to complete at home. We also created unique resources focused on family time to give parents specific things to do. When we did a series for teenagers about fighting for their relationships with their parents, we hosted a family experience event and gave parents clear instructions on how to engage with their teenagers during the series. We designed take-away objects that could be leveraged as activities in the home. If you are going to keep parents in the engagement loop, be diligent in creating and testing different initiatives.

These three issues help explain how the church can work in a unique way to partner with parents. They illustrate why it is so important to work from a different perspective if you hope to engage parents. As a leader, you have to learn the skill of leveraging repeated influence and creating relevant initiatives. It's a balance of action, and understanding how the loop of engagement works might best be described like a yo-yo.

In a simple yo-yo toss, the toy begins in your hand, is thrown outward, spins, and then loops back to your hand. At the top of the loop is the source of energy that gives the yo-yo enough power to return to your hand. As it drops and spins, it loses its original energy and must return to your hand for another boost. So it is with the families in your church. God is the source of all energy, so what I am really referring to is the instrument of that energy—the church.

When you establish a loop of engagement as family ministry, you are simply deciding that families need the church to be an energy source for their homes. The church has the potential to provide a clear programming strategy, repeated influence, and relevant information in order to reactivate the home. As a church, you establish environments or resources that serve as catalysts so the home can be reenergized as often as it needs to be.

See Concentrate 8.3

At the top of the loop are your family experiences, family small-group studies, parenting Web sites, baptism celebrations, and baby dedications. As a ministry team, you organize them strategically so they can systematically energize the family without causing burnout. When the families come to the source, they get influenced and challenged to live out their faith as a family. Then they leave, living out their initiatives as a family, until the force begins to wane. Then they go back to the top of the loop and get reactivated again.

Just like a yo-yo, the potential power is at the top. When it is released, it spins kinetically, goes through its rhythm, and cycles back up. There's a definite pattern: up to get energy; down to spin the message and be a demonstration. Up to get reactivated; down to live out an everyday faith.

And did you notice what guides the yo-yo on its path? One string. Not three strings, not four strings, just one. One single string, held by one integrated hand, makes sure nothing gets tangled.

In your church, you give families a regular source of energy with *repeated influence.*
You send them spinning along the path with *family initiatives.*
And they return to the source for more influence when they need it.

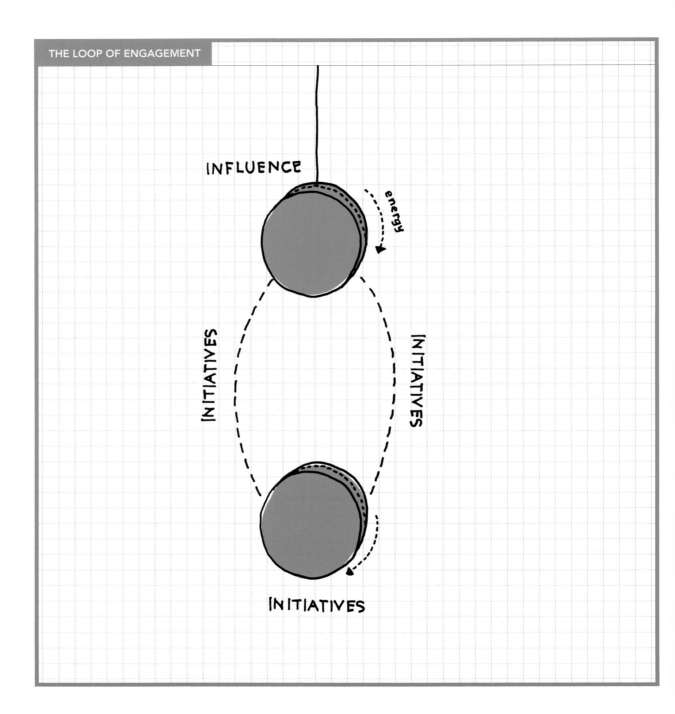

If you were to draw a diagram of the loop, you would write "influence" at the top, then follow the line to the bottom and write "initiatives." Keep those two words in front of you. They are critical for your team to understand how to keep families in the loop.

This model of family ministry requires your team to think through a series of questions that are relevant to the process in your specific context:

- Where do your families get their energy?
  What kinds of environments or resources work to give your families energy?
- What information do they need to keep them on track?
  Examine your initiatives to make sure they are working for the family.
- How frequently do they need to get energy from the source?
  When it comes to your programs or events, how often do you need to send them back to the top? What programs should be weekly, monthly, or occasionally?

This certainly isn't the only way to do family ministry. Some people prefer a different game altogether, playing by different rules. In their game, there is no string. There is no real system. Everyone is fighting for the same space. Everyone takes a turn to knock everyone else out of their territory. Everyone is positioned arbitrarily. The game is called playing marbles. And it has no rhythm. Instead of giving energy to each other, they drain it from one another and end up scattered.

## ACT LIKE EVERY PARENT YOU MEET IS COMING TO YOUR CHURCH THIS SUNDAY

What if the parents you met last week at the ball game showed up at your church this Sunday? What next step would you give them to connect them to a better strategy? Would you be ready to help them engage? Would they see your church as a source of energy for their families? The real question is, How do you see your role as a church when it comes to the family? Not only should you think Orange, you should start acting Orange.

You may have figured out by now that you have influence as a church. Just like you need to be wise in how you manage your time, finances, facilities, and resources, you must also be good stewards of your influence. Thinking Orange is thinking smarter. If you could leverage your influence to make the greatest possible impact, where would you leverage it? You have to consider the home in

SUNDAYS CAN BE THE CATALYSTS THAT GIVE FAMILIES NEW BEGINNINGS EVERY WEEK, MAKING EVERYDAY FAITH A REALITY.

the equation. If it is the only entity other than the church that God has specifically designed for influence, it is logical that combining the two makes a greater impact.

Carey Nieuwhof is a senior pastor from Canada who has been a proactive Orange thinker in the Toronto area. He had an Orange epiphany a few years ago as he was preparing to speak on a Sunday morning. "As I was thinking about the parents who lived in the community around our church, something dawned on me. They don't lie in bed at night wondering about the topic that I will speak about on Sunday. They don't even lie in bed at night thinking about God. They lie in bed thinking mostly about their kids."

**Remember the loop.**
The church is in a unique position to give the family hope and direction because most parents would love to know that people other than themselves think about their families. Sundays can be the catalysts that give families new beginnings every week, making everyday faith a reality. The power of the church is that it is a place where the family can start over and be reactivated through an ongoing cycle. The magic of the home is that it is a place where the family can start over with the same people every day.

Some parents are coming your direction to get in the loop. Think about that while you get ready for Sunday. You may be putting a large amount of time and energy into the top of the loop. You are writing, creating, organizing, designing, recruiting, and building so the loop can be perpetuated. It's what you do every week as a leader. Sure, it may seem like it's a routine. And sometimes you feel you are going through the motions. If you are honest, the closer Sunday gets, the less strength you have. You are putting all your energy into the top of the loop! Sometimes you wonder if it's really worth it. But don't stop doing it. Why? Because there are people who are going to get their everyday faith from you. There are people whose strength is waning. They are getting weaker and their faith is dissipating. And guess where they are coming? They are heading back to the top of the loop.

Parents who are wondering.
Parents who are wandering.

Parents who are worried.
Parents who are broken.
Parents who are tired.
Parents who are alone.
Parents who are hurting.
Parents who are hoping.
Parents who are determined.
Parents who are struggling to win the battle for the future and faith of their children.

I know what you do sometimes feels like a grind, but God promises to add His power to the fuel you give. He has designed us as a people who get energy from one another. It is the potential of what happens when we gather. It reenergizes our hearts. It refuels our hope. It reactivates our families. Our faith stays alive every day … as long as we stay in the loop.

### Put on the red hat.

As a parent, I need the church. I need other leaders in my life who will lean in and give me energy to keep doing this. I suspect that many of you who are wearing red and yellow hats realize that just because you are a leader doesn't mean you are exempt from needing leaders in your life as a parent. It really gets confusing sometimes.

Let's go back to Nehemiah's story. There is something in the text I had never noticed until a few years ago. It was a defining moment in the building of the wall. The work was about halfway done. People were tired. Morale began to drift. There had been some unrest and a few power struggles. The enemy, Sanballat, sensed the waning energy and saw an opportunity to start rumors, so he threatened an attack. The people began to panic, and Nehemiah recognized the danger of the situation. They had come too far not to finish, but it seemed like the risk of losing everything was becoming a probability. So Nehemiah did something that immediately rallied everyone. It became the turning point in the rebuilding of the wall of Jerusalem. His actions saved the city and immediately reactivated the families and leaders. This is what happened according to his journal:

*Therefore I stationed some of the people behind the lowest points of the wall at the exposed places, posting them by families, with their swords, spears and bows. After*

**AS PARENTS WE MAKE A DRASTIC MISTAKE IF WE STOP FIGHTING, YIELDING TO THE MYTH THAT MAYBE OUR KIDS DON'T NEED A RELATIONSHIP WITH US.**

*I looked things over, I stood up and said to the nobles, the officials and the rest of the people, "Don't be afraid of them. Remember the Lord, who is great and awesome, and fight for your brothers, your sons and your daughters, your wives and your homes."*[47]

Notice what he said: "Fight for your sons and your daughters, your wives and your homes." In one statement, he reminded them of the stakes and prepared them to fight.

Nehemiah's words ring true.

I have four children: a boy and three girls. One of the clearest lessons I learned about family was from Rebekah when she was in the seventh grade. Being the youngest, she has developed some pretty amazing verbal skills to survive her older siblings. One afternoon we were in her room having a conversation—a rather loud one. It was one of those "you're thirteen and you will do what I say and I am your father and you have to listen to me and that's just the way it is" kinds of moments.

That's when it happened. She took a verbal shot at me that totally caught me off guard. It hit me so hard I heard myself catch my breath. I had never dreamed one of my children would say what she said to me in that moment. (In all fairness to her, she had been trying to tell me something that had been going on and I had not been paying attention. So it was really an attempt on her part to get me to listen.)

I was so shocked. I had no comeback. It was so personal that I was extremely hurt.

I did the only thing I could think to do at that moment. I left. I walked out of the room, down the stairs, through the den, into the garage, got in my car, and drove off. Have I already said that I was really upset, and very, very personally offended?

I was driving down the road, feeling betrayed, when about fifteen minutes into the drive, my mobile phone rang. It was Rebekah.

"Dad, I'm sorry," she said. "You know I really didn't mean what I said." (It was one of those moments where the parent becomes the child.) Then she continued. "But why did you leave? Why did you walk out? I need to know that our relationship is worth fighting for."

I can't really prove this because I don't have any statistical information to back it up, but I think Rebekah verbalized what a lot of teenagers think at some point. They may not know how to articulate it, but they feel it. I have talked with college girls whose fathers have stopped fighting for their relationships with their daughters because they lost the battle for their marriages. I have talked to sons who have strained relationships with parents because they became disengaged relationally after conflicts in high school. As parents we make a drastic mistake if we stop fighting, yielding to the myth that maybe our kids don't need a relationship with us. Some of you who are both leaders and parents have gravitated away from making those relationships a priority because it's just too hard.

*See Concentrate 8.4*

Listen to Nehemiah, and "fight for your sons and daughters and your wives and homes."

All of us who are wearing yellow hats should accept our calling to partner with every parent, to help them keep fighting a real battle to win the hearts of their sons and daughters.

*See Concentrate 8.5*

If we don't help them fight, who will?
If we don't inspire them to reactivate their family, who will?
If we don't create a place to reenergize their faith, who will?

Every parent needs you as a partner. Start acting like it.

ESSENTIAL #4

# ELEVATE COMMUNITY

WHEN YOU
COMBINE 2
INFLUENCES, YOU

## INCREASE THE ODDS

# 9

## ELEVATE COMMUNITY
CONNECT EVERYONE TO A CARING LEADER
AND A CONSISTENT GROUP OF PEERS

Many people know that in 1891 Dr. James Naismith invented the game of basketball. Not a lot of people know, however, about the contribution of Tony Hinkle in the late 1950s. Hinkle made it easier for spectators and players to see the ball by making it orange. Today, basketball is the only sport that has an official orange ball.

My oldest daughter, Hannah, loved basketball, and I learned a lot just from watching her play the game. Primarily, I discovered that playing basketball is harder than it looks. Any winning team has to meet on a frequent basis to practice plays, learn strategies, and increase personal skills. The right coach can make all the difference. The next time you watch a basketball game, focus on the head coach moving along the sidelines with the players, giving constant instructions.

Maybe the most mysterious part of the game is how the players seem to have supersonic, laser-focused hearing. They can actually filter out the echoes of the gym floor, the roar of the crowd, and the shouts of their own parents to tune in to the solitary voice of the coach.

I remember watching Hannah shoot eight three-pointers during one particular high school basketball game. In a magical moment at the end of the game, I did what all proud fathers do—I ran up to her excitedly because I just knew all she wanted was my affirmation and approval. I began to lavish her with compliments about her playing skills and focus.

As we got in the car, I continued telling her all the things she did right until she interrupted me.

"Dad, did my coach say anything to you about how I played?"

**EVERYONE NEEDS TO BE BELIEVED IN BY SOMEONE, AND EVERYONE NEEDS TO BELONG SOMEWHERE. TRUE COMMUNITY PROVIDES BOTH.**

I said, "What does it matter what your coach said? Your father is here!" I was pumped.

"But, Dad, did Coach Brown say anything?"

Suddenly, it dawned on me that my daughter had crossed a line. She was more concerned about what the coach thought than she was about what I thought.

**When you elevate community, you recognize the need for multiple voices.**
The reality is that a time comes in all children's lives when they seem to care more about what another adult says than they care what their own parents say. That's why it's important to start early in a child's life establishing the right coaches.

When we talk about elevating community, we are talking about strategically placing coaches in the lives of our children and teenagers. Growing up in this generation requires some pretty significant relationships. Children and students need the skills to navigate through difficult obstacles and the right voices to give wise direction. Everyone needs to be believed in by someone, and everyone needs to belong somewhere. True community provides both.

You provide community when everyone is connected to a caring leader and a consistent group of peers.

*How do we implement?*

If you look back over your own life, you will probably notice that certain individuals stand out over time because of the impact and influence they had in your life. It's the power of significant relationships. When churches embrace this principle, they help parents by meeting the needs of children and teenagers to have older mentors to guide and encourage them in their faith. One of the greatest gifts your church can give its families is a consistent network of leaders and friends who are there to help them win.

In fact, whether or not a student remains involved in a faith community is tied to the number of adults who influence that person spiritually. In his research, Mark Kelly observed, "Teens who had at least one adult from church make a significant time investment in their lives … were more likely to keep attending church. More of those who stayed in church—by a margin of 46 percent to 28 percent—said five or more adults at church had invested time with them personally and spiritually."[48]

Community matters.

When we create this sense of community, several things can happen:

*See Concentrate 9.1*

- Parents feel supported, not alone, in trying to have moral and spiritual influence with their children.
- The church is characterized by meaningful and significant relationships, not superficial ones.
- We reproduce a generation of Christians who are able to develop authentic relationships easily.
- Students will pursue counsel from Christian mentors rather than from unhealthy relationships.
- Productions or programs are positioned as a step in a process rather than the whole answer.
- Leaders discover their potential to make a lasting investment in someone's life.

**When you elevate community, you cooperate with how God grows people spiritually.**

The team that started North Point had an epiphany several years ago when we were debating how to help people grow in their relationships with Christ. After discussing a variety of programming ideas and core principles, Andy flipped the dialogue. He suggested that maybe we had been asking the wrong question. Instead of trying to figure out how to help people grow in their relationships with Christ, we should ask ourselves how we grew in our own relationships with Him.

For the next few hours we told our stories. We recounted the defining moments in our lives when our faith was stretched to a new dimension. We talked about people who influenced us, principles we learned, pain we had encountered, answered prayers, and ministries that had challenged us.

At the end, we were surrounded by pieces of our life stories that represented mile markers where our spiritual growth had escalated. Then there was the epiphany. As we looked at our stories we realized that although they were very different, there were similar patterns. It's almost as if God had used the same chords over and over in every one of our lives to write different songs. We began to refer to them as "the catalysts for spiritual growth."

When you or I grow spiritually it is usually because of one or more of the following:

- a life-changing truth that helps us understand who God is or how to live
- a spiritual discipline we develop that puts us in tune with God's Spirit or voice
- a personal ministry that stretches us to tap into God's power and purpose
- a significant relationship that God uses to prompt or encourage us
- a pivotal circumstance that causes us to depend on God in a new way

These catalysts are key to helping others grow spiritually. A lot of churches are built around the idea that one or two of these are the most important. The reality is when it comes to programming, many churches act as if *truth* is the most important part of discipleship. Teaching and content become the most important things that happen in every environment. We begin to think that discipleship is a class or a curriculum. What if discipleship is as much about serving in ministry as it is about Bible study? What if discipleship is as much about being in a consistent, caring relationship as it is about praying? When churches say to me they can't or won't provide a consistent leader in the life of a child, I believe they are settling for a style of ministry that teaches truth, but not a model that disciples a life.

If we want to help someone grow spiritually, we should think about how we can cooperate with all the catalysts. They are all critical: life-changing truth, spiritual disciplines, personal ministry, significant relationships, and pivotal circumstances. A few years later, I had another awakening as I was working through these concepts. I realized that if we were going to be strategic in helping people grow spiritually, we needed to answer a question related to the five catalysts. In light of the five catalysts, who has the most strategic position of influence? The answer to me seemed obvious. It was two people: a small-group leader and a parent.

One of the reasons I believe so strongly in elevating community is the potential it provides for small groups and small-group leaders to participate in God's plan for spiritual development and discipleship. Jesus set the example of living in a consistent community—why should we live any other way? Ministries where children and students are connected to different leaders every time they come

SIGNIFICA

SPIRITUAL DISCIPLINES

TRUTH

PERSONAL MINISTRY

LIFE-CHANGING TRUTH

SPIRIT

PIVOTAL CIRCUMSTANCES

SIGNIFICANT RELATIONSHIPS

MIN

**LIFE-CHANGING TRUTH**
**SPIRITUAL DISCIPLINES**
**PERSONAL MINISTRY**
**SIGNIFICANT RELATIONSHIPS**
**PIVOTAL CIRCUMSTANCES**

# Catalysts for Spiritual Growth

Reoccurring themes in people's life stories suggest that God uses five catalysts to define and grow us as believers. As a leader your primary role in the lives of others is to leverage what God is already doing to help them grow as Christians. What if you organized your ministries around these five key issues?

### LIFE-CHANGING TRUTH
What is your role in teaching or amplifying spiritual truth for them?

### SPIRITUAL DISCIPLINES
What can you do to help them develop personal spiritual habits?

### PERSONAL MINISTRY
How can you encourage them to establish a personal ministry?

### SIGNIFICANT RELATIONSHIPS
How can you be more effective at using your life to influence those you lead? How can you mobilize other leaders to pursue meaningful relationships with children and teenagers?

### PIVOTAL CIRCUMSTANCES
What is your responsibility when it comes to crisis or difficult situations in their lives?

can only have so much impact. These relationships rarely, if ever, move beyond a classroom-teaching environment. On the other hand, discipling kids through long-term relationships requires that we do more than just provide them with information. We need to specifically place leaders into the lives of our children and teenagers who partner with their parents in the work that God is doing. These relationships will invariably have a greater and more lasting impact.

Over time, community is how people grow.

Children learn in the context of relationships, when their lives intersect with the lives of others. While the most significant relationships in a child's life are the relationships at home, children have a better chance of understanding and interpreting life-changing truth when multiple influences in their lives are all saying the same thing. When parents and leaders work together to teach the same principles, it gives a child a better chance to make wise decisions in the middle of challenging situations.

In order for leaders and parents to work together at communicating similar life principles, it's important for churches to develop a common language. This is why we have created what we call "Five Faith Skills" that allow leaders and parent to use common language to help children learn to navigate the Bible, personalize Scripture, dialogue with God, articulate their faith, and worship with their lives. No matter how deeply involved parents are with their children, some learning experiences may take place outside the home, away from their parents' care:

- the first time a child prays publicly
- the first time a child witnesses God's work in the lives of people outside of his family
- the first time a child has an opportunity to share her faith with others

When there is a consistent leader in the life of a child, parents know they have someone trustworthy to guide their children through these important experiences.

When you elevate community,
you help kids or students navigate through critical life situations.
Many children will walk out of your building and face experiences you never

dreamed they would face. Having caring adults around them who will listen and help them navigate those traumatic events will be critical to their spiritual growth.

A while back, our team at reThink received an e-mail that drove this principle home for us. The e-mail came from a church that had made it a priority to have consistent leaders in the lives of their children. They sent the message to us to ask for prayer because one of the fifth-grade boys in their church had died after being hit by a car. The leaders shared about the challenges they faced in ministering to the family as well as to the other children in the church. Nothing could change the hurt and pain of the situation. But in the middle of the hurt, listen to these words from one of the church leaders:

> One thing we know for sure is that Brandon is with Jesus. God gave me the awesome privilege of sitting in his small group before he was in the accident. We, of course, were talking about that month's virtue: courage. The small group activity was to write their top ten fears. One of the kids wrote "death," and I asked the question, "What is there to fear about death?" That's when Brandon shared that he has no fear of death because he knows and loves the Lord and was living for Him.
>
> Wow! Looking back, I know that was a gift from God. I was able to stand at the foot of his hospital bed and tell his hurting mother about that day as I held her in my arms. It was also a gift for the kids in his small group. None of them have to question for one second whether or not their friend is in heaven. God is so good!
>
> That moment would not have happened without your vision for small groups. This would have never happened in a Sunday school classroom setting. It's about building relationships and being able to hear the heart of God's precious children.

When you buy into the idea of community, you tap into the power of relationships. You are thinking Orange by offering families another trusted adult to help their sons and daughters interpret life situations. You are offering them a built-in support system for when life hurts. By elevating community, the church offers children and teenagers a safe place to run to.

NAVIGATE THE BIBLE

ARTICULATE YOUR FAITH

WORSHIP WITH YOUR LIFE

NAVIGA

ULATE YOUR FAITH

WORSHIP

DIALOGUE WITH GOD

BIB

ALIZE SCRIPTURE

**NAVIGATE THE BIBLE**
**PERSONALIZE SCRIPTURE**
**DIALOGUE WITH GOD**
**ARTICULATE YOUR FAITH**
**WORSHIP WITH YOUR LIFE**

# Faith Skills

We at the reThink Group believe there are five basic things children and teenagers need to be able to do so they can own their faith and make it personal.

NAVIGATE THE BIBLE: **survey, locate**
To learn where they can go to find verses that will help them with specific questions

PERSONALIZE SCRIPTURE: **memorize, apply**
To remember Scripture when they need it most and apply it in everyday situations

DIALOGUE WITH GOD: **public, private**
To encourage them to practice talking with God

ARTICULATE YOUR FAITH: **share, defend**
To be able to discuss and wrestle with what they believe so children and teenagers can make their faith their own

WORSHIP WITH YOUR LIFE: **serve, invest**
To know how to give back to God and to serve Him in the way they live their everyday lives

*When you elevate community,*
*you recruit and nurture a different breed of spiritual leaders.*

When Nehemiah made the decision to rebuild the wall around Jerusalem, he realized that he had a monumental task in front of him. Not only did he need to convince King Artaxerxes to grant him protection, materials, and time off for his project, Nehemiah also needed to launch one of the greatest volunteer campaigns of all time. He had a plan, but how could he convince hundreds of people to work with him every day for fifty-two days?

When we started North Point, we had a vision for what God could do through small groups. We were absolutely convinced that the most optimal environment for life change was community. We knew we wanted to create community in small-group contexts for children and students, so we did some investigation. We asked other churches how small groups worked for them. What we discovered was there weren't many churches with legitimate small-group communities for children. Most of them had structures in which kids would go to a different table or classroom with a different leader every week.

While many church leaders agreed this was not ideal, they gave us two specific reasons why consistent community for children just wouldn't work:

- They never knew which kids would consistently attend.
- They couldn't expect the same leaders to volunteer every week for an extended amount of time.

We were informed that consistency in small groups was simply impossible, especially for a large church. After listening to the feedback, we almost gave up on the idea before we ever started. But we kept working through it because we believed in the importance of creating community for children and for students.

While we understood the reason behind our fight for community, we still faced the practical challenge of finding devoted leaders to disciple small groups on a consistent basis. Many churches told us we would never find volunteers who were willing to make this kind of commitment. In practice, however, we discovered the opposite was true. We found that volunteers who showed up knowing they would be disconnected from the kids as soon as the day or month was over had a tendency to be inconsistent. But when volunteers were connected

**IF YOU WANT A TEENAGER TO TRUST YOU, YOU HAVE TO EARN RELATIONAL CHANGE IN YOUR POCKETS OVER TIME.**

relationally to the same kids every week, week after week, their commitment level *increased*. When churches bought into the idea that volunteers were inconsistent and hard to come by, their self-fulfilling prophecy fueled inconsistent and unmotivated leaders. By shifting to a model that asked volunteers to be an essential part of authentic community for kids and students, the leaders felt a sense of connectivity and meaning. They were accountable to someone. They had a meaningful mission. Something magical began to happen. The number of small-group leaders in the church skyrocketed because, for the first time, volunteers began to find fulfillment and purpose in mentoring and discipling kids and teenagers.

What do you think might have happened if Nehemiah had changed his volunteer recruitment plan? What if he had gone to the people saying, "Okay. We need workers for this wall project. I know you are all very busy, and you have a lot going on right now, but if you could sign up to give one hour of your time every other month that would really help me out." It's just not compelling. By being bold in his vision, Nehemiah created a place where people did more than just volunteer for his project—they put their hearts into it. They were sold out to seeing the completion of the wall. He offered a way to literally change history by committing to a project that was much bigger than they were. He invited them to play a role in God's story.

When you elevate community,
you do something that nothing in culture can match.
This is an important principle because it is true for every church, regardless of size. As you create environments and productions for your ministry, here's something I know is true: You will never outproduce Hollywood or Disney. You will never create a production or have a band that will compare with what the world can do.

When we first started North Point, we knew that we wanted to build the kind of environments that would attract unchurched people in our area. At first our budget was very limited, but as the church grew and more people caught the vision, the budget expanded. We were able to create environments none of us would have ever imagined possible. But no matter how professional and impressive our environments might be, right around the corner a rock concert or other production would come into town that could spend millions compared to our thousands. It's just a reality that the church will never outproduce culture when it comes to putting on a good show.

But here's the good news: Culture can never outdo churches with respect to creating community. No matter how much the culture tries to mimic community by creating false environments and shallow relationships, the culture can never be a consistent, personal presence in the lives of parents and children. Creating community is something every church can do regardless of size or budget simply by placing another consistent adult in the life of every child and student in your ministry. When this happens, children and students know they have a place where they can have a safe and meaningful spiritual discussion with an adult who cares. When that happens, nothing can compete.

This is going to change everything. When we focus on creating community, kids subconsciously recognize the value and move into adulthood knowing that community is something they need and want. If you believe in community, everything you do should move children and teens into the context of a small group where they can experience life change. And when you believe that, you'll see a couple of changes.

First of all, it's going to change the way you lead *strategically*. You're going to look at everything differently, and your priorities in ministry are going to be different. Do you know why? It is because your priorities will not simply be to buy the newest equipment or to figure out how to do the latest trend. You'll begin to realize your focus shifts from doing *more* toward doing things *well*. Your main concern in ministry will be to find the right kinds of leaders to invest in your children and in your students.

Once you find those leaders, you will look for ways to invest in them as they work on the front lines of ministry to disciple your children and students. This is also why it's important to have a graduated system in which leaders transition from one grade to the next with the same children. It takes time to establish a relationship, and even more so as you move toward middle school and high school. As children grow older it becomes increasingly important for them to have consistent leaders who walk with them across multiple years. A small child will trust and confide in an adult because adults are "big" people. If you want a teenager to trust you, you have to earn relational change in your pockets over time. That's why we believe it's critical for high school leaders to commit to the full four-year experience. Even if every leader doesn't complete the four-year commitment, you accomplish three things:

- You recruit a different caliber of leader.
- You guarantee that some will connect for four years, and many others will invest for at least a few years.
- They discover a different kind of perspective and motivation that comes with a long-term commitment.

When you give leaders the opportunity to connect with a group of teenagers over four years, the leaders grow as much as the students. The power of this kind of graduated system may be most evident when a high school senior graduates and begins to navigate the transition to the next phase of life.

What if we take the concept and carry it out another year or two? I know it sounds crazy, but just think about it for a minute: When do most students drop out of church? The decline of participation in church and faith starts to escalate in college. All the statistics I read suggest that when students leave the church at graduation, the overwhelming majority do not make a transition to a community of faith beyond high school.

*See Concentrate 9.2*

For the past few years I have spent a lot of time working with college students and dialoguing about this transition. One evening a college student explained it this way: "When we go off to college, everything is new. There is too much to figure out. You are wrestling with a new environment and new friends, trying to decide between majors and schedule, part-time job, budget, campus activities. It is a confusing and crazy time in your life. Add the idea of trying to figure out where to connect in a church, and it's all just too hard."

So what does the typical church do? When students graduate, we give them a devotional book and wave good-bye. Or we hand their names off to a college minister and try to connect them to leaders they don't know. What if, instead, we ask leaders who are working with twelfth-graders to step out of student ministry for a year or two and stay connected with their students during this critical transition? There is a difference when a leader says to a student who is leaving, "I am here if you ever need anything," and when he says, "We are going to stay connected as a group for the next year." The latter creates an expectation and encourages an intentional relationship at one of the most critical times in the student's life. Social networks like Facebook make this even more feasible. When you consider the amount of life change that occurs in the world of college students, you recognize how important it is for them to be connected to a leader who has history with them.

When you decide to elevate community, you will also begin to look at your ministry programs in a different way. You won't see them as one-time or annual experiences that exist only to jump-start your activities. Instead, every program becomes a step in the process that moves your children or students toward community. This one thing will change the way you evaluate your budget, manage your priorities, and plan your programming. Everything will be working strategically to move toward community. When you build community, you will view everything through a different lens. You'll listen to everything through a different filter. You will evaluate your success in ministry by the stories you hear from small-group leaders and by the stories you hear from parents whose kids are connected. It fundamentally changes the way you do ministry.

*See Concentrate 9.3*

When you elevate community, you'll see evidence of these benefits everywhere:

- Children and students meet in an organized way with a consistent group of peers and with leaders who assume a high level of responsibility for their spiritual formation.
- Small groups are valued and championed at every age level as a crucial environment to help kids grow spiritually.
- An effective group or community experience is a primary goal of every ministry, and programs are viewed as steps toward that goal.
- Staff and volunteer positions are organized to ensure the effectiveness of a small-group strategy.
- Parents value small-group leaders as partners in teaching and modeling truths to their children, and small-group leaders see their role as assisting and supporting parents.
- Small-group leaders are encouraged to graduate into older age groups with the same kids and students.

**When you elevate community,
you provide reinforcement to the parent.**
Not only will elevating community change the way you lead strategically, it will change your families. As a parent, I believe that one of the greatest gifts the

**THE MOST POWERFUL THING YOU CAN DO FOR PARENTS IS TO PROVIDE KIDS IN YOUR MINISTRY WITH ANOTHER ADULT WHO WILL SAY THE SAME THINGS IN THEIR KIDS' LIVES THAT THEY'RE TRYING TO SAY AS A PARENT.**

church can give me is community for my children. I want them to know that the church is a place where they can show up and be safe, a place where they can have meaningful dialogue with another trusted adult, and a place where they can ask difficult questions.

I am personally amazed that some leaders suggest parents are the only influences a child or teenager needs to have a dynamic faith. I disagree. As kids grow older and move toward independence, it is critical to establish another clear voice in their lives, especially in a culture that challenges their faith at every level. Some leaders even use Deuteronomy 6 to challenge the role of other Christian leaders in the lives of teenagers. Instead, parents and leaders both need to recognize how important it is for these two influences to partner. The Hebrew culture described in Deuteronomy naturally promoted this kind of relationship. We're challenged to *rethink* our understanding of family, as the Fuller Youth Institute explains:

> A family in the Old Testament would have included parents, children, workers, perhaps adult siblings with their own spouses and children. In fact, households could be compiled of as many as eighty people. These texts, such as Deuteronomy 6, are discussing the communal raising of children. Our own cultural distance from these passages may cause us to put undue pressure on parents alone.[49]

As a leader, when I put on a yellow hat, I need to recognize how important it is for me to make sure parents don't have to do this alone. As a parent who wears a red hat, I need to remember I can't do this alone. I want my children to know that church is a place where they can go to talk *about* me if they need to. When my children get frustrated with me, I would much rather they take that frustration to a place where they are surrounded by Christian friends and a good leader than to someone who has no loyalty to me as a parent. When churches aren't thinking strategically about community, students tend to pursue advice in unhealthy relationships. The most powerful thing you can do for parents is to provide kids in your ministry with another adult who will say the same things in their kids' lives that they're trying to say as a parent. This is the essence of Orange: two combined influences having a greater impact than just two influences.

**Give parents the gift of community.**

I haven't always felt this way about parenting. In fact, there was a time when I believed that my kids would always talk to me about everything. I thought they were never going to talk to somebody else about stuff they wouldn't share with me. As parents, we think this way when our children are young because we are naive. But inevitably it will happen. I know this because there were times when *I* talked to other people beyond *my* parents.

This became evident to me when my son, Reggie Paul, turned sixteen. We were going through a real tug-of-war and it was all connected to—you might guess—a girl he was dating. I remember that thinking somehow his years of experience with me as a father would make him pay more attention to me than to some girl he just met. But I was wrong. I couldn't compete.

*See Concentrate 9.4*

One night when he came home past curfew I confronted him in his room. I said something that probably wasn't the wisest thing for a father to say. I don't even know why I said it. I said it perhaps because my parents said it to me. Even though I knew it hadn't worked on me back then, I thought maybe it would somehow work on Reggie Paul.

I told him, "You are late coming home from a date, and I just need to know what's going on in your relationship, and I need to know now. I want you to tell me everything."

He looked at me and said exactly what you'd expect him to say: "No. I'm not going to tell you that."

Then I said, "You have to tell me; I am your father."

He said, "No, I'm not going to tell you *because* you are my father. You make the rules."

I was so flustered. I felt paralyzed. I didn't know what to do.

The next day, I showed up at Andy Stanley's office and said, "I just don't understand it. I'm trying to get my son to tell me what's going on, and he won't tell me anything."

Andy thought for a second, then with his gift of mercy said to me, "Well, did *you* tell *your* father everything?"

*See Concentrate 9.5*

The next day I went back to Reggie Paul. I said, "I talked to Andy and he said he didn't tell his father everything either, and I should understand why you won't tell me everything. I'm trying to be okay with that. But here's the question: If you won't tell me, then who will you tell?"

His response was easy. He said, "That's fair. I'll tell you who I'll talk to." He named someone.

As soon as he said the name, I felt a huge sense of relief because the person he named had been a lifelong friend of mine. I knew this friend loved our family, respected me, and had the same values that we have. This friend, one of Reggie Paul's small-group leaders, would be a safe place to go. I knew then more than ever what a gift it was for me to have this other adult in my son's life. I didn't worry about what this friend of mine would tell Reggie Paul because I knew he would be saying the same kinds of things that I would say.

What if the parents in your ministry were to have that conversation with their son or daughter? When they asked the question, "Who are you going to talk to?" would the son or daughter have a name? Would it be a name the parent trusted?

Thinking Orange is about being church leaders who provide parents with that kind of community for their children. It's about truly partnering with families so that when these moments happen, these children and students immediately know who they can turn to. The conversations they prompt can have an eternal impact.

ESSENTIAL #5
_____

# LEVERAGE INFLUENCE

WHEN YOU
COMBINE 2
INFLUENCES, YOU
_____
MOBILIZE GENERATIONS

# April:

## The Myth of the Perfect Parent

# 10

## LEVERAGE INFLUENCE
### CREATE CONSISTENT OPPORTUNITIES FOR STUDENTS TO EXPERIENCE PERSONAL MINISTRY

Think about this for just a second. Let's say you're going to teach a class on mountain climbing. You tell the students all the details of what it's like to climb a mountain, what rock configurations to look for, and what footholds to use. You even tell them what the experience is like when you get to the top of the mountain—the feeling of having climbed for hours and being awed by the breathtaking view before you. You create an exciting picture of what it's like, but the students in your class never get to experience climbing a mountain for themselves. How motivated do you think they are to climb after just listening to you talk?

But let's just suppose instead that you take them to a place where they can experience just a little bit of mountain climbing and you take them up the mountain as you teach. They get to apply all the information they are hearing. Do you think the impact will be different? Sure, it will be.

So what do you think would be more exciting—going to classes that teach you about mountain climbing, or actually standing at the summit after a hard climb to get a firsthand look at the view? Imagine sitting for several years and listening to someone describe the adventures related to climbing mountains. How would it affect you if you never really climbed a mountain yourself? Do you think you would be more or less motivated to climb?

Here is a profound question: Do you think climbers climb just because they have heard about climbing or because one day they started climbing?

Here are a few realities. If you never actually climb,
you will miss the wonder that comes with seeing the view,
you will miss the discovery of personal capacity,
you will miss the passion of engaging with the mountain.

**WE'RE ALL DESIGNED TO LIVE INSIDE A STORY ... TO PLAY A ROLE IN A STORY.**

But this is about more than just mountain climbing. The same principles hold true for the kids and teenagers who grow up in our homes and churches. Somehow we believe that if we only talk about the importance of faith and teach them how to show faith, they will automatically grow in their faith.

At what point do you think it is appropriate for students to grab some rope and start heading up the side of a mountain? Most churches spend a lot of energy trying to get students to come to programs where they talk about growing as a Christian, but they forget that the way you grow is by experience.

The way we do family and church has the potential to stunt or fuel children's future faith.

It's important to understand how closely spiritual formation is connected to the act of serving. If we fail to help kids make a practical investment of their time and energy in serving others, their hearts will never mature to care for others. This is an important principle to understand in the home and church because it requires an intentional shift in how ministry happens as students transition toward high school and into adulthood. Too many churches teach as if students should sit and listen instead of actually experiencing hands-on ministry. If we really want students to head to college as competent climbers, we need to start handing them some rope. We don't need to teach them about climbing; we need to take them up the mountain and help them experience it firsthand. Students need consistent opportunities to develop their faith, to see God show up as they do ministry and find out what He wants to do through them to influence others.

*experience = learning*

Leaders who are thinking Orange must decide something about discipleship. While you need to refine the message in a way that ensures they get it, that's not all you need to do. Beyond that, there comes a time when a child or a student needs to begin experiencing certain things if those things are going to stick, especially as they move toward their teenage years. When student ministries or churches buy into a classroom mentality, I think they set themselves up for failure. Why? Because the children or students are going to walk away thinking what we're teaching is irrelevant to their everyday lives if they are never given the opportunity to *experience* it.

## THE POWER OF A BIGGER STORY

Nehemiah was convinced that the generations of God-followers around him needed to experience something that would move their faith beyond its present condition. Think about what happened. Everyone in the community experienced the wall at some level. The text implies that assignments were made to families and tribes. Remember the people of God were "in disgrace," suffering from the loss of their reputation and respect. The context of the story created a backdrop for all of the people to see what God could do through them.

Here's another critical thing to think about when you are trying to raise a generation who find their identity in the story of God:

Make people feel significant by giving them something significant to do. A couple of years ago at our Orange Conference, Donald Miller shared a story about a friend of his who was having problems with his daughter. The dad was worried because the daughter had gotten involved in a Gothic lifestyle and was dating a guy who was bad news. As a frustrated dad, his technique for dealing with the situation was to yell at her and make her go to church. When he came to Don for advice, Don told him, "I think what your daughter is doing is choosing a better story."

He went on. "We're all designed to live inside a story. Your daughter was designed to play a role in a story. In the story she has chosen, there is risk, adventure, and pleasure. She is wanted and she is desired. In your story, she's yelled at, she feels guilty, and she feels unwanted. She's just choosing a story that is better than the one you're providing. Plus, in the midst of placing her in an awful story, you make her go to church. So you're associating a bad, boring story with God, who has a great story. Don't do that anymore. You have to tell a better story."

The dad became inspired, and within a week he had made contact with a small village in Mexico that needed an orphanage. The orphanage was going to cost about $20,000, so he proposed to the family that they raise the money. He painted the picture for them: "Here's the deal, you guys. I found this village in Mexico that needs an orphanage. Awful things may happen to these kids if they don't have a place to go, so I think we need to build this orphanage as a family. It's going to cost over $20,000, and I know we don't have any money, but we need to do it within two years."

He brought out a whiteboard and asked his family—who all thought he had lost his mind—for ideas. His daughter piped up and said, "I have a MySpace page and lots of friends; maybe we can use that." His son added, "We're going to have to go to Mexico because if we're going to do this, we need to see the village. And we'll need passports."

What's happening here? They were getting caught up in a real story with risk and adventure. Within three weeks, the girl had broken up with her boyfriend. Why? Because she found a better story, one in which she gets to play the heroine. She gets to sacrifice and give of herself to accomplish something that's great, and she's wanted and needed in this story.

*The heart will gravitate toward whatever offers adventure and significance.*
The bottom line is that everybody needs to experience something bigger than themselves. Whether we provide them the opportunity to do so or not, they will look for a way to participate in something adventurous. The question is not whether they will find these elements in the story they choose. The question is whether the story they choose will be God's story. Will it have wonder, discovery, and passion? If they miss the wonder, they will miss God doing something beyond their capacity. If they miss the discovery, they will miss who it is that God wants them to become. If they miss the passion, they will miss the chance for love and compassion that comes only from engaging the God who redeems this broken world.

One of the reasons some students are walking away from the church is that they have found something more exciting—they have discovered what seems to be a bigger story. When they look back at their church involvement, it was static and noneventful. They have never experienced the intoxicating kind of faith that comes when they allow God to work through their lives. They didn't have a hands-on encounter with ministry that gave them a personal sense of God's mission. They missed out on the passion that results when you collide with humanity to care for someone in a crisis situation. When there is nothing dangerous or adventurous about your style of faith, you begin to drift toward other things that seem more interesting and meaningful. Be honest, what does the average teenager in the average church really experience? When do we stretch their faith? When do we push them into ministry situations where they have to depend on God to do something in them and through them? When do we consistently give them opportunities to develop a personal ministry? The average high school teenager can get a job, drive a car, apply to college, and open a bank account, but we rarely allow them to lead or serve in a ministry inside or outside the church.

**What makes us think that students will do ministry when they leave us if they never do ministry while they are with us?**
I think that somewhere along the way we've missed an incredible opportunity to engage teenagers in personal ministry. There seems to be a window of time when students should be mobilized to serve. They are wired to engage and experience instead of digesting more information and presentations. If what they have heard doesn't move from their heads to their hands, it will probably never make it to their hearts. In fact, we are in danger of losing their hearts if we don't throw open the door for them to start experiencing their part in God's story. Keeping our children insulated means we are keeping them boxed in and separated from the real world around them. We can unknowingly damage their capacity to experience the wonder they were created to experience, the discovery they were intended to encounter, and the passion they were formed to demonstrate to the world around them. If we offer a story to our kids without these three elements, we are offering a story that will not capture their imaginations or affect their emotions. We either kill the wonder, discovery, and passion in them or we ignore it, implicitly encouraging them to go find it elsewhere.

How many of you have taken teenagers on a mission trip to get involved in another state or country and watched them come *alive*? Isn't it true that you see something happen in them that seems to ignite their passion? Some of your students came back ready to charge hell with a squirt gun because they felt like they could change the world. That's what happens when you finally experience the power of God's Spirit working through you. These same students will return to your church, engaged with God's story, in sync with His desire to use them. Then in about three or four weeks their passion dwindles and dies. It seems like someone put cold water on it and they all get back to normal again, back to how they were before they left on their mission trip. Why do you think that is?

I have a theory. Maybe it's because when we return home from that exciting mission, we put them right back in a classroom. For a while they had opportunity to experience what God designed them to be.

*w/our Children's ministry. How to expose younger ages?*

*keep it alive ...? how*

**IF WHAT THEY HAVE HEARD DOESN'T MOVE FROM THEIR HEADS TO THEIR HANDS, IT WILL PROBABLY NEVER MAKE IT TO THEIR HEARTS.**

But now they are back home, the experience is over, and they are back to being taught.

What would happen if we simply decided that our best resource for unleashing this generation and volunteerism is found in our teenagers. Here's a novel idea: Let's try saying to our students, "Here are the ropes. Here is a class or here's a small group, or a worship platform and some technical equipment. Here are some things you can do to be part of rescuing a generation, and we want you to plug in. You are enough of an adult now that you need to begin developing your skills and you need to begin seeing what God wants to do in and through you."

I think that kind of mentality sets a teenager up in a way that nothing else does. From what I've seen over the last thirty years, if I had it to do all over again as a student pastor, I would create more opportunities for them to serve. I would think in terms of what I could do to make sure that life change happened. I would try to design environments where they not only sense God, but where they experience what God wants to do *through* them.

Students should get the chance to realize what they are capable of doing when God is moving in them. If they experience God at work in them, they'll have a hard time getting over it.

One of the best ways to stimulate faith is to give someone an opportunity to have a personal ministry.

*See Concentrate 10.1*

At North Point we decided we were not going to create programming for teenagers on Sunday mornings. We weren't going to create any classes where they would to sit and have Bible study. Instead, we were going to treat them like any other adults on Sunday morning (we didn't have classes for adults either). We decided we would give them opportunities to serve with us on Sunday morning. We wanted them to serve not simply because we needed their help, but because it would be critical to their spiritual growth.

Think about it. When did you grow as a leader? Didn't most of us get jump-started in our faith when we plugged into a ministry and served? If most of us grew more when we assumed ministry responsibility, what makes us think that wouldn't be true for teenagers as well?

Here's another thought: What if service is also a catalyst for initiating faith in someone's heart? It is not unusual for students who are not believers to be rallied to participate in a missional effort that captures their heart. They begin with reservations about God, and somewhere along the way something is ignited that draws them into a meaningful relationship with God. The Bible says we are all created in the image of God. I think that's why people who are not believers still do positive things to help others. They are simply tapping into their God image, whether they intend to or not. When students engage in something bigger than themselves and they see God working in the lives of others around them, it can be a powerful force to confront their personal need for a relationship with Christ. In some ways, it may be more advantageous to involve nonbelieving kids in a mission effort than it would be to draw them to church with a secular concert so we can present the gospel.

Remember the mountain-climbing illustration? It highlights a principle about discipleship that a lot of churches miss. Discipleship isn't just about worship, it isn't just about prayer, it isn't just about Bible study, and it isn't simply about establishing a devotional life. Discipleship is as much about serving and *doing* ministry as it is anything else. There needs to be a radical shift in the design of most student ministries. Teenagers need to be given responsibility to leverage their influence in the lives of others and to own an area of ministry for themselves.

*See Concentrate 10.2*

Engaging a teenager in ministry is the best way to ensure …
a dynamic faith in God. (That's wonder.)
a personal identity in Christ. (That's discovery.)
a responsive heart toward others. (That's passion.)

Isn't that what we want to see happen in the life of every teenager who walks away from our churches? Every parent and every leader desires for God's Greatest Commandment to show up in the lives of their kids. We want them to believe …

*Wonder:* I am created to pursue an authentic relationship with my Creator.
*Discovery:* I belong to Jesus Christ and define who I am by what He says.
*Passion:* I exist every day to demonstrate God's love to a broken world.

If children believe this by the time they leave home, the family wins. If these three things become a reality, we as a church have done our job.

**YOU DON'T BEGIN TO SERVE WHEN YOU FEEL COMPASSION, YOU FEEL COMPASSION AS YOU BEGIN TO SERVE.**

What happens when students don't learn how to leverage their influence and serve others? If churches and homes don't make this a priority, if serving doesn't become a primary focus of leaders who work with teenagers, a number of things will potentially be sabotaged in the heart of a student.

*authentic*

Not giving them the opportunity to serve will hinder the development of a compassionate heart. You don't begin to serve when you feel compassion, you feel compassion as you begin to serve. Without a sense of compassion students and families never <u>experience</u> <u>a sense of calling and mission</u> to make others a priority.

Not serving can leave kids paralyzed in their capability to do ministry. They will always be afraid to take the next step. They don't know what they are capable of, or what they have to offer the world around them. Consequently, they see only what the world can offer them rather than what they can offer the world. They become adults who live as though they are the center of the universe. In terms of the church, they have a consumer mindset. What can the church do for me?

Finally, and probably most important, when students are not given the opportunity to serve, they never learn the power of loving someone simply for the sake of love. They become more concerned with the utility of changing a person without taking the time to love and care for them first. Without this kind of love, the students' perspective on the church, on themselves, and their relationship with God hangs in the balance. They will question their significance and the reality of how God can really change someone.

*Wonder* fades.
*Discovery* is eclipsed.
*Passion* is extinguished.

## WHAT HAPPENS WHEN WE *RETHINK* THE VALUE OF PERSONAL MINISTRY?
### We move toward a holistic model of discipleship.
We've noticed a handful of things that are catalysts for spiritual growth. It is important for those who lead kids, including parents, to understand and cooperate with the process of spiritual growth. Most churches, by design, focus on teaching

or presenting truths. Personal ministry or service needs to be viewed by every leader and parent as a priority when it comes to discipleship.

A number of churches I know have rearranged their Sunday morning schedules in order to allow high school students a consistent opportunity to serve. Depending on their spiritual maturity, they can be mobilized to do anything from technical support, to drama, to greeting, to leading worship and/or small groups. Small-group leaders understand that mobilizing kids for ministry is just as important as teaching them. Opportunities for service are expanded to go beyond the context of weekly programs. As students seek service options, other departments and adult leaders are part of the plan to mentor teenagers as they assimilate into various roles in the church. Parents participate as well, finding common ground as mission projects are arranged so that families can engage together.

*See Concentrate 10.3*

H.S

Q: How?
A: short term/ local missions including our children?

**We move toward an experiential and relational approach to curriculum.**
Jesus did not teach the disciples to do ministry. He did ministry with the disciples while He taught them.

I recently asked a group of seasoned leaders from around the country this question about spiritual formation: "If you had six ninth-grade boys or girls for four years, what would you do to disciple them?"

They each talked about different projects and mission endeavors. Some mentioned the amount of time they would devote to building the relationship. Some brought up authors they would want to read together. Toward the end of the conversation we realized that no one had brought up taking them to any kind of classroom presentation.

I'm not suggesting that there is anything wrong with traditional programming. But too often churches define discipleship in a context of a presentation-driven method. Instinctively, though, many leaders recognize something more relational and experiential is required for spiritual formation. The goal is not to cover a body of information, but to engage young people in a process that results in life change. It's one thing for your student to understand and defend their faith as it relates to a handful of primary truths; it's another to expect every student to win a Bible trivia contest.

**JESUS REACHED THE WORLD BY LEVERAGING THE INFLUENCE OF COMMON PEOPLE AND EMPOWERING THEM TO DO UNCOMMON THINGS.**

*Our Goal*

I know students who can quote the Beatitudes and list the twelve disciples but still don't have an interest in pursuing a growing relationship with God. Truth is an important part of discipleship, but our faith doesn't simply grow because we know more; it grows when we serve more. As you observe the stages of development from preschool to college, the need to experience ministry becomes more intense as kids get older. A curriculum that incorporates a balance of learning with relevant experience and ministry opportunities is much more likely to encourage students to become responsible for their own spiritual maturity and development.

### We find a new way to measure ministry.

Senior leaders, parents, and student pastors have to be intentional about changing their priorities. They should *rethink* the pressure that is put on the average student ministry to define success by the amount of programming or attendance. Instead of asking, "How many came last week?" they should ask, "What percentage of students are engaging in ministry?" Student ministry in our culture is a moving target and is extremely difficult to evaluate. We can, however, measure the impact of a practical plan to give students an opportunity to serve.

Another issue related to success in ministry is an intentional approach to recruit the B-team. Many leaders focus on reaching students who are popular or in influential roles with other students. The theory is that the more well known a student is, the more influence he will have over other students. The reality is that the untapped power of influence in a student ministry are those students who are not as well known.

Someone could make the case that Jesus seemed to have a similar approach. Instead of leveraging the influential religious elite, He recruited a host of rather ordinary men.

*Who needs/craves the attention*

Think about it this way. If you give a popular, well-known student a hundred dollars' worth of attention, it will probably seem like ten dollars. If you give a student who is not in the mainstream of popularity a hundred dollars' worth of attention, it could seem like a thousand. Jesus reached the world by leveraging the influence of common people and empowering them to do uncommon things. The point is not that you shouldn't disciple everyone, but that you make sure you don't overlook the potential of the average student. You just never know who may be on the sidelines waiting for an opportunity.

Have you ever heard of Matt Williams? Texas Tech football players, fans, and coaches hadn't either until September 20, 2008. On that particular day, Williams won a promotion for the chance to attempt a thirty-yard field goal between the third and fourth quarter of a home game. The prize was free rent in a local apartment complex. In shorts and sneakers and trying to remember technique from when he played for the Weatherford High School Kangaroos, Matt Williams made the field goal. Fifty thousand people were watching. So was Texas Tech's head coach, Mike Leach. Leach said, "I grabbed an equipment guy and said, 'Go get him.'"

As Williams started back to his seat in the stands, the equipment manager chased him down. Five weeks later, Matt Williams was named ESPN All-America Player of the Week in his first start for the undefeated Texas Tech Red Raiders. Another week later, Williams kicked two field goals in Texas Tech's 39–33 upset over the nation's top-ranked Texas Longhorns. Matt Williams went from the sidelines to the headlines. Matt's experience is the stuff of boyhood dreams and Hollywood movies. An average small-town boy, not much more than ordinary, ends up making a huge difference.[50]

What if Matt's story could be the story of a student in your ministry? Is it possible that on the fringes of our ministries, untapped potential is just waiting for the opportunity to be given a chance? It could be that in your most unlikely student, influence is waiting to happen. Matt Williams started in the bleachers and ended up on the field. The point? You never know who is sitting on your sidelines. You never know who is observing from the stands. Everyone has potential and possibilities. We should start organizing our ministries to leverage the influence that every student has to make a difference.

## PROGRAMMED TO OVERPROTECT

Most moms and dads are ready to fight the battle for their children's safety and future as soon as they are born. Parents will buckle them into car seats that fit like plastic straitjackets, construct beds and play zones with prison bars, hook their arms to an expandable leash to walk through the mall, and install video surveillance systems so their children can be monitored from every room. Parents

*Volunteers... = good team members*

are programmed to protect and provide. They feel responsible to make sure they have the kind of boundaries that will keep children safe. Over time parents become convinced their primary job is protection, so they make rules, set limits, and put up fences because that is what they are supposed to do. They are parents. They will insulate, isolate, and segregate their kids from everything they think might be a threat. In some cases that mindset translates to the church. Parents and leaders are more comfortable with a version of church that operates from a protectionist perspective.

As parents and leaders, it may be terrifying to think of a son or daughter mountain climbing. We might be tempted to a reactionary approach that guards children from the potentially dangerous and risky business of mountain climbing. In other words, we care more about their safety than we do their faith. We would sacrifice the things they would learn and the things they would experience to protect them. The tragedy is that we are actually okay if they never climb the mountain, if it guarantees they never get hurt. But living this way and parenting this way demands the question, What happens one day when they are on their own? When they leave for college? When they enter the working world? When they get married? They were meant to be a part of an adventurous story. This is a mission that requires us to engage with culture in order to rescue a generation of hurting and disconnected people. In some ways it would be better for sons and daughters to get hurt and learn lessons while they are still with us than to launch on their own without any experience in climbing. Remember if they never learn to actually climb while they are with you, they may never try at all. Then what happens to their passion? What happens to their heart? What if they were made for something more? If you are a leader or parent remember this:

The family and church were designed ultimately not to protect children, but to set them free to demonstrate God's love to a broken world.

## THE FAMILY REDEFINED

In the Hebrew culture, systems of faith converged automatically with systems of family. They didn't have to work at being Orange. A belief in God was central to every custom and lifestyle. It was intertwined seamlessly into routines, celebrations, and feast days. Every leader, parent, priest, prophet, and family operated from the same context of belief and religious practice.

At some point, however, this all changed. It changed when Jesus stood on a hill and told His disciples, "Go into all the world." He told them to do what He had done. He had entered Hebrew culture as God in the flesh. Now He was urging them to go into foreign cultures to tell His story. He sent them as missionaries into communities where people did not operate from the same context of the Hebrew family.

Church leaders were called to understand and connect with pagan cultures, to translate the story of God's redemptive plan in their language and to present the gospel in new terms. The goal was not to force conformity to Jewish family traditions but to lead all people, from all cultures, to understand God's story. No wonder Paul said he would be all things to all people.[51] Because of Jesus' directive to take the church beyond the original Hebrew culture, how faith and family intersect would have to be redefined.

So now let's go back to Moses, recognizing that our goal is not to stay there. We should go back in order to understand that the Hebrew family insulated itself in order to preserve the remnant that portrayed God's love to an outside world. But now God's people are called to invite others into the spiritual family and to declare God's story to every culture. One represents a subculture that was passive about reaching other cultures, while the other actively influences them. What does this have to do with anything? It changes the way we see the partnership between church and family. The definition of both will be affected by various cultures that we are called to reach. But the transferable principles that Moses taught about loving God and transferring faith still hold true. He was an Orange leader. He rallied everybody to partner for the sake of a generation's future. He understood the potential for family and faith in leveraging a generation to *be* the church.

Many modern models of family and church lean heavily toward creating an insulated protective bubble around both. Although it may not be their intent, they seem to be defining something that attempts to align with the practice of the Old Testament culture instead of a New Testament mission. Just remember that thousands of years of history took on a different meaning once Jesus started inviting people who were on the outside to participate in His story. As leaders and parents, our primary calling is not to keep our children in the church, but to lead them to be the church. When we simply protect and preserve,

AS LEADERS AND PARENTS, OUR PRIMARY CALLING IS NOT TO KEEP OUR CHILDREN IN THE CHURCH, BUT TO LEAD THEM TO BE THE CHURCH.

we make the same mistake the one servant made in the parable of the talents. We cover our children with our fear and lack of faith. We hinder their potential to make the kind of difference in the kingdom that they were designed to make.

Churches have the potential to turn a generation around by handing them the keys to ministry and saying, "Guess what? Not only do we need your help, but God designed you and God created you for this very reason. You were called to use your gifts just as much as the pastor was called to use his. Each one of us has a personal responsibility to be the church, and if you recognize that, it will revolutionize your life."

*See Concentrate 10.4*

As an example of this principle of influence, let me tell you about a note we received from one of the small-group leaders at a church that is implementing our reThink curriculum. She wanted to talk to us about a boy in her sixth-grade class. Here's what she wrote:

> This is my first year teaching my fifth- and sixth-grade small group. One thing I'd like to share with you is in regard to a sixth-grade boy I have in my class, Seth.
>
> To say that he's been a challenge is an understatement. Each week, he tested my patience to the limit and unfortunately had to be removed from class once because he was being so rude and disrespectful to me. I tried to cut him some slack, but each week it was a struggle not to lose my cool with him in front of class.
>
> Lo and behold, when I introduced the Compassion project in November, this kid was on fire! I already sponsored a child named Rashid with Compassion, so I brought in his pictures and letters. My problem child was hooked immediately and began naming off all the ways he was going to be able to help and all the things he was going to be able to send Rashid. He was disappointed to learn that we couldn't send a box of gifts each month, but I said that we could send money to him instead.
>
> Seth said he was going to shovel snow this year to earn money and he wanted to send it all to Rashid to help him and his family. This past Friday we got our first snowfall of the season, all ten inches of it. I'm here to tell

you it wasn't easy shoveling. On Sunday, Seth was bursting at the seams to tell me that he had earned $65 shoveling snow, and he wanted to give it all to Compassion. I'm not sure he'll be allowed to give it, but that's what he wants to do with it.

Seth is a changed kid. Each week, he asks if I've heard from Rashid and has become the designated pen pal from my class. I took pictures of the class to send to Rashid, and Seth wanted to be in each one of them so Rashid would learn his face. I also used newsprint for the class so that they could draw pictures and write some short notes for Rashid. Seth is in charge of that, too.

I don't know what it was that triggered such an interest in Compassion. Okay, so maybe I do. But the transformation in Seth is remarkable.

I think God created the children and students in our ministries to experience what He designed them to do. When we allow them to leverage their influence, we give them the weapons to rescue a generation. In doing so, we influence a generation to participate in the call of David:

*Tell the next generation the praiseworthy deeds of the LORD, his power, and the wonders he has done…. so the next generation would know them, even the children yet to be born, and they in turn would tell their children. Then they would put their trust in God.*[52]

That is what we mean by leveraging influence. When we give them the keys to ministry, we are helping them *become* the church. God has wired them as His lampstands, to shine a light so we can see Him, others, and ourselves in the way He intends. It affects us spiritually, personally, and socially.

It incites wonder.
It provokes discovery.
It fuels passion.

The greatest calling of the church and the home is to lead our sons and daughters into a growing relationship with Jesus Christ.

The best gift we can ever give them
is to enable them to play an active role
in His story of restoration and redemption.

Orange Essentials

INTEGRATE STRATEGY
REFINE THE MESSAGE
REACTIVATE THE FAMILY
ELEVATE COMMUNITY
LEVERAGE INFLUENCE

# Orange Essentials

There are five issues that are essential to designing a ministry that is effective in partnering with parents.

INTEGRATE STRATEGY
Leaders and parents are leading with the same end in mind.

REFINE THE MESSAGE
Core truths are crafted into engaging, relevant, and memorable experiences.

REACTIVATE THE FAMILY
Parents actively participate in the spiritual formation of their own children.

ELEVATE COMMUNITY
Everyone is connected to a caring leader and consistent group of peers.

LEVERAGE INFLUENCE
Consistent opportunities are created for students to experience personal ministry.

# ORANGE-ALITY

I am like many of you. At times, I've worn a yellow hat. At other times, a red hat. I often wear both at the same time. Sometimes I have interchanged them so often I became confused about which one I was wearing.

I am convinced that no other entity is more strategically positioned to illuminate God's grace to our culture than the church. At the same time, no other entity has more potential to demonstrate unconditional love than the family. God initiated them both as part of His design to show the world who He is. Both have taught me a lot about my relationship with Him.

One of the reasons I have been nervous about writing this book is that I'm not sure I have ever felt qualified to lead ministry or to be a parent. According to *StrengthsFinder 2.0*, I am a self-assured, futuristic, communicative, and a strategic maximizer. The more difficult side of those qualities suggests that I am sometimes moody, introverted, and insecure. Throw in a little attention deficit disorder, and you have an interesting mix. I owe the staff at North Point, reThink, my wife, Debbie, and my family more than you can imagine. They are proof that God uses church and family to build your faith in Him. It really is amazing how becoming a parent teaches you things about God's character.

Thinking red has been an incredible adventure for me. When my daughter Sarah was four years old, I had been working through some frustrating situations over a period of a several months. Candidly, I was not in a good place emotionally. I left the house to go for a long drive to sort through some issues, and Sarah insisted on going with me. She had the same relational sensitivity then that she has now. I had been wrestling with a number of critical decisions, and during the drive I became hyperfocused and preoccupied with thinking through my stuff. It was almost like Sarah was tuned into to the fact that I was stressed, because during the entire ride (somewhere between two and three hours), she remained completely quiet and still in the passenger's seat. I tried to analyze my situation from every possible angle that day, but when I looked at it from any direction, it left me feeling kind of hopeless and empty. I'm ashamed to admit that I actually forgot Sarah was in the car.

I pulled into our driveway with everything still unresolved, opened the car door, and began to get out. Then I heard her voice for the first time since we left the house. It was such an interruption to my state of mind that it actually startled me.

"Daddy," she said. "Don't forget me. I have to get out through your door!"

The door on her side of the car was too heavy for her to open, so we had this routine. I would open my door, and she would crawl out across my lap while I held it. She had said those words to me many times before, but that day it was almost as if God was reminding me about my relationship with Him. It may have been the first time I understood what it really meant to look at God as my Father.

I remember walking into the house and going straight back to my bedroom. I closed the door, dropped to my knees, and prayed out loud, "God, I don't think I have understood how You love me as Father. I need you to know that the door on my side is too heavy for me to open. I need You to show up for me today. I need You to open a door that only You can open. I have to get out through Your side."

I had an overwhelming sense of relief and peace when I realized that God was actually my Father, and He felt the kind of love for me that I felt for Sarah.

I am not sure how a parent could not believe in God. Most parents instinctively realize being a parent has redefined their relationship with God because it gives you a different perspective on everything. As church leaders, we cannot underestimate how children can shape their parents' faith and how parents can shape their children's faith.

## THINK YELLOW

My transition to becoming a church leader is directly connected to my parents. My dad grew up Baptist and my mom was a Methodist. I never remember a Sunday as a child when church was not a priority. Thinking yellow, or understanding the role of the church, was integrated into my personal culture by their love for the church.

My dad and I are very different. He was born in the Great Depression, and his dad farmed cotton. Dad joined the Air Force when he was a teenager to get away from some things.

He's reserved. I'm emotional.

He doesn't say a lot. I talk too much.

He's a saver. I'm a spender.

He can fix or build anything. I had a mechanical bypass.

He's a little stubborn, strong-willed, and opinionated. I'm … well, we are different in *most* ways.

I remember sitting down a few years ago and pondering how my dad turned the spiritual dial in my life and influenced my faith. I was only one year old when he and Mom decided to move us to Memphis. During that time, a group of Christian couples became friends with my parents, and Mom and Dad rediscovered church. I can remember growing up in Sunday school and hanging out with those Christian families every Sunday night after church—long before anyone told us about the importance of being in a "group." They encouraged my parents to stop smoking and drinking because of the impression it might make on my brother and me.

I watched him get ordained as a deacon when I was eight. It was one of only two times I saw him cry. I was baptized that same year, and Dad started auditing a few Bible college classes just to learn more about the Bible. He would pass along tapes from his professors and let me listen to what they said about creationism, the existence of God, and a host of other issues I had questions about as a teenager. I remember vividly a season in my life when I was wrestling with some private thoughts and temptations. It was one of those times when I really didn't know anyone I could trust with my questions. One night he "accidently" left a cassette tape on the desk in my room called "The Cry of an Unhappy Christian." Its message contained a life-changing truth for me that helped answer some of my many questions.

When I decided I wanted to be in full-time ministry, Dad sold a number of things from the house, including our pool table, to buy audio equipment to use when I traveled. I bet you are thinking my dad was some kind of saint, but the funny thing is I never thought of him that way. He struggled like anyone else. But in his own way, he figured out how to turn a God-dial in my life. Although a number of men have made an impact in my faith, his influence was different. Why? He was my dad. I cannot tell you where I would be spiritually if not for my parents.

The key to their spiritual influence, I believe, was the couples in the church who became my parents' friends. Their connection to my parents demonstrates the power church and community can have in some families. Looking back, I am convinced that those couples are probably some of the main reasons I am doing what I am doing in ministry today. They were the first good role models either of my parents had of a Christian marriage or family. And the truth is, parents today are not that different from parents forty years ago.

They still need some light.
They still need positive models.
They still need someone to partner with them to influence their children.

## THINK ORANGE
I wish you and I could sit down at a restaurant and talk about what all this means. We could share our stories. Some would be similar, and some would be very different. I am assuming you have a story about your faith journey. Whether or not your parents had a positive impact on your spiritual growth, you still realize the powerful role they played. Intuitively as leaders, you recognize that a parent's faith can make a huge impression on a son or daughter. Regardless of how you feel about anything you have read in this book, you know this is true.

This next part is a little harder. You have to figure out how to take that belief and apply it to your ministry. You have to sort through some of the information in this book and customize it for yourself and your church. Stop for just a second. I want to remind you that I do not believe I am an expert on everything about the family or the church. Please remember what I said at the beginning of the book: It's okay to disagree with me about a lot of what I have said. At my age, I am aware of my potential to be wrong. But I do not believe I am wrong about …
the influence churches have to be a *light*,
the influence parents have to show unconditional *love*,
the impact they can both make if they *combine* their efforts.

I hope you will at least agree with me about the most important things, and primarily that no other entity has more potential to influence the home than the church. I am so thankful to have been a part of churches who dare to think orange, to be a light to their communities, and to encourage parents to nurture an everyday faith in the hearts of their children. This is something any and every church can do. *Regardless of the size, denomination, doctrine, or structure of your church, you have incredible potential to partner with the family for the sake of a generation.* As a Christian leader, I hope you would purpose to do the following:

1. Synchronize leaders and parents to build
   an authentic faith in children and teenagers.
2. Refine your message so it clearly
   communicates God's story of restoration.
3. Help parents be more intentional about
   nurturing an everyday faith in their kids' lives.
4. Give every child and teenager a spiritual coach or leader
   who can reinforce what a Christian parent would say.
5. Fuel passion in the hearts of this next generation
   to be a demonstration of God's love to a broken world.

If that's as far as you can get in agreeing with what we have written in this book, this effort was still worth the time it took. Rewrite the principles in your own words if you want, and make sure you put them somewhere where they can be a reminder.

After traveling to a number of churches around the country, I am aware there are many different views and questions about how to partner with parents. The good news is a huge network of Orange thinkers has entered into the conversation. Over the past several years, we have met a number of incredible leaders who are constantly discovering new insights about implementing Orange ideas. Those of us at the reThink Group feel extremely fortunate to have the opportunity to be inspired by their stories every week.

We are celebrating the renewed sense of urgency everywhere to *rethink* how the church and family should partner. The shift to a more family-friendly approach is happening faster and faster. A number of entities are weighing in on the issue. Depending on who you talk to, everyone has an opinion on how to reorganize ministries to better partner with the family. There is a growing debate that excites me. The fact that the conversation is intensifying is a positive thing. Regardless of the size or style or cultural setting of your church, the issue of family is universal. Churches and ministries are waking up to the principle that they can and should do more to engage parents in the process of spiritual growth.

It's a natural inclination to want to evaluate how parents feel about children and student ministries in their local churches. While there is valuable information in how parents respond to these kinds of surveys, it is also important for church leaders to realize they are called to rally a new generation of parents that are more actively involved.

We should go a step beyond and start interviewing the parents who are no longer attending the church to find out why they left. Better yet, we have to ask hard questions about the large number of students who have dropped out of the church altogether. While we should guard against minimizing the work that churches and parents have done to impact the next generation, we should also challenge each other to embrace a holy dissatisfaction that will allow us to make important shifts in our ministries so we can do more.

There are many indicators that the church and home can reinvent themselves to make a greater impact in the next generation. The bottom line is that we as church leaders are called to *influence* parents to become active partners in the process of their children's spiritual formation. Something needs to shift in our churches so we begin to see what happens in the home is just as important as what happens in the church. It's good that parents seem satisfied with the church's programming for their kids, but what if that programming serves the family as a placebo, falsely convincing them that everything is okay?

The church and family are at a pivotal time, and there is incredible opportunity for us to redefine how we do ministry. I know a lot of parents and church leaders give their best to their kids, but some of their best resources, time, and programming could be reallocated in the light of a more effective system. I don't want to be an alarmist, but the reality is leaders everywhere all agree that something needs to change about how churches partner with the family.

Consider the following information released by the Barna Group:

Almost nine out of ten parents of preteens (87 percent) say they are satisfied with the quality of ministry and counsel their young ones receive from their church.... Thus, parents are happy, children receive some religious instruction and experiences, and churches are serving people. This sounds like a wonderful win-win situation except for one issue: *The approach is completely unbiblical!* When a church—intentionally or not—assumes a family's responsibilities in the arena of spiritually nurturing children, it fosters an *unhealthy dependence.*[53]

Ivy Beckwith made this statement:

> The church's ministry to children is broken.... It's broken when church leaders and senior pastors see children's ministry primarily as a marketing tool.... Something's broken when we trivialize God to our children.... It's broken when we depend on our programs and our curriculum to introduce our children to God—not our families and communities.... And perhaps most importantly, it's broken when the church tells parents that its programs can spiritually nurture their children better than they can.[54]

Group Publishing released an article suggesting there are a lot of churches doing good things in the area of family ministry. The student ministry section of that report also indicated that shifts to partner with parents should be a priority:

> The days when youth ministry focused only on teenagers are over. Since youth mirror the faith of the adults who love them, parents and congregations need sustained and intentional models for Christian maturity. Parents are a key.[55]

Over the last few years I have had several meetings with leaders of the Willow Creek Association who say their Reveal research suggests there is a gap between what parents need in the home and what the average church is doing. I am thankful for their influence in the kingdom and the way they unselfishly give so many different leaders a voice to promote the idea of a strong partnership between the church and family.

Every one of these organizations and leaders are incredible. All of them have capable and expert staffs who have given their lives to help churches. It is obvious that different leaders have different opinions about what a better partnership with parents should look like. Whether you agree with the approach of any of these leaders doesn't really matter; often they don't agree with each other. What matters is that leaders begin to understand how to make partnerships between the church and home a priority in their local churches. Most leaders I know are beginning to ask harder questions about what is really working in the church and what isn't. The very fact that the conversation is changing suggests that most everyone generally agrees that more can be done to harness the influence of the home to develop a child's faith. The decisions we make as church leaders should have less to do with "customer satisfaction" and more to do with our responsibility to lead and inspire parents. It all boils down to each individual leader's understanding and awareness of his or her unique situation.

That's why you can't miss this critical question:

*Do you believe your church can do a
better job at partnering with the family?*

If the answer to that is "yes," then the next logical question is …

*What are you going to do about it?*

If you are reading this as a leader, you are probably in one of three situations:

- You are already acting Orange and you want to go to another level.
- You are ready to start acting Orange and you want to know the next step.
- You are content to think yellow.

I honestly hope that if you are in the first category, you are beginning to network with other leaders who are also passionate about thinking Orange. Synergy can happen when there is true collaboration and collective learning.

If you are in the second category, I would invite you to go on a discovery journey. Convince your core decision makers to start meeting. Find the appropriate resources and take the first step by getting in a room together to begin a dialogue. Begin the process to make whatever changes are necessary.

## MAKING THE SHIFT

As I have stated, I believe the church and family are at a crossroads. Things are shifting around us rapidly, and the test for many leaders will be in how quickly and completely they are willing to make a change.

I have loved photography all my life. I picked it up in ninth grade when I was invited by my football coach to become the team photographer. I guess my football skills were so exceptional it intimidated the other players, so he asked me if I wanted to shoot the games instead.

I've been obsessed in recent years with the shift the medium has made from film to digital. The first digital camera was made by Kodak and released in 1991. It weighed eight pounds and cost $13,000. Nikon, however, was the first company to make a digital SLR, a single-lens reflex camera, and it was released in 1999. The SLR allows a photographer to use interchangeable lenses on the same camera, and it helped Nikon strategically dominate the market of professional film photographers. They designed a camera body that could be used with all their existing lenses so those photographers wouldn't have to purchase new lenses. It made sense, but it meant Nikon needed to use a smaller computer chip to capture images.

Canon took a different approach. Canon completely reinvented the digital SLR camera, releasing the EOS D30 in 2003. It required all new lenses, but it had a larger chip and better technology. Can you guess what Nikon customers did? They dumped their Nikon gear and jumped to Canon, making Canon the new leader among professional photographers.

By 2003, Kodak was struggling technologically and financially, even though they had been the first to introduce a digital camera. They severely miscalculated how fast the shift to digital would happen—Kodak executives had estimated the shift from film to digital would take about eight years. In 2005, digital cameras outsold film cameras for the first time. Kodak missed the estimate by six years and almost completely lost the company.

The problem with Kodak was *speed*.
They just didn't make the shifts they needed to make fast enough.
So they lost the potential to reach a number of customers.

The mistake Nikon made was a lack of *commitment*.

They made only a partial shift; they went only halfway.

In an attempt to keep their customers happy, they gave their customers what they wanted. They were afraid too much change might alienate loyal Nikon users. Instead, they lost some of their most faithful fans. (Just for the record, I am an avid Nikon user. They have effectively reinvented themselves over the past several years.)

Canon was right on target.

They took a risk and made the change.

They didn't try to put old lenses onto new cameras because their priority was quality, not convenience. They were focused on the future. They were not preoccupied by the customers they were trying to keep, but instead took a risk so they could ultimately reach new customers. They didn't react to change; they led change.

Has it ever occurred to you that the very parents in your church who complain about the changes you make may also blame you one day if you lose influence with their kids? Many of them would jump at the chance to go somewhere else if it might potentially increase their ability to influence their own children. Leadership doesn't mean giving parents what you think they want; it is giving them what you as a leader know they need.

This book is a call for churches to make a shift for the sake of a generation,

A shift that integrates your strategy
A shift that synchronizes your message
A shift that reactivates the family
A shift that elevates community
A shift that leverages the influence of the next generation
and mobilizes them to *be* the church.

If you really believe two combined influences
will make a greater impact than just two influences,
then maybe it's time to make the shift.

# FAQ

This book is the beginning of a dialogue. In it, you've seen the concepts and the framework that make Orange what it is. We hope these principles will catalyze discussion and help you *rethink* what the church and family could be. That's what our purpose in writing it has been: to outline the principles of Orange.

If you want greater detail on the practical side of Orange, a companion workbook for *Think Orange* will soon be available, and you'll want to join us at one of our live venues. The Orange Conference and Orange regional gatherings feature numerous sessions that deal with the nuts and bolts of our strategy.

A third level of dialogue happens online. OrangeLeaders.com links hundreds of church leaders from around the world who are implementing the Orange strategy. Best practices, forums that deal with specific issues, and personal relationships are built there that facilitate the kind of discussion that can answer almost any question.

As we've spent time on the road and online and had hundreds of conversations with church leaders, we've heard tons of great questions, some of which are listed on the next page. Get answers to these and post some of your own questions at OrangeLeaders.com.

We look forward to advancing the conversation with you.

## INTEGRATE STRATEGY
- How do we cast vision for senior leadership?
- How do we transition to be more Orange?
- How do college-age students fit into the strategy?
- What does a staff organizational chart look like at different stages?
- How do I implement Orange in a start-up church?

## REFINE THE MESSAGE
- How do you engage middle and high school students?
- Should we get everyone in the church on the same topic?
- In elementary ages is it more important to teach the Bible or to teach character?
- What would a sample schedule look like if we were more family-friendly?
- How does salvation fit into this?

## REACTIVATE THE FAMILY
- How do we cast vision for parents to engage in the strategy?
- How do I fit Family Experiences (FX) into our schedule?
- How can I get families to reinvent family time?
- How do I engage unchurched parents?

## ELEVATE COMMUNITY
- How do I get consistent leaders in small groups?
- What do small-group leaders do?

## LEVERAGE INFLUENCE
- How do we train leaders?
- When do we start plugging children in to serve?
- How do we engage students to serve?

# Steps to Orange-ify

It's one thing to dream. It's another to do.

No doubt the concepts behind Orange will trigger ideas and more than a few ambitions. But how do you go from imagination to implementation, from where you are to where you sense you need to be? And as you move toward implementation, how much *rethinking* will you actually have the courage to do?

Here are seven steps that helped us become an Orange church:

1. **Discover.** This is where you may be right now. Explore the concepts. Put this book into as many hands as possible. Explore your preconceptions. Engage your team. Pray, discuss, probe, and ask enough questions to get a comprehensive analysis of your current situation and the possibilities that lie ahead for you.

2. **Define an Action Plan.** After you've explored big ideas and specific approaches at length, it's time to create a plan. Clarify your strategy. Clarify your wins. What will victory look like in your community? Identify the programming and leadership shifts that need to take place to make the change happen. Do the hard work—it's critical that your team get onto the same page.

3. **Communicate.** I like to think of communication as an ongoing process that happens in concentric circles. Debate and dialogue with your core team. Once your plan is in pencil, expand the circle one level and communicate your ideas with your wider leadership circle for testing and input. When done, share the results, take it out one more level, and cast vision with your congregation and community. Never stop doing that. The more you communicate, the more you will become what you believe.

4. **Reorganize.** This is the time to finalize your plan. Begin to reassign staff, budgets, and resources around your new strategy. Don't just think addition, think subtraction. Part of moving to Orange will likely include shutting down things that compete with an Orange strategy. Celebrate past successes and future possibilities well, and give people new positions in the new structure.

5. **Develop.** Train your staff and volunteers in the model and the programming that goes with it. Don't just develop skills, develop people. Leaders do this best when we don't just talk about *what* we are doing or *how* we're doing it, but when we talk about *why* we do what we do.

6. **Promote.** Dream about how to communicate what you are doing at new levels. Plan a message series. Design or adopt a small-group curriculum. Create some online strategies. Share your passion with people at a deep level, and watch it become contagious.

7. **Launch.** Some leaders launch too quickly, implementing only partially digested ideas. Some leaders think plenty but launch nothing. Both have disappointing outcomes. As a strong leader, launch well. Take the time you need to work through the first six steps, and then launch with passion, joy, and attention to detail. Keep your ears open for feedback and midcourse correction. Make sure you celebrate the wins that happen. What you celebrate gets repeated!

CAREY NIEUWHOF  Connexus Community Church – Barrie | Orillia | Bracebridge, Ontario

# Family Ministry Models

We've noticed three distinct approaches to family ministry. The one that your church adapts—intentionally or unintentionally—will set the tone for how parents and families understand the change you're trying to make.

The first approach is a **supplemental** approach. Each ministry department interjects family ministry components into already-planned programming, sometimes even hiring an additional staff member to make sure the children's ministry has a family element or that the student ministry is parent-aware. Each ministry determines how to approach outreach and training for families, as long as a basic goal of family ministry is acknowledged.

The second approach is a **departmental** approach. A new staff position, usually called a "family minister," is added. The family minister works independently of other ministries, kind of connected but not integral to planning and strategy. The family minister does programming for families and parents, while the student ministry focuses on students and the children's ministry focuses on children. Each age-group department and possibly even other departments plan activities and programs for families independent of each other. It's nice when they work together, but they would be able to accomplish the basics without ever meeting or talking together.

Both of these approaches create competing systems. Calendars quickly fill up with events designed for individual members of the family. Dollars disappear into divergent programs that divide the family instead of bringing it together. Programming is usually characterized as being random and haphazard instead of strategic and intentional.

The third approach is an **integrated** approach. Age-group department leaders function as one team to manage and plan a comprehensive strategy for the family that impacts each member of the family individually.

In an integrated approach, someone (who may or may not be called the "family minister") is charged with leading and facilitating this family ministry team. He or she may be specifically hired for that purpose or may be an age-group leader who is acknowledged as a leader among his or her peers.

Whether you are a larger church with paid staff or a smaller church with volunteer directors, it's important to develop a family ministry team concept. All members of this family ministry team work together, functioning as a leadership/management team to oversee age-group and family programming. They work together to design a calendar that makes sense and values family time. They communicate plans and priorities so budgets reflect thoughtful process and the guiding strategy.

Usually, there's one telltale sign to indicate if a strategy is integrated: Do age-group directors meet together? If they meet together weekly or biweekly to dialogue and work on strategy, then they know what's going on and how each ministry fits together instead of working against each other. When those who lead children and students get together in the same room, they're more likely to be aligned with the vision and strategy of the ministry.

If your staff can't agree on and implement an integrated strategy where everyone is on the same page, how can you expect parents to synchronize with your strategy? If you can't get your staff on the same page, how can you ever expect to get parents on the same page?

# Integrating Your Team

A year and a half ago, our church shifted to an integrated family ministry strategy and combined our preschool, elementary, teens, and college ministers into one cohesive leadership team. The first time we sat around a table as a newly "integrated" team, we weren't sure what we were actually going to do together. As the leader, I quickly had to create the type of meetings that connect multiple departments into one unit. Some of the ideas worked, and others failed. We're still in progress, but here are five things any team can try.

1. **Hold weekly meetings with an agenda and rotating participation.** Weekly meetings are important for creating community. If you only meet once a month or every other week, you are communicating to the team that they don't actually need each other's input. Rotate responsibilities so everyone has a chance to lead devotions, book studies, and prayer.

2. **Have a standing agenda item for ideas and challenges.** Make a schedule so different team members own this, bringing an idea or challenge to the team each week. After they introduce the idea or challenge, no discussion takes place immediately. Over the next week, each member of the team has a fifteen-minute appointment with the presenter, during which the team member offers feedback. The week after all discussions have taken place, the team addresses the idea or challenge as a group. Everyone on the team has a chance to speak, then the presenter wraps up, and the team makes a decision.

3. **Obtain team leader buy-in.** In order to create a strong team, the leader must commit his or her time and resources to the projects that are most important to the team members. In order for team members to fully buy in, they need to see a leader who supports their ideas, works hard for them, and fights for the necessary resources to accomplish the job.

Team members need to know the leader values fairness and doesn't play favorites by consistently giving one ministry more attention or money. As the leader, you have to leverage your influence toward the accomplishment of the team's goals, not just your own.

4. **Schedule one-on-one appointments.** I have committed to thirty-minute weekly meetings with the people working directly for me. When I first started this, I made sure they knew this was not an attempt to squeeze all our working together into just thirty minutes; I hoped we'd have hours each week for collaboration and dreaming. But we all know how busy we get, so it's good to have a regular time on the calendar. This is a great way for a leader to communicate, "You and your ministry are too important to me to let a week go by where we didn't get at least thirty minutes to connect." Overall, these meetings are proactive rather than reactive.

5. **Communicate weekly to all staff members.** I send a newsletter at the end of each week called "The Staff Loop." Its purpose is to encourage our staff members as well as to keep the vision right in front of them. I want them to know that I'm accessible to them and involved on many levels.

SCOTT AUSTIN  Next+Gen Ministries Pastor | Community Bible Church | San Antonio, TX

# Family Ministry Threads

There are certain threads that tie the family ministry team together and establish a code that is the basis for meeting agendas and interdependent relationships. These are topics the team should discuss, debate, and decide together, and they should be revisited in some way at every meeting. They will help determine how effectively the team drives toward the mission of combining the influences of churches and families. Regardless of the size of your church, these common threads should connect the individuals who lead preschool, children, and students.

**The Group Thread** Age-group leaders believe a small-group context is the best possible environment for life change. Across all ministries, they resist a "classroom" mindset and establish a graduating system that features a relationship with the small-group leader as pivotal. The team works to develop an organization driven by community.

**The Parent Thread** Parents are not seen as sidelined supporters of the ministry but as partners. Since most moms and dads parent children of multiple ages, church leaders should strive to create interconnectivity. As a team, leaders constantly clarify a unified plan that cuts across all departments to protect the family and programming from competing systems.

**The Production Thread** The learning curve accelerates when team members share resources and discoveries related to technology, video, programming, and other elements. Occasional collective planning can stimulate creativity and provide a great venue to evaluate the relevance of each other's ministry.

**The Transition Thread** Churches traditionally look at transition between grades as something that happens on the first Sunday of a new school year. Instead, the transition should be planned creatively months before it happens, and leaders may cross over into other areas to help manage the communication and changes smoothly.

**The Content Thread** The goal of a family ministry team is to establish a comprehensive plan that builds content, consistent relationships, and core experiences into the lives of kids and teenagers. The team has to consistently evaluate and monitor the quality of the environments that communicate principles and provide meaningful experiences.

**The Volunteer Thread** A cohesive message to volunteers about how they fit into the big picture of spiritual growth for a child is essential. If staff doesn't work closely together, volunteers will feel disconnected. A meeting to clarify a master plan for training and developing volunteers keeps everyone on the same page.

**The Learning Thread** It is important for key age-group leaders or directors to adopt a continual learning approach to ministry. The accountability that can happen within a family ministry team allows them to become better specialists in their age groups and to develop as generalists to oversee all ministries.

When the family ministry team meets together on a consistent basis, the team …

- values the interdependent relationships that are critical to success
- draws lines between healthy competition and unhealthy competition
- makes collective learning and input a priority
- provides a platform for the unfiltered debate that is necessary to improve systems
- allows focus of resources to make a powerful impact

# Action Verbs for Age-Group Volunteers

A few years ago our team was casting vision for a group of leaders who worked with preschool, children, and teenagers. We wanted them to understand the unique contribution they each made to a specific age group while also knowing the role they played in a comprehensive plan from preschool to high school. I gave them a biblical word picture and one action verb to remind them of the significance of their roles.

### For Preschool

We gave the word **EMBRACE** to those who worked with preschoolers. It depicts the idea of a young child holding out his or her arms to a mother or father. Those who work with preschoolers have the opportunity to do something no one else does: They give children their first impression of a heavenly Father who loves them unconditionally.

The Old Testament tells the story of Jonathan's son Mephibosheth. He grew up as a cripple in exile because he was dropped as an infant when his family was fleeing David's army. Mephibosheth lived most of his life believing David was his enemy until he was discovered by David's men years later. Because of David's covenant with his father Jonathan, he had been looking for Mephibosheth so he could let him live in his kingdom as a son of the king. This story reminds me that we don't want children to grow up not knowing that God wants to be their friend. The goal of every preschool leader is to help young children start their lives embracing the wonder of a heavenly Father's love.

### For Children

We gave the word **TRUST** to those who worked with elementary-age children. It described how we want children to grow in their relationships with Jesus. The elementary years are the time most people make a decision to trust Christ and understand how God's principles can be trusted in their everyday lives.

Jesus told a parable about a loving father and two sons. The younger son left home prematurely to "discover" himself, wasted his inheritance, and ultimately ended up alone. He came back home as a broken person because he "remembered" how his father had treated him. He knew he could trust his dad to love, forgive, and accept him. The goal of every leader who works with this age group is to create a place where children discover they can trust God with their lives. We hope they will grow up knowing they can go to God and the church to be restored and loved, no matter what happens.

### For Students

We gave the word **EXPERIENCE** to teenagers. They are at a place where what they have heard has to be solidified in their hearts. As they are transitioning from children to adults, it is important they learn to become self-feeders and responsible for their own spiritual growth.

Paul's letters to Timothy are a great example of the coaching or mentoring this age group needs. He personally guided Timothy through a host of situations. He encouraged him to experience a personal ministry and an authentic relationship with God. It is important during the teenage years to help students clarify their spiritual priorities as they step into the next chapter of their lives. This is a critical window of time when they need to begin experiencing what it means to be the church.

# Synchronizing Your Content

The idea of synchronizing content is critical if you hope to get parents on the same page with what you are teaching their children. But just to be clear, it does not mean you should try to get everyone in the church talking about the same thing at the same time. Although that may work every once in a while, you need to be careful that you don't sacrifice unpacking the core truths that are critical for each age group to understand.

Churches often ask how to manage the tension between the synchronization and the relevance of their content. On one hand, they want to identify and teach a clear set of important principles for every stage of life. On the other hand, they want to synchronize everyone in the church to be on the same page when it comes to the message being taught. It is a delicate balance.

If the pendulum swings too far toward relevance, churches may end up customizing different content for every grade level. This presents a host of problems, including the fact that parents are forced to keep up with a different curriculum for each of their children. It also creates a cumbersome process for churches to manage, as leaders of different age groups become disconnected and segmented in their approach.

If the pendulum swings too far toward synchronization, churches might assume that everyone in the church—from preschoolers to empty-nesters—should be discussing the same principles every week. This process creates a number of problems, the most significant of which is that relevance is sacrificed. When you attempt to teach everyone the same set of truths at the same time, only one group will have the relevance advantage, and everyone else will be forced to adapt. For example, the pastor may determine that the church needs to focus on spiritual warfare, and it's left to the children's minister to adapt that message for five-year-olds. It is like trying to make David wear Saul's armor.

We at reThink try to manage the polarity that exists between the two approaches. We have designed unique content for three major age divisions: preschool, elementary, and students. Although they have supplemental information that may target a specific part of an age group (e.g., activities for kindergartners or high school seniors), each curriculum is built around major truths that are relevant to that group. Applications are separated, but the direction is the same in each group.

We have three curriculums, one for each age group, that are based on a comprehensive strategy that weaves together wonder, discovery, and passion. We amplify these concepts so parents and leaders can understand the overall plan for the three age groups. But each age group has specific core truths that they focus on.

# The Right Mix

Radio DJs recognize the importance of a strong playlist. Putting songs on the right rotation and selecting the right mix of music not only creates a great mood in your environment, it also has the potential to reinforce your strategy and message.

The right mix complements the core message and drives it home. There are four kinds of songs we use to enhance environments:

- **Faith** songs that are Christian in theme but are not the same as contemplative worship. They are designed to celebrate faith and a relationship with God.

- **Bible** story songs are done in a variety of styles and can be featured with weekly emphasis or during a monthly series. They are designed in a creative way to make key stories memorable.

- **Virtue** songs are usually "crossover" songs. They can be used in any home, church, or even school to help reinforce a positive atmosphere. They are designed to teach or reinforce a principle that relates to character.

- **Activity** songs are neutral and may be even nonspecific in message. They may aid in transitions during the production, or children can sing and dance along with them as an activity. They are produced primarily just because they are fun. They are designed to engage children's imaginations and keep their attention.

Several years ago we realized most songs designed for kids were underproduced or targeted for the youngest children, so we went Orange with our music. We decided when it came to elementary-age kids, our music would target middle school stylistically, stay energetic, reflect cultural trends, and remain parent-friendly. We believed something significant could happen in the home and even in the car if the entire family enjoyed listening to the music together.

If kids are able to listen to and learn songs at home, the participation and engagement level significantly increases when they are at church. We've designed a unique Web site called AmberSkyRecords.com to help church leaders and parents access a wide variety of music they can use to enhance their environments. It allows leaders to download scripts, devotions, video, and songs that enhance the worship experience for kids. Additionally, the site also teaches leaders dance moves for the songs.

Think like a DJ. Add at least one new song every week so you can keep rotating something fresh into the mix. A strong playlist with the right music can create a positive mood and add energy to your environments. Help parents learn how to build a strong library of music to teach and inspire their sons and daughters.

# Strategy, Not Curriculum

A curriculum provides information, but a strategy teaches with the end in mind. There are key things a child needs to learn at each age from birth to graduation—age-specific core concepts, principles, and experiences to have a real, growing, and personal relationship with Jesus Christ. By having an overall strategy, a master plan exists that keeps the end result for a child in mind.

**A curriculum equips leaders,
but a strategy develops them.**

A strategy helps leaders focus on the right things—developing volunteers into leaders, connecting with the home, connecting with kids and students. This shift in focus allows you to concentrate your time and energy on growing those in your ministry and allows you to grow as a leader.

**A curriculum facilitates a meeting,
but a strategy prioritizes community.**

The role of the small group is elevated when you have age-specific strategies. Every teen should have a trusted adult leader in his or her life who is communicating the same things the teen's parents are communicating. We believe that small groups are the primary place where truth is being processed because it's where students have relationships. It's the place where they feel safe to ask questions and internalize truth.

**A curriculum replaces parents,
but a strategy connects with them.**

A strategy seeks to create an alignment between the church and the home. As much as we try to maximize the impact we have on this generation, the time a student spends at home plays a huge role in his or her spiritual development, not just in the hours spent there, but because of the fundamental relationship between a parent and a child. That's why it's important to be strategic in how we connect with parents and champion the parent-student relationship.

**A curriculum provides information,
but a strategy mobilizes students to
experience what they are learning.**

We believe in transitioning students away from a lecture-based format to one where students can actually experience the core truths. From our perspective, this is a key component to their faith becoming part of their DNA. We believe students should be active in ministry, getting a chance to be a part of the local church now and not waiting until that "someday" when we think they will suddenly desire to be a part of it, without ever having experienced it for themselves. A key and integral part of spiritual growth is service.

TIM WALKER  Editor, XP3 | The reThink Group

# The Master Plan

*"'Love the Lord your God with all your heart and with all your soul and with all your mind.' This is the first and greatest commandment. And the second is like it: 'Love your neighbor as yourself.'"*
*Matthew 22:37–39*

We believe in this verse so much that we have connected every curriculum and resource to these key relationships. Three words remind us how important these relationships are: Wonder | Discovery | Passion

These three issues are the priorities of our strategy and help determine a win for those who teach or lead children.

## WONDER

What if children grew up amazed with the *wonder* of their heavenly Father and how much He loves them? What if they understood God is big enough to handle whatever they will face in life?

## DISCOVERY

What if children were provoked to pursue a lifestyle of *discovery*, where their identity is determined by a personal relationship with Christ and they are guided by His Spirit?

## PASSION

What if kids developed a sense of *passion* that mobilized them to do what Jesus did on earth? What if they understood they are designed to personally participate in God's story to show His redemptive plan to every generation?

Each of the three relationships Jesus highlighted in Matthew 22 has a different level of relevance to the stages of a child's development. Picture the concepts of wonder, discovery, and passion as three separate dials.

**Wonder** is the most natural dial to turn during the formative years. We spin our content around truths that teach young children about God as a loving Father and Creator.

During the elementary years, we add the **discovery** dial and spin our content to help them see how His truths should be the compass for their decision making. We also begin tuning in the passion dial, encouraging older elementary-age kids to serve and challenging them to make others a priority.

When kids move into the teenage years, we turn up the **passion** dial. It is critical for teenagers to personalize what they learn, but they need consistent opportunities to do ministry so they can understand how to be the church. Middle and high school students feel significant when we give them something significant to do.

Content is arranged and focused around these concepts:

Preschool—birth through age four
- **God made me (wonder)**
- **God loves me (wonder)**
- **Jesus wants to be my friend forever (wonder)**

Elementary—kindergarten through fifth grade
- **I can trust God no matter what (wonder)**
- **I need to make the wise choice (discovery+)**
- **I should treat others the way I want to be treated (passion)**

Students—sixth grade through twelfth grade
- **I am created to pursue an authentic relationship with God (wonder)**
- **I belong to Jesus Christ and define who I am by what He says (discovery)**
- **I exist every day to demonstrate God's love to a broken world (passion+)**

# Family Initiatives

How does a church leader who wants to help families establish a rhythm in their homes find a way to work with the natural times a family already has?

There is a way to accomplish this that is as old as Moses—literally. In Deuteronomy 6:7, Moses instructs parents to teach biblical virtues their children. "Talk about them when you sit at home and when you walk along the road, when you lie down and when you get up."

The reThink Group distributes several resources to help church leaders partner with families to ensure they focus on what matters most. The resources look different at each stage, but they are designed to do the same thing: help parents transfer a spiritual legacy to their children.

For preschoolers, we produce a SmallTalk card as a part of our First Look curriculum. This card reviews the weekly Bible story and provides a great conversation tool for parent and child.

For elementary-aged kids, the 252Basics curriculum has several complementary components:

- A **God Time** devotional card for children to use at home

- A **Refrigerator Door** card that summarizes for parents what was discussed at church

- The **Family Times Virtue kit** offers a resource for each of the times of day mentioned in Deuteronomy 6:7:

  – Morning Time: Blank cards are provided so parents can use them to write encouraging notes to their kids

  – Meal Time: Discussion starters built around the monthly virtue are included to help families start mealtime conversations

  – Drive Time: A CD that features a drama built

around the monthly virtue and a parent-only section that includes practical advice for parents

  – Bed Time: Bible story cards that creatively engage both parents and kids to help bring the weekly Bible story to life

In middle school and high school, we distribute a summary of each series written in especially parent-friendly language to help parents stay connected to what their children are learning. Each series comes with a short article written specifically for parents of teenagers, encouraging them in one of the five family values and reminding them of the importance of the role they play in their sons and daughters' lives.

Of course, you can use these resources or create your own. Some churches write small-group curriculums for adults that help parents focus on parenting issues. Others have created DVD-driven curriculums that families can watch together to spur discussions.

Regardless of what you do,

- Make sure how you encourage parents is synchronized with what is being taught on Sunday.

- Ensure that families are not overloaded with too many products, experiences, or events. Resources that fit into the flow of daily life will always have the greatest chance of effectively helping families.

Helping families start meaningful dialogues and create shared experiences at home will help equip parents to do what God has called them to do. When you do that, you're well on your way to thinking Orange.

# Styles of Family Experience

Regularly getting parents and kids together for a shared experience is a key element of an Orange strategy, but maintaining this kind of family experience doesn't have to break a budget or involve full-time circus performers on staff. At the most basic level, family experiences happen every day without any planning at all. Think about your experiences in parks, restaurants, homes, and schools and the way the family connects in these places. The best qualities of these times can be strategically adapted to create an environment where churches and families partner to influence children.

Building an environment that reflects the idea that what happens at home is more important than what happens at church can become more manageable when you lay out some options for a practical next step.

Every church has a different style and schedule. The principle of having a family experience suggests that you create an opportunity for parents and kids to share a learning environment in the same room. This experience should be interactive, should include other families, and in some cases may even involve a level of production. The goal is for every size church to determine how to create some type of experience that will engage the family. Here are some ideas:

### HomeFX

Four or five families with elementary-age kids who meet on a regular basis with the intention of encouraging each other and growing as spiritual leaders for their kids. Each element of the event is leveraged to focus on a specific theme or virtue. Food, movies, and activities all contribute toward creating teachable moments for kids and parents.

### WeeklyFX

A multimedia large-group production featuring live storytellers, comedic performers, short videos, and high-energy music. A weekly production allows church leaders to leverage what is taught in elementary-age small groups as an active tool for parents. Each week's production can use current community news and trends as a springboard for building families' relationships with each other and with God.

### MonthlyFX

A multimedia event similar to the weekly event, although the monthly version often features a brief time to directly address parents without their children present. This vision-casting/encouragement time is combined with the spectacle of a full-family production to maximize impact for both parents and students. (We call it a place where kids take parents to learn about God.) Additional video segments can be used so not as many stage volunteers are needed.

### FX Event

Consider the community-transforming power of a Christmas presentation at a mall, an outdoor summer picnic, or even a Trunk-or-Treat Halloween event in a local parking lot. The structure can be either heavily or frugally produced depending on the resources available. Stage lights, sound, and performers might be worth the extra investment since this special event can generate a lot of attention and energy simply from the fact that it is a unique treat for the audience. Volunteer efforts can also be leveraged to creatively maximize the production value.

**GREG PAYNE** Writer/Director | The reThink Group

# Baby Dedication

North Point Community Church has a commitment to celebrating the significant milestones in a family's life. From the time children are born, to the moment they accept Christ, to a family celebration of their baptism, to recognition as they graduate from high school, the significant events in children's lives should be celebrated.

Baby dedication was very popular, but we knew the experience could be much more. We realized we were missing an opportunity at the very beginning of a child's life to partner with parents in a significant way. Although we knew how to throw a great party, we were missing the mark when it came to casting vision for what our relationship with them could look like. So here's what we did.

- **We stopped doing the event.** Sometimes you need to stop doing something, even if it is successful, in order to get the space you need to create something better.

- **We enlisted the insight of experts.** We led brainstorming meetings with parents and ministry leaders who were further down the road in parenting their children, but not so far they'd forgotten what that new-baby stage of life was like.

- **We narrowed our focus.** We had too much good information we wanted to share. We narrowed the focus of what we wanted to accomplish with this first step.

  First, we wanted to get parents thinking with *the end in mind*. We wanted to them to realize these early years would pass quickly, and before they knew it they would be helping their children pack up for college.

  Second, we wanted them to know that as their church, *we had a plan*. Dropping the kids off in our preschool ministry is not about the church providing great child care while parents go to the service. Instead, it's designed to make a first impression of the heavenly Father on the heart of every child who is placed in our care.

- **We created something more intentional.** Our intention is to keep handing them tools when they are ready for them and when they need them, all along the way.

Here's what "BabyD" looks like now:

**Step 1:** Parents visit our Web site and listen to a series of three talks. We ask both mom and dad to listen to these messages and complete a simple homework assignment. The homework helps parents establish the habit of setting aside a small amount of time and talking about what they feel is most important for their child.

**Step 2:** Attend a thirty-minute orientation about our preschool ministry. We want to cast vision for partnering with parents. We want to walk them through our plan and introduce them to the central message we will be teaching.

**Step 3:** Sign up online to attend the Baby Dedication Celebration. This is a time for parents to share with their closest friends and family their commitment to put God first in their home. It is also a time of celebration! God has created a new life in this world, and that is definitely something to celebrate. We have lots of cake and punch and a photographer to help mark this day.

KENDRA FLEMING Multi-Campus Director Preschool and Children's Ministry | North Point Ministries | Alpharetta, GA

# Mile Markers

My twelve-year-old son and I went on a special camping weekend to discuss and celebrate together the gift God was giving him—puberty. I see it as God's way of saying, "Welcome—you're officially a newbie adult in training." As his parent, I'm not convinced it's a gift yet. I'm still terrified by the thought, not to mention the smells, of my boy becoming a man. The trip was an intentional chance for my son to ask questions about guy and girl stuff, and I was able to share what God has in mind in making him a man. Coming home, we celebrated the future God has for us as father and son.

According to Deuteronomy 6, as moms and dads live out their lives with God, they naturally model and teach their children about God and His character. It takes a little more effort to unpack His plan for them and unique ways they can contribute to the world. This organic transfer of knowledge, wisdom, and faith occurs in both the rhythm of daily life and in specific moments as children grow into adulthood. I consider these moments milestones because they mark the path of growing up.

Milestones, then, are significant moments in the life journey of a parent and child that offer a unique opportunity to reinforce truth and celebrate a growing relationship with God.

What if …

the birth of a child

entering kindergarten

becoming an adolescent

obtaining a driver's license

taking a first job

graduating high school

… became intentional moments to assist parents in exploring and celebrating God's purpose for their children?

In adopting an Orange strategy at Ada Bible Church, we celebrate the traditional spiritual milestones like child dedication, salvation, and baptism with our families. A smart church sees these events as an opportunity to engage nonbelieving parents with truth and wisdom; to enlist parents in passing on faith to their children; and to teach, encourage, and train parents. But we also work to create environments that help families maximize other significant moments in the journey of parents and children.

We host a special weekend event for parents of fourth- or fifth-grade students to explore wisdom and character with their kids. We also provide a take-home resource that guides parents through discussing sexuality and puberty with their sons and daughters. Another event we're excited about is a time during which we guide parents in passing their faith stories on to their students, which helps them develop a legacy of their own. Our graduation weekend celebrates high school seniors, and we encourage parents to write a letter of reflection and encouragement to their students as they transition to a new chapter of life.

By helping parents celebrate and understand these transitions in their children's lives, we help them strengthen the relationships within their homes and reinforce the influence of the church.

BRIAN VANDERARK  Senior Pastor of Family Ministries | Ada Bible Church | Ada, MI

# High School Milestones

When it comes down to it, the most practical level of partnership between the home and the church exists between the small-group leader and the parent. But in order for an effective partnership to take place, it's important to get them both on the same page.

One way to do this is to implement a system that puts a consistent leader in the life of a student over multiple years. This not only helps small-group leaders build relational change in their pockets with the students, it also allows them to build a relationship with the parents over time. Another way to align parents and small-group leaders is to create message series with content that can be leveraged both for students and parents, engaging the entire family. A third way to work toward alignment is to create a language for small-group leaders and parents that will help them understand the primary developmental stages and milestones within each year of the student's life. Here are a few of the key issues students face:

**9th Grade:** *Belonging*

When freshmen enter high school they enter a new world of possibility. There are new people to become friends with. There are new clubs to join. There are new teachers to impress. But the most pressing issue is waiting to see where they will land in the social spectrum. With a new school (even if it's next door to the middle school/junior high) comes the opportunity for a new start. If they are going to switch social groups or branch out, now is the time. Their primary drive is for acceptance and belonging.

**10th Grade:** *Freedom*

Sophomore year is when students are first old enough to get a job, have a learner's permit, and work toward a driver's license. Many of the belonging issues from freshman year have been settled and they have a consistent group of peers. They know where they fit in, and they're pretty sure high school is going to last forever. Now they are exploring the newfound freedom of being able to drive to the grocery store and pick out what they want to eat, or meet friends at the movie theater and watch what *they* want to watch. The most basic concern of sophomore year is what to do with the freedom they have been given.

**11th Grade:** *Identity*

This is the year of Advanced Placement classes for some students. For others, it's the golden year on the sports team—students are now upperclassmen and they know it. It can be a year of philosophical processing as they spread their ideological wings. Maybe they are really communists after all; or perhaps they do believe in partial-birth abortion; or maybe they decide Kabbalah is the most reasonable religion. It's the year when they are most likely to argue and debate as they figure out what they really believe—and it's probably not going to line up with Mom and Dad (right now).

**12th Grade:** *Direction*

Senior year—high school is almost over! Life is pushing these students forward whether they feel ready for it or not. Now is the time to decide: Where will I go to college? Will I keep dating him? Who will I room with? What do I want to major in? This can also be a sentimental year for some. But the main questions center on the question, "What's next?"

KRISTEN IVY  Assistant Editor, XP3 | The reThink Group

# Group Leader Characteristics

The small-group leader is the single most important volunteer in our ministry. It's true that every volunteer role is important, but let's be honest: The relational and spiritual impact we desire for our students won't happen unless adults choose to invest themselves into the lives of our children and students. Understanding this places a huge responsibility on leaders to know what to look for when recruiting small-group leaders.

Early in my career as a leader, this picture of the ideal leader was the grid by which I recruited volunteers. I knew that if I recruited the right people, I would not always feel the need to be in training mode. Over the years I have made some interesting discoveries that have redefined what I look for in a leader.

**First, a good small-group leader must have time.**

It doesn't matter how good you are with students or how much charisma you have if you don't make the time to invest relationally. What happens outside the church's walls is every bit as important (if not more important) as what happens inside the building. Don't get me wrong—our Sunday afternoon program is pivotal to the spiritual formation of a student and serves as a potential springboard for what can happen during the week. But there is a problem when the leader does not use that springboard to connect relationally. The leader who shows up every Sunday night but does not connect during the week does not have the same influence that a relationally invested leader possesses. The conversations over dinner or a late-night phone call after attending a football game together is where those life-changing, direction-altering conversations consistently take place.

**Second, a good small-group leader knows how to make good decisions on the fly.**

Dating, sex, school, parties, college, drinking, and choosing good friends are pivotal issues for high school students, and your leaders are navigating these waters every day. You simply can't be there for every student in every situation, so it is important to have leaders who can be there. How your leaders respond, react, forgive, celebrate, and confront directly impacts their ability to have long-term influence on their small groups.

**Finally, a good small-group leader knows how to be real.**

This is more important than looking or dressing a certain way—as counterintuitive as that may feel. I tried to recruit young, hip adults almost exclusively. I know this was pretty shallow and I admit that I underestimated our students. I have learned that students have a keen sense of who is real and who is not, and they place a high value on authenticity. Young or old, single or married, thin or overweight doesn't seem to matter quite as much as having a leader who genuinely cares enough to spend time investing in them.

KEVIN RAGSDALE Multi-Campus Director of High School Ministry | North Point Ministries | Alpharetta, GA

# High School to College

As a high school small-group leader at my church, I approached last May with mixed emotions. Graduation marked the end of my service as a small-group leader, yet the transition didn't feel right. Even though the church prepared a good-bye, served a graduation dinner, and handed me a gift card as a sign of gratitude for the past four years, I couldn't help but feel that my time with this group was still incomplete.

After talking with the youth minister at my church, I decided to commit to an extra year with my group. Some of the girls are still living at home and have jobs in the area. Some of the girls have gone to local state universities, and others are now in private and public schools around the country. We no longer meet weekly after a large-group session. Needless to say, our group looks different than it did a year ago, but the constant thing is that I am committed to pursuing them.

Last semester I visited each of their college campuses within driving distance to spend time with the girls in their new environments.

- I set up a day each week to send messages on Facebook to connect with and encourage them.

- When the girls are home on holidays, I plan times for us to meet over coffee or have dinner.

- This Christmas break we had a reunion sleepover that was our group's most well-attended event in five years.

Part of my commitment to this group of girls includes replacing myself. The goal of my continued commitment is not to hold on indefinitely but to love them through this crucial transition time and to help them take the next step in their faith journey. I've gone with them to a local college ministry since there wasn't one on our church campus, and I regularly check in with them to get a feel for how they are connecting to ministries in their new locations. For those who are still at home, I look for ways to connect them to service opportunities in our church where they can meet other young adults and experience true community.

A lot of what I have done over the past seven months has been both systematic and organic. Each girl is experiencing transition in her own unique way, and the way I pursue her and the amount of time I remain actively committed to pursuing her depends a lot on her situation.

I wish all church leaders who work with youth would take a look at the system they have for graduating seniors. Even when they have checked out of some of the programming, seniors are still relationally present. Nevertheless, there are two critical issues to consider:

- In most churches it seems like we are disconnecting when the stakes are the highest.

- We are not tapping into the relational influence when the felt need is the greatest.

With all the growing statistics about the drop-off rate for college freshmen and young adults, we need to reevaluate how we determine success in high school ministry. What might happen if every high school leader decided that graduation simply wasn't the end of the story?

KRISTEN IVY  Assistant Editor, XP3 | The reThink Group

# College-Friendly Churches

As a pastor, I want what's spiritually best for those I lead. I want them to understand God's will from a spiritual perspective, and my goal in ministry is ultimately to present them mature in Christ. This spiritual focus can require me to tackle tough decisions or conversations, but it definitely requires a strategy for lifelong discipleship.

To develop that strategy, here are some concepts we must embrace:

First, we have to understand that God has chosen the body of Christ as the means by which He brings believers to maturity (Eph. 4:11–14). Put another way, people cannot become spiritually mature unless they stay intimately connected to other believers.

Second, we must strategically develop church structures that promote intimate connection. The first step is making sure our structures support people through all life stages.

Third, we have to face the reality that the college-age years are the biggest disconnecting point for people. Church leaders talk about this problem, but few have developed a strategy that bridges the disconnection.

Some leaders have attempted to build a bridge for this disconnection by developing another church service. But even if this attracts hundreds of college-age people, it doesn't necessarily solve the core problem. In fact, from a college-age person's perspective, this approach could contribute to further disconnection. This model actually exposes all the differences between people, not the similarities. In order for true connection to take place we have to have another approach, a lasting one.

There are churches that truly engage college-age people. These churches have a structure that's strategic, beyond a separate service. They've developed a lifelong discipleship process by intentionally connecting people of all generations. Because college-age people stay connected to the people in the church, the outcome is a continuous flow of growing believers. These churches embrace at least seven crucial characteristics:

- Leaders place a high priority on cross-generational relationships.

- Leaders cultivate a heart in older mature believers for discipleship of younger believers and hold them to this standard (2 Tim. 2:2; Titus 2:3–4).

- Student ministry leaders express respect for older adults in the church. There is mutual respect between the ministers of children and youth, and ministers who work with the adult congregation.

- No leader is on an island. They view themselves as a small part in the lifelong discipleship of people.

- Leaders work alongside parents and strategically do so from the nursery through the college-age years.

- College-age individuals have a leader who works in an assimilation role to connect college-age people with more experienced believers.

- College-age individuals have a leader who understands the search for identity, intimacy, meaning, pleasure, and truth during the college-age years and is able to disciple people toward biblically mature conclusions in each area.

CHUCK BOMAR Senior Pastor | Colossae Church | Tigard, OR

# Mentoring Boys

"My father left when I was a toddler, and right about the time I was breaking into houses, a man at my church invited me to a morning book study and took me under his wing. He befriended me. His role was simple. He played catch with me, invited me over to eat with his family, and even gave me a shot at writing for a local newsletter. That one affirming voice in my life, I believe, kept me out of jail. I created The Mentoring Project as a thank-you to my mentor growing up. And I know there are millions of men like him who simply need an official program they can sign up for in order to mentor a young man in a situation similar to my own."

With those words three years ago, I started The Mentoring Project to encourage mentoring relationships for young men growing up without fathers. Why? Because fatherless boys with mentors are less likely to drop out of school, experiment with drugs, or end up in our prison system.

At the time we started TMP, we did not know of a single mentoring program being operated in a church. But we think churches are an amazing resource for this very kind of thing. There are 360,000 churches in America today. This means the infrastructure for a radical change in American culture is already in place. The volunteers are on hand as well. As we equip churches to start these programs, we see lives changed almost immediately.

The first church involved in the mentoring project was my own church, the Imago Dei Community in Portland, Oregon. Through Imago, about fifteen children are currently being mentored. The Mentoring Project works by pairing kids with individual mentors and in larger groups, engaging the children in lifelong friendships with not just their mentors but also other men in the group.

I'm often asked what mentoring looks like, and the answer I give can sometimes come as a surprise to those asking the question. Mentoring happens in the context of the friendship. Essentially, mentoring is

- playing catch,
- going fishing,
- attending a baseball game,
- having conversations while on a hike,
- group camping trips,
- and mostly just hanging out.

Our desire is to spread beyond the Pacific Northwest in the coming years. We have set a goal of equipping a thousand church-based programs that will mentor at least ten thousand fatherless boys. Our corollary vision is to see a statistical drop in crime that can be attributed to the efforts of the church in America and its work at building relationships with young boys without fathers.

If you'd like to start a Mentoring Project program at your church, visit our Web site at www.TheMentoringProject. org to learn more. There you will be able to find the resources you need to get started.

# Spiritual Growth Catalysts

Spiritual growth can be mysterious. Everyone values it. But how does it happen? When you ask the question, the conversation gets fuzzy pretty quickly.

It has become increasingly clear that mere attendance doesn't bring spiritual growth. Lots of people participate in student ministry, children's ministry, or adult worship but wouldn't say they are growing. And scores of people have privately read their Bibles and prayed for years but still long for something deeper. So what gives?

When you investigate people's faith stories, some common threads tie them together. These recurring themes suggest God uses five catalysts to define and grow our faith:

### Life-Changing Truth

Surprisingly, information alone doesn't change people, nor does great teaching. What changes lives is teaching that is *applied*. Small groups are the best environments in which to apply truth. In a group, a leader knows each child's or student's story, and truth can be applied in a context that is personal and relevant to each group member.

### Spiritual Disciplines

*Discipline* is a word most of us don't like, but many of us can talk about something that started as a discipline but became a passion over time. What we used to resent became an important part of our lives. Prayer, reading Scripture, giving, journaling, and even fasting are disciplines that can deepen our relationships with God.

### Personal Ministry

The pervasive message of our culture is that we gain by getting. The story goes like this: We acquire more possessions, more influence, more power, and we "arrive." But Jesus' radical message is that we grow not by getting but by *giving*. It's the opposite of what we'd expect. In turn, our faith and trust is stretched and we grow.

### Significant Relationships

Most of us can look back over our spiritual journeys and recall people who had a positive spiritual impact on us: teachers, coaches, neighbors, bosses, church leaders, or friends. Looking back, we'd probably conclude that God used human relationships to grow us closer to Him. When church leaders elevate community and groups-based ministry, we give people a chance to form significant relationships that can help them grow closer to God.

### Pivotal Circumstances

God takes each of us to pivot points, moments of decision or events that change everything. For example, most of us never ask for God to bring difficult circumstances into our lives. But when they inevitably come, they are always pivotal points. Hardship either grows our faith or shrinks it. Most of us pray for and even expect our lives to get easier, but consider this: Very few of the people we meet in the Bible had easy lives. It seems like God let them live through difficulty, and in the process they learned to trust Him. It sounds surprising, but one of the greatest seasons of growth in faith can happen when circumstances look the worst. A supportive community can help us follow God's hand during hard seasons. These pivotal circumstances don't necessarily have to be difficult times. It might be making a team, receiving a promotion, determining a key decision, or personalizing a new discovery that becomes a pivot point for growth.

# Mobilizing Students

With nearly twenty thousand high school students gathering on Florida beaches for Lanny Donoho's BigStuf camps, the potential for life change on an individual level is remarkable. When Lanny looked at those crowds, he saw a monumental force for worldwide change and realized that this potential could reach a global level.

"I was trying to think of a way to train the college students who serve as BigStuf interns," Lanny explained. "I wanted something different, something more real than sitting in a hotel conference room talking about what it means to do ministry." Reality rushed in when he took those interns to Kenya to see firsthand how God provides and how lives are changed.

"I realized that even while we were having an impact just by being there, the college-aged kids with us would never be able to look at the world the same way. They were going to be right in the middle of the action."

How does Lanny's experience in Africa translate to Middle America?

"I think church leaders can join with parents to be intentional in expanding the influence of students in their own communities and around the world."

Lanny suggests a few things to try:

1. Ask small groups to do something outside the church at least once a month. "Some churches do occasional mission projects, but make it monthly so kids understand it's part of the expectation for the group."

2. Do a series twice a year challenging students to take risks. "Students are ready to go way beyond their comfort zones, but we usually settle for an experience which makes them feel right at home."

3. Create opportunities for weekly ministry. "We expect students to go to athletic practices, church group, and even to jobs every week. How can they be encouraged to make a weekly commitment to someone or an organization in need?"

4. Inventory students to assess their passions and skills. "The best way to find the hidden potential in your group is to ask the right questions. Everyone has a gift or an interest waiting to be deployed."

5. Match students with mentors or models. "Ideally, each student has a consistent mentor who can guide him to implementing his calling. Even a one-time lunch with a leader or to visit a local or international mission field can inspire a kid for a lifetime."

6. Expect more of parents. "Parents will make or break a student's experience in serving. They need to be prepared to invest time and money in their student's experience. On the other hand, the kid's got to own it personally. It can't be Mom and Dad's mission."

7. Take them on a mission trip. "Not to be obvious, but when you take students into the laboratory of international travel and new people, they'll have an overwhelming experience with the totality of who God wants them to be. They think they're going to serve, but they come back having a more in-depth experience themselves because they see people who have next to nothing who still have joy and peace. They build real relationships with real people. That's what makes the difference, not only there, but here at home."

LANNY DONOHO Founder & President | BigStuf Camps, YMR | www.410bridge.com

# The Job Only Students Can Do

What happens when you ask students to accomplish a mission that only they can accomplish? When we talk about deploying students for ministry, the ideal is to match their gifts and experience with a need specialized for their ability.

For dozens of American teenagers, that journey takes them to Russia each spring. Students who weren't even born when the Berlin Wall fell are taking a unique skill set to the former Soviet Union: the power of social networking and peer friendships.

On the Russian side, students from elite Russian public schools compete for the opportunity to attend a week-long camp where they'll hone their English skills with American conversational teams. The Americans serve as peer counselors in groups of six or eight during the day. At night, cultural differences dissolve as they play together, worship together, pray together—just like most U.S. church youth groups. Except most of the Russian students aren't Christians. Yet.

The fact is, American adults wouldn't be the best candidates to accomplish this mission. The supervising adults are tolerated by the Russian kids, but as teachers, not as friends. With tightening religious restrictions, church leaders have limited access. The mission can't be made up. It's got to be a legitimate cultural exchange. And since the Russian language students show up to learn "pop culture" English, who better to talk with than the across-the-ocean teens who know that language best?

When they say their good-byes at the end of the week, both sides have talked about what it means to have a relationship with God. And thanks to the Internet, cell phones, and Facebook, those conversations are just the beginning. Instead of a once-in-a-lifetime mission trip, the students build lifelong friendships. Instead of a long plane ride,

they're back in an instant via text or Web. American kids are discipling their Russian peers, all online. And even though the online communication is powerful, the kids who've been before are the first ones on the plane when it's time to go back for the next English camp.

The distinctive is that opportunities like this aren't about getting teenagers to do something the adults don't want to do, or creating artificial experiences so students will think they own the ministry. Find something they can do better than anybody else. They just might change the world.

MIKE JEFFRIES Associate to the Senior Pastor | FBC Fort Lauderdale, FL

# Connecting Students to Their Story

Churches learning to think Orange often face the significant challenge of bridging the generations. People from different age groups simply have a hard time seeing the world in the same way, and based on my research at Barna Group, I believe this gap is expanding, not narrowing. What can be done?

Make it a priority, and then get creative.

I came across a great idea recently from a youth worker I know. He and his youth group created a visual history of their church, which had launched in the 1960s. The teens talked with some of the original members of the church and captured interviews with the current senior pastor and several retired staffers. They found newspaper clippings, dusted off blueprints from building projects, and learned more about the history of the community at the time of the church's founding. Taking all they discovered, they compiled this into a short film and magazine.

What these students got was an understanding for the sanctity of history while using their aptitude for story, image, media, and relationships, and utilizing the latest software and gadgetry. The outcome was more than just a DVD of interviews and clips. It was a bridge that got a younger generation talking to and appreciating an older generation, creating a dialogue between individuals that otherwise would never have happened. The most profound impact was that the older adults in the congregation were not only awed by the technological abilities of the teenagers, they couldn't help but take more interest in the youth. This experience opened the door for more potential interactions between generations and raises some interesting questions for any of us at churches with varying ages. Are older adults involved in student ministry, or are there adult small groups to mentor young leaders? Do grandparents realize the influence available to them in their own families? Imagine the potential at hand.

What could you do to help teens see your church and community through different eyes? How could you spark greater concern and affinity among older adults toward teenagers? I bet you have other innovative and practical ideas that would build generational bridges. Start by admitting that such connections are important, and then try something intentional.

You often hear young people described as history-makers. Just think: They might also be history-*keepers*.

**DAVID KINNAMAN** President | Barna Group

# Nerve to Serve

It was the summer of 1999 when I first noticed we had a problem. I had been the children's pastor at Seacoast Church for two years, and while our adult ministries had begun to focus heavily on meeting the needs of our community, our children's ministry was falling behind. Each year we collected shoe boxes filled with items for needy kids overseas and raised money for orphans in Africa.

At the beginning of school we collected school supplies for those that couldn't afford them. While these were good projects, I suspected the kids weren't really getting it. I watched as the parents brought the boxes or supplies and put them into their kids' hands, or handed them money out of their pockets to put in the offering boxes as an afterthought. As a result I began to ask myself some questions.

Did the kids in my ministry know what it meant to really *be* like Jesus?

Did they understand who He was and how much He loved them?

I wanted desperately for the kids to know and understand the servant heart of Christ. But I felt I wasn't giving them the opportunity to learn.

In the summer of 2000, we kicked off our first children's service club, Nerve to Serve. We aimed the club at fourth- and fifth-graders, who came one day a week to spend thirty minutes digging into their Bibles, learning about the character of Jesus, and then doing an hour of hard work. We used many Bible stories, but we often came back to our anchor verse, Matthew 20:24, "That is what the Son of Man has done: He came to *serve*, not be *served*—and then to give away his life in exchange for the many who are held hostage" (MSG).

The kids pulled weeds on the church grounds, took cold drinks and thank you notes to our area fire stations, and wrote letters of encouragement to prisoners in a nearby prison, praying over the list of names given to us. One particularly hot day they handed out icy bottles of water to complete strangers shopping at an outdoor mall.

We asked our kids what things Jesus would do if He lived in Mount Pleasant. What needs would He see? The answers the kids gave us were astounding. They thought of things we never would have on our own. They didn't stop with projects in our community, but began to think bigger. They began to understand the impact of serving others.

Since that time, our church has expanded to thirteen campuses in three different states. Most campuses have their own version of Nerve to Serve. Some of the clubs happen during the summer, some during the holiday season, and some all year round. Many have branched out to encompass kindergarten through fifth grade, and some campuses make it a family event where moms, dads, and kids serve together. Depending on the campus, each club operates differently but with a common goal: having a heart to serve as Christ did.

SHERRY SURRATT Director | Women's Initiatives, Leadership Network

# ENDNOTES

Chapter 2: Bright Lights
1   C. S. Lewis, *Mere Christianity* (New York: HarperCollins, 1952), 199.
2   N. T. Wright, *Simply Christian* (New York: HarperCollins, 2006), 200.
3   Anne Lamott, *Traveling Mercies: Some Thoughts on Faith* (New York: Anchor Books, 2000), 100.
4   Craig Van Gelder, *The Essence of the Church: A Community Created by the Spirit* (Grand Rapids, MI: Baker Books, 2000), 98.
5   Revelation 1:20.
6   John 12:32.
7   John 18:36–37.
8   Revelation 2:5.
9   Revelation 2:4.
10  Verse 10.
11  Verses 9, 11.
12  Verse 19.
13  Lifeway Research, "LifeWay Research Uncovers Reasons 18 to 22 Year Olds Drop Out of Church," http://www.lifeway.com/lwc/article_main_page/0,1703,A=165949&M=200%20906,00.html (accessed January 19 2009).

The Essence of Family
14  Deuteronomy 6:4–12
15  Verses 21–24
16  Chap Clark, *Hurt: Inside the World of Today's Teenagers* (Grand Rapids, MI: Baker Academic, 2004), 110.
17  Joyce A. Martin, MPH et al., "Births: Final Data for 2006." *National Vital Statistics Reports,* 57, no. 7 (January 7, 2009), http://www.cdc.gov/nchs/data/nvsr/nvsr57/nvsr57_07.pdf (accessed January 10, 2009).
18  Roy B. Zuck, *Bibliotheca Sacra* 121 (1965), 228–235.
19  If you'd like to check out the resources yourself, see "The Importance of Family Dinners" study series conducted by Columbia University and the National Center on Addiction and Substance Abuse. Access the study online at http://www.casacolumbia.org/absolutenm/articlefiles/380Importance%20of%20Family%20Dinners%20IV.pdf.
20  Madeline Levine, *The Price of Privilege: How Parental Pressure and Material Advantage Are Creating a Generation of Disconnected and Unhappy Kids* (New York: HarperCollins, 2006), 215–216.
21  Deuteronomy 6:2.
22  See Exodus 34:26; Leviticus 19:19; Leviticus 22:28; and Deuteronomy 22:8 for a few examples.

## Chapter 4: Orange Glow

23  I recently heard a leader announce online that he was going to "champion the movement" of family for today's church. That is misleading for a number of reasons. First, you can't appoint yourself to be a movement champion. Secondly, there have been a lot of pioneer thinkers before you who have fought for this issue for a long time, including Moses.

24  George Barna, *The Barna Update.* "Parents Accept Responsibility for Their Child's Spiritual Development but Struggle with Effectiveness," *Barna Update,* May 6, 2003.

25  Penny Edgell, (Professor of Sociology at the University of Minnesota, *Religion and Family in a Changing Society* (Princeton, NJ: Princeton University Press, 2006), 47.

26  George Barna, "Parents Accept Responsibility."

27  Andy Stanley, Reggie Joiner and Lane Jones, *Seven Practices of Effective Ministry* (Sisters, OR: Multnomah Books, 2004).

## Chapter 6: Essential #1 Integrate Strategy

28  Nehemiah 2:17.

29  Nehemiah 4:20.

30  Matthew 22:35–36.

31  Patrick Lencioni. *Silos, Politics, and Turf Wars: A Leadership Fable about Destroying the Barriers That Turn Colleagues into Competitors* (San Francisco: Jossey-Bass, 2006), 143.

32  Sue Miller with David Staal, *Making Your Children's Ministry the Best Hour of Every Kid's Week* (Grand Rapids, MI: Zondervan, 2004). Sue was the founding innovator for Willow Creek's Promiseland. She now works with reThink and has been instrumental in "refining our message" on how to reach children.

## Chapter 7: Essential #2 Refine the Message

33  Deuteronomy 6:9.

34  "And Jesus grew in wisdom and stature, and in favor with God and men" (Luke 2:52).

35  Ephesians 4:15.

36  Matthew 4:19.

37  Matthew 19:14.

38  John 4:13–14.

39  Luke 18:25.

40  Matthew 6:3.

41  Matthew 19:30.

42  John 8:12.

43  John 14:9.

44  Matthew 5:13–14.

45  John 14:6.

### Chapter 8: Essential #3 Reactivate the Family

46  Malcolm Gladwell, *The Tipping Point* (New York: Little, Brown and Company, 2002), 96.

47  Nehemiah 4:13–14.

### Chapter 9: Essential #4 Elevate Community

48  Mark Kelly, "LifeWay Research: Parents, Churches Can Help Teens Stay in Church," LifeWay Christian Resources, http://www.lifeway.com/lwc/article_main_page/0%2C1703%2CA%25253D165950%252526M%25253D200906%2C00.html (accessed October 1 2008).

49  Meredith Miller, "Family Ministry: Good Things Come in Threes," Fuller Youth Institute, 5 September 2007, http://fulleryouthinstitute.org/2007/09/family-ministry/ (accessed February 3 2009).

### Chapter 10: Essential #5 Leverage Influence

50  Austin Murphy, "Texas Tech Is the Surprising Feel-Good Story of the 2008 Season," Murphey's Law, *Sports Illustrated*, November 7 2008, http://sportsillustrated.cnn.com/2008/writers/austin_murphy/11/07/tech/index.html (accessed February 20 2009).

51  1 Corinthians 9:22.

52  Psalm 78:4–7.

### Orange-ality

53  George Barna, *Transforming Children into Spiritual Champions* (Ventura, CA: Regal Books, 2003), 79, 81.

54  Ivy Beckwith; Renee Altson; and Spencer Burke, *Postmodern Children's Ministry* (Grand Rapids, MI: Zondervan, 2004), 13–14.

55  Kenda Creasy Dean, "Expand the Umbrella," *Group Magazine*, Jan/Feb 2009, 60.

# ABOUT THE AUTHOR

Photo by Ken Hawkins

Reggie Joiner is the founder and CEO of the reThink Group, a nonprofit organization providing resources and training to help churches maximize their influence on the spiritual growth of the next generation. The reThink Group provides innovative resources and training for leaders who work with preschool, children, families, and students. They have partners throughout the United States and eight other countries. The reThink Group is also the architect and primary sponsor of the Orange Conference and the Orange Tour, which provide national training opportunities for senior pastors, church leaders, and ministry volunteers.

Reggie is also one of the founding pastors, along with Andy Stanley, of North Point Community Church in Alpharetta, Georgia. In his role as executive director of Family Ministry, Reggie developed the concepts of ministry for preschool, children, students, and married adults over the course of his eleven years with the church. During his time with North Point Ministries, Reggie created KidStuf, a weekly environment where kids bring their parents to learn about God, as well as Grow Up, an international conference to encourage and equip churches to create relevant, effective environments for children, families, and teenagers.

Reggie is the coauthor of *7 Practices of Effective Ministries* along with Lane Jones and Andy Stanley. He and his wife, Debbie, live in Cumming, Georgia, and have four grown children: Reggie Paul, Hannah, Sarah, and Rebekah.

orange

Orange - The Event

Three conferences in one; the only
place to bring your senior leadership,
student ministry leaders, and children's
ministry leaders together.

www.TheOrangeConference.com

3 age-appropriate curriculums built around one strategy.
3 stages of life.
1 end in mind.

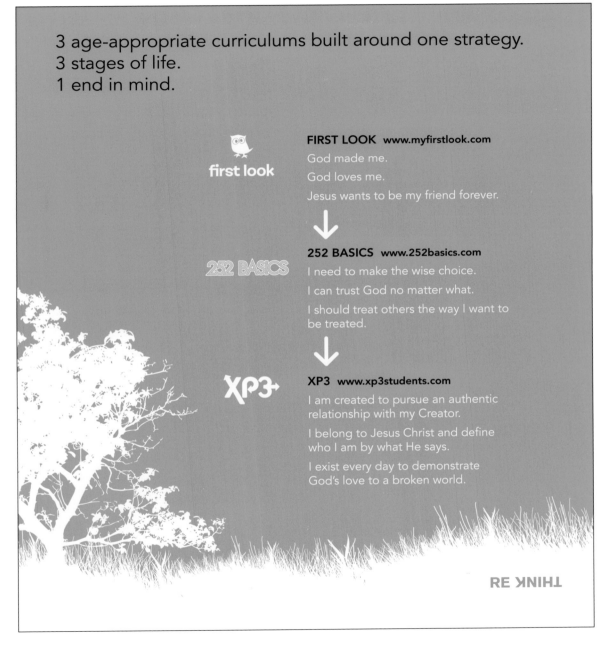

FIRST LOOK  www.myfirstlook.com

God made me.

God loves me.

Jesus wants to be my friend forever.

252 BASICS  www.252basics.com

I need to make the wise choice.

I can trust God no matter what.

I should treat others the way I want to be treated.

XP3  www.xp3students.com

I am created to pursue an authentic relationship with my Creator.

I belong to Jesus Christ and define who I am by what He says.

I exist every day to demonstrate God's love to a broken world.

RE THINK

What if there was a network
devoted to equipping staff and
volunteers to be better leaders?

**OrangeLeaders.com** meets that need. This
innovative curriculum provides ongoing
training materials for volunteers in every
age-group ministry as well as personal
development for staff members.

orange

www.OrangeLeaders.com

# THE RETHINK GROUP STORE

## www.therethinkstore.org

Visit the reThink Group online store to purchase these products and to find quality products to enhance your ministry, train your leaders, and develop volunteers.

## FAMILYTIMES®

With activities designed to help parents make the most of everyday moments together—MealTime, DriveTime, BedTime, and MorningTime—this monthly resource equips parents to take an active role in the growth of their children's faith and character.

## THE GOOD FIGHT

All families fight. But what if, instead of fighting over differences, we began to fight *for* relationship? The Good Fight series encourages students to stay in the fight and never give up on their relationship with their parents.

RE ʞNIHⱢ

# THINK
# AGAIN
## THE COMPANION WORKBOOK!

Integrate your strategy, refine the message, elevate community, reactivate the family, and leverage influence. Imagine the impact when your church activates the strategies of THINK ORANGE.

THINK ORANGE

JOINER

**THINK ORANGE**

IMAGINE THE IMPACT WHEN CHURCH AND FAMILY COLLIDE ...

**COMPANION WORKBOOK**

REGGIE JOINER

**orange**

available fall 2009